T0277888

It's easy for readers to feel intimidated by the works of England's greatest puritan theologian. But this new book shows how much of Owen's writing has a devotional purpose—and, in daily readings of two or three paragraphs, allows readers to build theological stamina over time. *Daily Readings in John Owen* is a beautiful gift for the church.

CRAWFORD GRIBBEN
Professor of history, Queen's University,
Belfast, Northern Ireland

John Owen is one of the greatest ever English-speaking theologians—a theologian whose concerns were always to magnify the grace and glory of God in Christ and serve the pastoral needs of the church. Yet sometimes his seventeenth-century prose can be a bit off-putting. So Lee Gatiss has done us a great service in producing an accessible collection of bite-size chunks of the rich diet offered by Owen. By tracking Owen's life this book provides a great introduction to Owen and his thought. But best of all it enables us to marvel afresh at our glorious Saviour.

TIM CHESTER
Senior Faculty, Crosslands Training

What a splendid idea! The abundant riches of John Owen's writings have been long neglected, partially because of Owen's difficult writing style. Thanks to Lee Gatiss, we can now draw from these riches daily in a form that is accessible and easy to absorb. The introduction to the book gives a brief overview of Owen's life, while the short introductions to each month take us on a journey with him through the progression of his thoughts, from his earliest writings to his latest, as we grow and learn with him to keep our eyes fixed on Christ.

SIMONETTA CARR
Author of the Christian Biography for Young Children series,
which includes John Owen

JOHN OWEN
DAILY READINGS

EDITED BY
Lee Gatiss

CHRISTIAN HERITAGE

Copyright © Lee Gatiss 2022

Softback ISBN: 978-1-5271-0720-5
Ebook ISBN: 978-1-5271-0979-7

Published in 2022
in the
Christian Heritage Imprint
by
Christian Focus Publications,
Geanies House, Fearn, Tain, Ross-shire,
IV20 1TW, Scotland, UK
www.christianfocus.com

Cover design by Daniel van Straaten

Printed and bound by FLB group

INTRODUCTION

John Owen (1616–1683) was one of the leading Puritans of the seventeenth century. He was a Christian statesman, a fine scholar, a thoroughgoing Protestant, a Reformed theologian, and a prodigious Bible commentator. He was also a pastor and preacher, both at a national level (as Chaplain to Oliver Cromwell and a Parliamentary preacher) and at the local level (pastoring congregations in Essex and London at different stages of his ministry). He left behind him several thousand pages of published material, from tracts and treatises to books and sermons, as well as a massive commentary on the epistle to the Hebrews, which is around two million words in length. All this means that there is a huge amount of material for us to choose from if we want to engage with and learn from this prince of the Puritans.

Owen was born to Puritan parents within the Church of England in the year that William Shakespeare died. In terms of his public influence, Owen was a rising star in the 1640s and at the height of his power in the 1650s. As Vice Chancellor of Oxford University, he wielded a significant amount of power and influence within the short-lived English Republic. Famously, he was the chosen preacher to the House of Commons the day after Charles I was beheaded in January 1649.

Yet Owen eventually found himself on the losing side of the epic struggles of the seventeenth century and was ousted from his position of national pre-eminence. After the Act of Uniformity in 1662 effectively barred him from any position within the established church, the academy, or the state, he remained one of the most influential leaders among the nonconformist dissenters. Yet his vision for church and state had effectively been vanquished.

He did not struggle during the subsequent period of persecution in quite the same way as John Bunyan and other dissenters did, being well-provided for financially and in terms of 'friends in high places'. Yet his personal life was not easy. When his first wife Mary died in 1676, only one of their eleven children was still alive (and the unhappy marriage and early death of that remaining daughter would also bring considerable sorrow). He was afflicted with various liver, kidney, and eye troubles, along with much opposition and many enemies. 'These things are apt to make us faint, to despond, and be weary', he admitted, 'I know not how others bear up their hearts and spirits. For my part, I have much ado to keep from continual longing after the embraces of the dust and shades of the grave, as a curtain drawn over the rest in another world.'

The 'Protestant work ethic' played an important part in his make-up. He certainly considered those who are industrious in their affairs to be far more amiable and desirable than the idle rich: 'Industry in men's callings is a thing in itself very commendable' he wrote, 'If in nothing else, it hath an advantage herein, that it is a means to preserve men from those excesses in lust and riot which otherwise they are apt to run into.' Strenuous intellectual exertions may distract the mind and prevent a plunge into darkness and a melancholic longing after 'the shades of the grave'. Alongside preparation of two or three substantial sermons each week as a pastor, his concurrent literary output was staggering, but it may well have been good for his mental health.

It would be tempting to present the following extracts from Owen in thematic order, as most editions of Owen's works do. However, I have chosen to approach things differently, and having recently re-read his works *chronologically*, I have elected to present his thoughts that way. So we will begin the year with his earliest published thoughts, and end with his more mature reflections, hopefully gaining a sense of how his life and ministry changed and unfolded in the process. Given his well-known tendency to be somewhat opaque to the ordinary modern reader, I have assumed some liberty to update Owen's language here and there, so that it is more readily understandable today, and to abridge what he wrote to fit within the confines of a single page here. Much of his work was aimed against alternative systems of theology, and though there is a time and a place for such writing, I have tried to focus here on his more positive and less polemical contributions, though that inevitably leaves out a great deal of no less useful material.

Over the course of the year we should, however, catch an authentic glimpse of Owen, not abstractly but as he developed and grew in his walk with the Lord and understanding of his ways. I pray that you also will develop and grow in your walk with the Lord, as I have, by engaging with the teaching of this fallible but faithful man of God.

LEE GATISS
Cambridge

Translation of Latin words and works is mine. Scripture references at the start of each day are taken from the English Standard Version (ESV) Anglicised Version, and used by kind permission of Crossway and Harper Collins. Scripture within each extract has been updated from Owen's original seventeenth-century English to more closely approximate or match the ESV.

HOW TO USE THIS BOOK

There are many ways you might benefit spiritually from reflecting carefully on the contents of each page. Here are four ideas:

1. The related scripture verse at the top of each page, that I have selected for that day — might you memorise it and repeat it morning, noon, and night?

2. Is there an arresting word, a phrase, an image, or a thought in the extract from Owen, which you can turn into prayer?

3. Are there other verses referred to which you could look up, pondering their connection to Owen's main thought?

4. Might the title of each day be something to meditate on throughout the day, to fuel and frame your thoughts and prayers?

As Owen said, 'These duties of private communion with God are the means of receiving supplies of spiritual strength from him. Hence our Saviour lets us know, what a man is in secret, in these private duties, that he is in the eyes of God, and no more.' So remember to pray before you read, that God would enlighten the eyes of your heart, teaching, correcting, rebuking, and training you.

JANUARY

This month we will be engaging with John Owen's early works from 1643–1647, when he was starting out as a writer and pastor aged twenty-seven to thirty-one. His first published work was *A Display of Arminianism*. Here, he sets out his vision of God and the gospel, in distinction to an alternative theology which most of the Puritans considered spiritually flawed and (in the regime of Charles I and Archbishop Laud) politically repressive. He shows how it is novel, un-biblical, and against the established Reformed doctrine of the Church of England. For this book, Parliament rewarded Owen with a pastorate at Fordham in Essex.

After this, Owen confessed himself to be of the Presby-terian persuasion and published a short book in 1644 on *The Duty of Pastors and People Distinguished*, in which he discusses 'the means to be used by the people of God … for the increasing of divine knowledge in themselves and others.' Joseph Caryl said at the time that this was 'written with much clearness of judgment and moderation of spirit'.

In the second half of this month, we will hear Owen the preacher extolling before Parliament the greatness of *A Vision of Unchangeable Free Mercy* (1646). To this he also attached a brief *Country Essay* on church government and toleration. Then, he expounds on 'rules of direction for the walking of the saint in fellowship, according to the order of the gospel', in a short book called *Eshcol, A Cluster of the Fruit of Canaan* (1647), published shortly after he formed a Congregationalist church in Coggeshall, Essex.

During this time, Owen also published two short catech-isms which were used to instruct people in the principles of the doctrine of Christ.

JANUARY 1

Glory to God Alone!

The light shines in the darkness, and the darkness has not overcome it.

JOHN 1:5

The soul of mankind, by reason of the corruption of nature, is darkened with a mist of ignorance, meaning it is unable to comprehend divine truth. It is also armed with prejudice and opposition against some parts of that truth, which are either above or contrary to false principles which we have framed for ourselves.

A desire for self-sufficiency was the first cause of this infirmity, and mankind still languishes in the pride of this. There is nothing we contend for more than independence from any supreme power which might either help, hinder, or control us in our actions. This is the bitter root from which have sprung all those heresies and wretched contentions which have troubled the church—contentions concerning the power of mankind to bring about its own happiness, and its exemption from the overruling providence of Almighty God.

All these wrangling disputes of carnal reason against the word of God come down in the end to this question: whether the first and chiefest part in ordering things in this world ought to be ascribed to God, or humanity? People, for the most part, have assumed this pre-eminence to themselves. All the innovations of such people against the received doctrine of the Reformed churches aim at these two ends: they wish to exempt themselves from God's jurisdiction, and to clear human nature from the heavy imputation of being sinful and corrupted. And so at length, with much toil and labour, they declare that the sacrifice of praise for all good things should be divided between God and their free-will.

JANUARY 2

Rejoice in God's Decrees

God saved us and called us to a holy calling, not because of our works but because of his own purpose and grace, which he gave to us in Christ Jesus before the ages began.

2 TIMOTHY 1:9

Christians have always believed, upon infallible grounds, that all the decrees of God are eternal and therefore unchangeable and irrevocable. To ascribe the least changeability to the divine essence was ever accounted transcendent atheism in the highest degree. All God's works from the beginning are 'known from eternity' says James (Acts 15:18). From this, it has up until now, been concluded that whatever God in time brings to pass, that he decreed from all eternity so to do.

Consider this particularly in the decree of election, that fountain of all spiritual blessings. When one has a saving sense and assurance of this, it effects a spiritual rejoicing in the Lord. 'He chose us before the foundation of the world' (Eph. 1:4), and his 'purpose of election', before we were born must stand (Rom. 9:11). His purpose in our salvation by grace, not according to works, was 'before the ages began' (2 Tim. 1:9), an eternal purpose, proceeding from such a will that none can resist.

Whatever God has determined to be accomplished, according to the counsel of his wisdom and the good pleasure of his will, stands sure and immutable to the praise of his glory. So, the immutability of God's nature, his almighty power, the infallibility of his knowledge, his immunity from error in all his counsels—all these show that he never fails in accomplishing anything that he proposes for the manifestation of his glory.

JANUARY

Anchor of Hope

In Christ we have obtained an inheritance, having been predestined according to the purpose of him who works all things according to the counsel of his will.

EPHESIANS 1:11

When wicked robbers had stolen all Job's property, that holy man concluded, 'The LORD gave, and the LORD has taken away' (Job 1:21). The working of God's providence is so mighty and effectual, even in and over those actions in which the devil and human beings do most maliciously offend, that it may be said to be his work.

Nothing in the world is independent of his all-disposing hand; yes, Judas himself betraying our Saviour did nothing but 'whatever God's hand and plan had predestined to happen' (Acts 4:28). God works nothing by chance or accidentally, but all things determinately, according to his own decree or 'the counsel of his own will' (Eph. 1:11). Consider the prophecies in Scripture—especially those concerning our Saviour—how many free and contingent actions did concur for the fulfilling of them. The same may be said of other predictions, such as of the destruction of Jerusalem by the Babylonians, which though in regard of God's foreknowledge it was certainly to come to pass, yet they did it most freely, not only following the counsel of their own wills, but also using divination for their direction (Ezek. 21:21).

All this we believe to be a good part of the foundation of all that consolation which God is pleased to afford us in this vale of tears. Amidst all our afflictions and temptations, under whose pressure we should otherwise faint and despair, it is no small comfort to be assured that we do nor can suffer nothing but what his hand and counsel guides to us. This is a strong motive to patience, a sure anchor of hope, a firm ground of consolation.

JANUARY 4

Providence and Prayer

Turn my eyes from looking at worthless things; and give me life in your ways.

PSALM 119:37

Providence is an ineffable act or work of Almighty God, by which he cherishes, sustains, and governs the world, moving all created things in accordance with the natures that he gave them, to those ends which he has proposed.

It is not troublesome to God to take notice of all that he has created. 'Not a sparrow falls to the ground without our Father' and 'even the hairs of your head are all numbered' (Matt. 10:29-30). Behold his knowledge and care of all! He powerfully overrules all events, arranging them to certain ends for the manifestation of his glory. So Joseph tells his brethren, 'As for you, you planned evil against me; but God planned it for good, to bring it about that many people should be kept alive, as they are today' (Gen. 50:20).

In innumerable places, it is clear that his providence rules in the counsels of mankind and their most secret resolutions. The working of his providence is effectual even in the hearts and wills of individuals to turn them whichever way he wants, and to determine them to this or that in particular.

Sometimes the saints of God pray that God would be pleased thus to determine their hearts, and bend their wills, and wholly incline them to something. So David says in Psalm 119:36, 'Incline my heart to your testimonies, and not to unjust gain!' This prayer being his may also be ours, and we may ask it in faith, relying on the power and promise of God in Christ that he will perform our petitions (John 14:14)—not just by a general influence, but by a powerful bending of the heart and soul.

JANUARY 5

Secret and Revealed

The secret things belong to the LORD our God, but the things that are revealed belong to us and to our children forever, that we may do all the words of this law.

DEUTERONOMY 29:29

The secret will of God is his eternal, unchangeable purpose concerning all things which he has made, to be brought by certain means to their appointed ends. He himself affirms, 'My counsel shall stand, and I will accomplish all that I please' (Isa. 46:10). Some call this the absolute, efficacious will of God, the will of his good pleasure, always fulfilled. This is the only proper, eternal, constant, immutable will of God, whose order can neither be broken nor its law transgressed, so long as with him there is neither change nor shadow of turning.

The revealed will of God contains not his purpose and decree, but our duty—not what *he* will do according to his good pleasure, but what *we* should do if we will please him. This, consisting in his word, his precepts and promises, belongs to us and our children, that we may do the will of God.

'This is the will of him that sent me, that everyone who sees the Son, and believes in him, may have everlasting life,' says our Saviour (John 6:40). This is what his will has appointed. God's will is the rule of our obedience, and transgression of this will makes an action sinful; for 'sin is the transgression of a law' (1 John 3:4).

Now, God has not imposed on us the observation of his eternal decree and intention. It is utterly impossible for us to transgress or frustrate that. A master requires of his servant to do what he commands, not to accomplish what he intends, which perhaps he never revealed to him.

JANUARY 6

Chosen by Grace

God's firm foundation stands, bearing this seal: 'The Lord knows those who are his.'

2 TIMOTHY 2:19

The true doctrine of predestination has been clearly stated in the seventeenth article of our church: 'Predestination to life is the everlasting purpose of God, whereby, before the foundations of the world were laid, he has constantly decreed by his counsel, secret to us, to deliver from curse and damnation those whom he has chosen in Christ out of mankind, and to bring them by Christ to everlasting salvation.'

The article, in harmony with Scripture, affirms that it is an eternal decree, made before the foundations of the world were laid; so that by it we must need to be chosen before we were born, before we have done either good or evil. The words of the article are clear, and so also is the Scripture: 'He has chosen us in him before the foundation of the world' (Eph. 1:4). Now, from this it would undoubtedly follow that no good thing in us can be the cause of our election.

Secondly, the article affirms that election is *constant*—that is, one immutable decree; agreeably also to the Scriptures, that speak of the 'unchanging nature of God's purpose' (Heb. 6:17).

Thirdly, the article is clear that the object of this predestin-ation is *some particular people chosen out of mankind*; that is, it is such an act of God as concerns some people in particular, taking them, as it were, aside from the midst of their brethren, and designing them for some special end and purpose. The Scripture also abounds in asserting this truth, calling those who are so chosen a 'few' (Matt. 22:14), and 'a remnant chosen by grace' (Rom. 11:5); and those 'ordained to eternal life' (Acts 13:48).

JANUARY 7

Original Sin

Behold, I was brought forth in iniquity; and in sin did my mother conceived me.

PSALM 51:5

If anyone wants to know how serious the doctrine of original sin has always been considered in the church of Christ, let them consult the writings of those learned fathers whom God stirred up to resist, and enabled to overcome, the spreading Pelagian heresy. Or look into those many councils in which that heretical doctrine of denying this original corruption is condemned, cursed, and exploded.

Amongst the many motives they had to proceed so severely against this heresy, one especially deserves our consideration: it overthrew the necessity of Christ's coming into the world to redeem mankind. It is only sin that makes a Saviour necessary; and shall Christians tolerate such an error as, by direct consequence, infers the coming of Jesus Christ into the world to be needless? In this, some have fallen from the pure doctrine of the word of God, the consent of orthodox divines, and the confession of this church of England.

In the ninth article of our church, concerning original sin, I observe especially four things: first, that it is an inherent evil, the fault and corruption of the nature of everyone. Secondly, that it is a thing not subject or conformable to the law of God, but has in itself, even after baptism, the nature of sin. Thirdly, that by it we are opposed to God, and inclined to all manner of evil. Fourthly, that it deserves God's wrath and damnation.

All of these are frequently and evidently taught in the word of God. There is something in us, as soon as we are born, excluding us from the kingdom of heaven, so that unless we are born again, we shall not enter into it (John 3:5).

JANUARY 8

Original Perfection

God made man upright, but they have sought out many schemes.

ECCLESIASTES 7:29

It is not my intention to enter into any curious discourse concerning the state and grace of Adam before his fall, but only to give a faithful assent to what God himself affirmed of all the works of his hands—they were exceedingly good. No evil, no deformity, or anything tending towards that, came from that fountain of goodness and wisdom. Man, the most excellent work of his hands, the greatest glory of his Creator, was then without spot or blemish, endued with all those perfections his nature and state of obedience was capable of.

Nothing reveals more the deviation of our nature from its first institution, and declares the corruption with which we are polluted, than that propensity which is in us to everything that is evil. That inclination of the flesh which lusts always against the Spirit, which stirs up, conceives, hatches, brings forth, and nourishes sin; that perpetual proneness that is in unregenerate nature to everything that is contrary to the pure and holy law of God.

The Scripture, describing the condition of our nature at its first creation, intimates no such propensity to evil, but rather a holy perfection. We were created 'in the image of God' (Gen. 1:27)—in such a perfect uprightness as is opposite to all evil inventions. When to this image we are again in some measure 'renewed' by the grace of Christ (Col. 3:10), we see by the first-fruits that it consisted in 'true righteousness and holiness' (Eph. 4:24).

Our nature is now infected with an inclination to evil, and a lusting after that which is forbidden. Surely our nature was not at first yoked with such a troublesome inmate.

JANUARY 9

Christ's Precious Blood

He who did not spare his own Son but gave him up for us all,
how will he not also with him graciously give us all things?

ROMANS 8:32

Christians have, until now, believed that Christ made satisfaction for the sins of those for whom he died, that they themselves should not eternally suffer for them. Is God unjust, to punish twice for the same fault—his own Son once, and again the poor sinners for whom he suffered? I cannot conceive an intention in God that Christ should satisfy his justice for the sin of those who were in hell some thousands of years before, and yet still be resolved to continue their punishment to all eternity. No, Christ gives life to everyone for whom he gave his life.

We confess that 'blood of God' (Acts 20:28), of the 'Lamb without blemish or spot' (1 Pet. 1:19), was so exceedingly precious, of such infinite worth and value that it might have saved a thousand believing worlds. His death was of sufficient dignity to have been made a ransom for all the sins of everyone in the world. On this internal sufficiency of his death and passion is grounded the universality of gospel promises—which have no restriction that means they should not be made to all and everyone.

In some sense, Christ may be said to die for 'all', and 'the whole world'. The worth and value of his death was very sufficient to have been made a price for all their sins. And this word 'all' means some of all sorts (not for everyone of every sort), as it is frequently used in the holy Scripture. So where it is said that Christ 'died for all', it means either all the faithful, some of all sorts, or not only Jews but also Gentiles.

JANUARY 10

God's Work and Ours

Work out your own salvation with fear and trembling, for it is God who works in you, both to will and to work for his good pleasure.

PHILIPPIANS 2:12-13

In Deuteronomy 10:16, the Lord commands the Israelites to 'circumcise the foreskin of their hearts, and to be stubborn no more'. The circumcising of their hearts was a part of their obedience—it was their duty to do so, in obedience to God's command. And yet, in Deuteronomy 30:6, he affirms that 'the LORD your God will circumcise your heart ... so that you may live'. So, it seems, the same thing, in different respects, may be God's act in us and our duty towards him.

Ezekiel 18:31 says 'Make yourselves a new heart and a new spirit! Why will you die, O House of Israel?' The making of a new heart and a new spirit is here required under a promise of a reward of life, or a great threatening of eternal death. So this must be a part of their duty and obedience. And yet, in Ezekiel 36:26-27, God affirms that he will do this very thing that here he requires of them: 'I will give you a new heart and put a new spirit in you.' In how many places, also, are we commanded to 'Fear the Lord!'? No one will deny this is our duty. And yet in Jeremiah 32:40, God promises that he will put his fear in our hearts, that we shall not depart from him.

Faith and repentance are also expressly attributed to the free donation of God. He 'granted to the Gentiles repentance that leads to life' (Acts 11:18). Faith is 'not of ourselves, it is the gift of God' (Eph. 2:8). We pray that he would give us what he commands us to have.

JANUARY 11

Unbelievers' Destiny

I am the way, and the truth, and the life. No-one comes to the Father except through me.

JOHN 14:6

The ancient people of God did not obtain salvation without faith in Christ. Neither can we grant this happiness without him to those who never had their special revelations of his will and heavenly instructions. We confess that the poor natural endeavours of the heathen do not lack their reward—either in this life, by outward prosperity and inward calmness of mind, or in the life to come by a lessening of the degrees of their torments; as Christ says 'they shall not be beaten with so many blows' (Luke 12:47-48). Yet we absolutely deny that there is any saving mercy of God towards them revealed in the Scripture, which should give us the least intimation of their attaining everlasting happiness.

Consider the corruption and universal disability of nature to do anything that is good: 'without Christ we can do nothing' (John 15:5). Consider the sinfulness of their best works and actions: 'the sacrifice of the wicked is an abomination to the Lord' (Prov. 15:8) and evil trees cannot bring forth good fruit (Matt. 7:16-17). But even apart from this, the word of God is plain, that 'without faith it is impossible to please God' (Heb. 11:6).

Paul shows that none are glorified except those who are called (Rom. 8:30). He also declares that all calling is carried out by the preaching of the word and gospel (Rom. 10:14-15). Put these two places together and it appears that no salvation can be granted to people on whom the Lord has so far poured out his indignation by depriving them of the knowledge of the sole means of salvation.

JANUARY 12

Freedom

Everyone who practises sin is a slave to sin. So if the Son sets you free, you will be free indeed.

JOHN 8:34, 36

We do not absolutely oppose free will. About words, we will not contend. We grant people, in the substance of all their actions, as much power, liberty, and freedom as a mere created nature is capable of. We grant as large a freedom and dominion to our wills over their own acts as a creature, subject to the supreme rule of God's providence, is capable of. We are endued with such a liberty of will as is free from all outward compulsion and inward necessity, having a power to choose and apply itself to that which seems good to it, in which it is a free choice. It is, however, subservient to the decree of God.

Now, call this power free will, or whatever you please. As long as you don't make it supreme, independent, and boundless, we are not at all troubled. Even in spiritual things, we deny that our wills are at all deprived of their proper liberty: but here we say, indeed, that we are not properly free until the Son makes us free. We do not claim such a liberty as should make us despise the grace of God, by which we may attain true liberty indeed.

Let us now look at the power of our free will in doing that which is morally good. We shall find not only an essential imperfection, inasmuch as it is created, but also that it is corrupted. Scripture has no such term as free will. The expressions it uses concerning our nature and all the faculties of it in this state of sin and unregeneration seem to imply the opposite—that we are in 'slavery' (Heb. 2:15), and 'dead in sins' (Eph. 2:1).

JANUARY 13

Foolish Tyranny

Can the Ethiopian change his skin or the leopard his spots?
Then also you can do good who are accustomed to do evil.

JEREMIAH 13:23

Being by nature dead in trespasses and sins, we have no power to prepare ourselves for the receiving of God's grace. What ability, I pray, does a dead man have to prepare himself for his resurrection? Can he collect his scattered dust, or renew his perished senses? We are all 'ungodly', and 'without strength', when Christ died for us (Rom. 5:6). Our understandings 'darkened, being alienated from the life of God through the ignorance that is in us, because of the hardness of our hearts' (Eph. 4:18). So void is the understanding of true knowledge, that 'the natural man does not accept the things of the Spirit of God; they are foolishness unto him' (1 Cor. 2:14). We are nothing but confounded and amazed at spiritual things.

We are not only blind in our understandings, but captives also to sin in our wills. We are 'servants of sin' (John 8:34)—'free' only in our obedience to that tyrant (Rom. 6:20). Indeed, all our affections are wholly corrupted, for 'every imagination of the thoughts of their hearts were only evil all the time' (Gen. 6:5).

There is not only an *impotence* but an *enmity* in our corrupted nature to anything spiritually good. The things that are of God are 'foolishness to a natural person' (1 Cor. 2:14). There is nothing that people hate more than that which they account as folly. They mock at it as a ridiculous drunkenness (Acts 2:13). If only our days did not yield us far too many obvious proofs of the universal opposition between light and darkness, breaking forth into a contempt of the gospel and all ways of godliness!

JANUARY 14

The Sweetness of Grace

All that the Father gives me will come to me, and whoever comes to me I will never cast out.

JOHN 6:37

I would not assert such an operation of grace as should, as it were, violently overcome the will of a person, and force them to obedience. This would be damaging to our liberty. Rather, I assert only what consists in such a sweet effectual working as infallibly promotes our conversion, makes us willing who before were unwilling, and obedient who were not obedient, that creates clean hearts and renews right spirits within us.

We do not affirm grace to be 'irresistible' as though it came upon the will with such an overflowing violence as to beat it down and subdue it by compulsion to something it by no means inclined to. But if that term must be used, it means, in our sense, only such an unconquerable efficacy of grace as always and infallibly produces its effect. For who is it that can 'withstand God' (Acts 11:17)? The operation of grace is resisted by no hard heart—because it mollifies the heart itself. It does not so much take away a power of resisting as give a will of obeying, by which the powerful impotence of resistance is removed. This brings new light to the understanding, new inclinations to the will, and new affections to the heart.

This is the infallible efficacy of grace. Our conversion is brought about by a divine, almighty action, which the will of a person will not, and therefore cannot resist. It is a 'new creation,' a 'resurrection', a 'new birth'. He that creates us does not persuade us to create ourselves, and neither have we any power to resist him as he does.

JANUARY 15

Original Religion

To Seth also a son was born, and he called his name Enosh. At that time people began to call upon the name of the LORD.

GENESIS 4:26

Before the giving of the law, the chief men among the servants of the true God, everyone in their own families, performed those things which they knew to be required by the *law of nature*, *tradition*, or *special revelation* (the unwritten word of those times). They instructed their children and servants in the knowledge of their creed concerning the nature and goodness of God, the Fall and sin of man, the use of sacrifices, and the promised seed (the sum of their religion). This we have delivered concerning Seth, Enoch, Noah, Abraham, Lot, Isaac, Jacob, Jethro, Job, and others.

To me, it seems evident that there were no determinate ministers of divine worship before the law; for where do we find any such office instituted? Where are the duties of those officers prescribed? Or were they of human invention? God would never allow that in any regard the will of the creature should be the measure of his honour and worship. *The law of nature* a long time prevailed for the worship of the one true God. The manner of this worship, people knew at first from the vocal instruction of Adam, full of the knowledge of divine things. This afterwards their children received from them by *tradition*, helped forward by such who received *particular revelations* in their generation, such as Noah, who was 'a preacher of righteousness' (2 Pet. 2:5). So knowledge of God's will increased.

The sum is, that before the giving of the law, everyone served God according to the knowledge they had of his will. Public performances were assigned to none, farther than the obligation of the law of nature to their duty in their own families.

JANUARY 16

Progressive Revelation

Long ago, at many times and in many ways, God spoke to our fathers by the prophets, but in these last days he has spoken to us by his Son.

HEBREWS 1:2

The administration of God's providence towards his church has been various, and the communication of himself to it at 'many times' has been 'in many ways'. It pleased him not to bring it to perfection but by degrees, as the earth brings forth fruit: 'first the blade, then the ear, and then the full corn in the ear' (Mark 4:28).

Thus, the church, before the giving of Moses' law, seems to have had two main *defects*, which the Lord at that time supplied: one in *discipline* or government, in that every family exercised the public worship of God within itself, which was first removed by establishing a consistory of elders; the other in the *doctrine*, wanting the rule of the written word, being directed by tradition, the manifold defects of which were made up for by a special revelation. To neither of these defects was the church since exposed.

The lights which God made are sufficient to rule the seasons for which they are ordained. As, in creating of the world, God 'made two great lights, the greater light to rule the day, and the lesser light to rule the night' (Gen. 1:16), so, in the erection of the new world of his church, he set up two great lights: the lesser light of the Old Testament to guide the night, the dark space of time under the law; and the greater light of the New Testament to rule the glorious day of the gospel. And these two lights sufficiently enlighten everyone who comes into this new world. There is no need of the false fire of tradition where God sets up such glorious lights.

JANUARY 17

A Royal Priesthood

You are a chosen race, a royal priesthood, a holy nation, a people for his own possession, that you may proclaim the excellencies of him who called you out of darkness into his marvellous light.

1 PETER 2:9

All faithful ministers of the gospel, inasmuch as they are ingrafted into Christ and are true believers, *may*, as all other true Christians, *be called priests*. This is because they are members of Christ, not ministers of the gospel. It respects their persons, not their function, or not them as such (see Rev. 1:6, 5:10, 20:6 and 1 Pet. 2:5, 9).

In the Old Testament, we find the Lord thus speaking to his people, 'You shall be to me a kingdom of priests and a holy nation' (Exod. 19:6). So it seems that there was then a twofold priesthood: a *ritual* priesthood, conferred upon the tribe of Levi; and a *royal* priesthood, belonging to the whole people. The first is quite abolished and swallowed up in the priesthood of Christ; but the other is carried over to us under the gospel, being ascribed to them and us, and everyone in covenant with God.

We have this title with reference to those who are without: for as those who were properly called priests had a nearer access unto God than the rest of the people, especially in his solemn worship, so all the people who are in covenant with God have such access to him by that covenant, in comparison of them that are without, that in respect of it they are said to be priests. We also have an interest in this title of priests *by virtue of our union with Christ*. Being one with our high priest, we also are priests. There is a twofold union between Christ and us: the one, by his taking upon him our nature; the other, by bestowing on us his Spirit.

JANUARY 18

No Excuses

Out of the mouth of babies and infants, you have established strength.

PSALM 8:2

What is the duty and privilege of the common people of Christianity in sacred things? Everyone is so far a minister of the gospel as to teach and declare the faith to others, even if they have no outward calling to ministry. No excuses of disability or any other impediment ought to be made. The Lord can and will supply all such defects.

This was Moses' case in Exodus 4:10-11: Moses said to the LORD, 'Oh, my Lord, I have never been eloquent, either in the past or since you have spoken to your servant, because I am slow of speech and slow of tongue.' Then the LORD said to him, 'Who made man's mouth? Who makes him mute, or deaf, or seeing, or blind? Is it not I, the LORD?' So also was it with the prophet Jeremiah. When God told him that he had ordained him a prophet to the nations, he replied, 'Ah, Lord GOD! Behold, I don't know how to speak, for I am only a young boy.' But the LORD said to him, 'Do not say, "I am only a young boy"; because you will go to all to whom I send you, and whatever I command you, you shall say.' (Jer. 1:6:7) The prophet Amos also rested upon this truth when he was questioned, although he was unfit for that heavenly employment either by education or course of life (Amos 7:14-15).

Nothing can excuse anyone from going with the message of him who can perfect his praise out of the mouths of babes and sucklings.

JANUARY 19

I Must Speak

*Speaking the truth in love, we are to grow up in every way
into him who is the head, into Christ.*

EPHESIANS 4:15

Consider what our Saviour said to St Peter in Luke 22:32,
'When you have turned back, strengthen thy brethren.' This,
containing nothing but an application of one of the prime
dictates of the law of nature, cannot, ought not, to be restricted
to people of any particular calling as such. St James also says,
'My brothers, if anyone among you errs from the truth and
someone brings them back, let them know that whoever brings
back a sinner from their wandering will save their soul from
death' (James 5:19-20). From these and the like places, it
appears to me that here is a general obligation on all Christians
to promote the conversion and instruction of sinners, and
people erring from the right way.

Amos says, 'The lion has roared! Who will not be afraid?
The Lord GOD has spoken! Who can but prophesy?' (Amos 3:8).
Jeremiah adds, 'If I say, "I will not mention him, and I will no
longer speak in his name", there is in my heart something like
a burning fire shut up in my bones. I am weary from holding it
in, and I cannot.' (Jer. 20:9). Peter and John answered the rulers
of the Jews, 'If it is right before God to listen to you rather than
to God, you judge. For we are not able, given what we have seen
and heard, but to speak.' (Acts 4:19-20).

From this, it appears that truth revealed to someone carries
along with it an immovable persuasion of conscience (which
is powerfully obligatory) that it ought to be published and
spoken to others. Although none may take advantage of this to
introduce confusion into our congregations.

JANUARY 20

The People's Duty

The law of the LORD is perfect, reviving the soul; the testimony of the LORD is sure, making wise the simple.

PSALM 19:7

What should private Christians, living in a pure, orthodox, well-ordered church, do? How far should they interest themselves in holy, soul-concerning affairs, both in respect of their own particular souls and those of their brethren in the midst of whom they live?

First, let there be a *diligent searching* of the Scriptures, with fervent prayers to Almighty God for the taking away of that veil of ignorance which by nature is before their eyes. That they may come to a saving knowledge in and a right understanding of them, is not only *lawful* and *convenient* for all who profess the name of Christ, but also absolutely *necessary.*

Secondly, they may also examine and *try by them the doctrine that publicly is taught to them.* The people of God must not be like 'children, tossed to and fro, carried about by every wind of doctrine' (Eph. 4:14). All that is spoken in the pulpit presently is not gospel. Now, what shall the people of God do in such a case? Must they not beware of false prophets, which come unto them in sheep's clothing, but inwardly are ravening wolves?

In these evil days we live in, I hear many daily complaining that there are such disagreements among preachers, they know not what to do nor scarce what to believe. My answer is: Do but your own duty, and this trouble is at an end. Pin not your faith upon people's opinions; the Bible is the touchstone. That there is such diversity amongst teachers is their fault, who should think all the same thing; but that this is so troublesome to you is your own fault, for neglecting your duty of trying all things by the word.

JANUARY 21

Public Ministry

We ask you, brothers, to respect those who labour among you and are over you in the Lord and admonish you, and to esteem them very highly in love because of their work.

1 THESSALONIANS 5:12-13

For a *public, formal, ministerial teaching*, two things are required in the teacher: *first, Gifts from God; secondly, Authority* from the church (I speak now of ordinary cases). Those who lack either are no true pastors. For the first, God sends none upon an employment but whom he fits with gifts for it. And for the others, that want authority from the church, neither ought they to undertake any formal act properly belonging to the ministry, such as is solemn teaching of the word. The blessing on the word is promised only to sent teachers (Rom. 10:14-15). In a word, if our Saviour Christ be the God of order, he has not left his church to confusion.

No one, under a pretence of Christian liberty and freedom of conscience, should cast away all brotherly amity, and cut themselves off from the communion of the church. Christ has not purchased a liberty for any to tear his body in pieces. They will prove at length to be no duties of piety which break the sacred bonds of charity. People ought not, under a pretence of congregating themselves to serve their God, separate from their brethren, neglecting the public assemblies, as was the manner of some rebuked by the apostle (Heb. 10:25). There are peculiar blessings and transcendent privileges associated with public assemblies, which are not attached to private gatherings.

Ministers ought to have from us that regard, respect, and obedience, which is due to their labours in that sacred calling. Let not them who despise a faithful, careful minister in public, flatter themselves with hope of a blessing on their endeavours in private.

JANUARY 22

The Gospel Withheld

A vision appeared to Paul in the night: a man of Macedonia was standing there, urging him and saying, 'Come over to Macedonia and help us!'

ACTS 16:9

In this chapter of which we treat, the gospel is forbidden to be preached in Asia and Bithynia. This restraint, the Lord by his providence as yet continues to many parts of the world. Now, the reason and regulation of this is given in Romans 9:22, 'What if God, willing to show his wrath, and to make his power known, endured with much long-suffering the vessels of wrath fitted to destruction?' placed alongside Matthew 11:25-26, 'You have hidden these things from the wise and prudent. Yes, Father, for so it seemed good in your sight.' Acts 14:16 says he 'suffered all nations to walk in their own ways.'

God is no more the cause of their sins, for which they incur damnation, than the sun is the cause of cold and darkness, which follow when it is absent. He is not the cause of a man's imprisonment for debt, who will not pay his debt for him, though he is in no way obliged to do so. So, then, the not sending of the gospel to any people, is an act regulated by that eternal purpose of God by which he determines to advance the glory of his justice, by permitting some people to sin, to continue in their sin, and for sin to send them to their own place. A king not sending a pardon to condemned criminals shows that it is an issue of his purpose that they shall die for their faults.

When you see the gospel strangely, and through wonderful varieties and unexpected providences, carried away from a people, know that the spirit which moves in those wheels is that purpose of God which we have recounted.

JANUARY 23

Purpose of Grace

When the Gentiles heard the gospel, they began rejoicing and glorifying the word of the Lord, and as many as were appointed to eternal life believed.

ACTS 13:48

God's purpose is to save some in and by Jesus Christ, effectually to bring them to himself, for the praise of his glorious grace. God knows those who have the seal of the Lord stamped on them. He owns them as his, and to them he will cause his gospel to be revealed. Paul is commanded to abide at Corinth, and to preach there, because God had many people in that city (Acts 18:10). Though the devil had them in present possession, yet they were God's in his eternal counsel.

Have you never seen the gospel hover about a nation, now and then about to settle, and soon scared and upon wing again—yet working through difficulties, making plains of mountains and filling valleys, overthrowing armies, putting enemies to flight, and at length taking firm root like the cedars of God? Truly if you have not, you are strangers to England. Now, what is all this but the working of *the purpose* of God to attain its proposed end, of gathering his saints to himself?

In the effectual working of grace for conversion and salvation, why should it be directed to John, not Judas, and Simon Peter, not Simon Magus? Why, only from this discriminating counsel of God from eternity, to bring the one and not the other to himself by Christ? Their fore-ordination to eternal life gives them a right to faith and belief. 'The Lord added to the church such as should be saved' (Acts 2:47). The purpose of saving is the rule of adding to the church of believers. The purpose of God's election is the rule of dispensing saving grace.

JANUARY 24

Light after Darkness

The name of the LORD is a strong tower; the righteous man runs into it and is safe.

PROVERBS 18:10

Learn to look upon the wisdom of God in carrying all things through this wonderful variety, exactly to answer his own eternal purpose. He suffers so many mountains to lie in the way of reforming his churches and settling the gospel, that his Spirit may have the glory, and his people the comfort in their removal. It is a high and noble contemplation, to consider the purposes of God, so far as by the event revealed, and to see what impressions his wisdom and power leave upon things accomplished here below—to read in them a temporal history of his eternal counsels.

There are many things of light, for our good, which he has brought forth out of all that darkness with which we have been overclouded. If there had been no difficulties, there would have been no deliverances. Did we never find our hearts so enlarged towards God upon such advantages? Had there been no tempests and storms, we would not have made for shelter. Did you never run to a tree for shelter in a storm, and find fruit which you expected not? Did you never go to God for safeguard in these times, driven by outward storms, and there find unexpected fruit, the 'peaceable fruit of righteousness' (Heb. 12:11) that made you say, 'Happy tempest, which cast me into such a harbour'? It was a storm that occasioned the discovery of the golden mines of India. Has not a storm driven some to the discovery of the richer mines of the love of God in Christ?

JANUARY 25

Gracious Continuance

If the Lord of hosts had not left us a few survivors, we should have been like Sodom, and become like Gomorrah.

ISAIAH 1:9

No nation as yet enjoyed the word that deserved the continuance of the word. God always has something against a people, which makes the continuing of his grace to be of grace, the not removing of his love to be merely of love, and the preaching of the gospel to be free and undeserved. Though there was work and labour and patience for Christ's sake at Ephesus, yet there was a matter against Ephesus for which he might justly remove his candlestick (Rev. 2:4-5). If he does not remove it, that is due to the same mercy that first set it there.

He bears with our manners, whilst we grieve his Spirit. Look upon the face of this kingdom, and view the body of the people. Think of the profaneness, villainy, trampling upon the blood of Jesus, ignorance, contempt of God and his ways, despising his ordinances, reviling his servants, defaming the power of godliness, persecuting and tearing one another. And yet hear also the joyful sound of the word in every corner. You will quickly conclude that you see a great fight of God's love against our sins, and not of our goodness deserving his love.

God, in his just judgment of late ages, had sent upon the western world the efficacy of error, that they should believe lies, because they received not the love of the truth. How is it that this island glories in a reformation, and Spain still sits in darkness? Is it because we were better than they, or less engaged in antichristian delusions? Nothing but the good pleasure of God, and Christ freely coming to refine us, caused this distinction.

JANUARY 26

Gospel Famine

Those who seek the Lord lack no good thing.

PSALM 34:10

No one in the world needs help like those who lack the gospel. Of all distresses, lack of the gospel cries the loudest for relief. Those who lack the gospel may truly cry, 'Give us the gospel, or we die!'—and that not temporally with Ishmael, for want of water (Gen. 21:15-16), but eternally in flames of fire.

A person may lack liberty, and yet be happy, as Joseph was; a person may lack peace, and yet be happy, as David was; someone may lack children, and yet be blessed, as Job was; someone may lack plenty, and yet be full of comfort, as Micaiah was. But the one who lacks the gospel, lacks everything that should do them good. A throne without the gospel is but the devil's dungeon. Wealth without the gospel is fuel for hell. Advancement without the gospel is but a going high to have the greater fall.

When Elisha was minded to do something for the Shunammite woman who had so kindly entertained him, he asked her whether he should speak for her to the king or the captain of the host. She replied that she did not need those things. But when he found her to want a child, and spoke to her about that, she was almost transported. Ah! How many poor souls are there who need not our word to the king or the captain of the host, but yet being gospel-less, if you could tell them of that, would be even ravished with joy!

Think of Adam after his fall, before the promise, hiding himself from God, and you have a perfect portrait of a poor creature without the gospel.

JANUARY 27

Avoid Heresies

I appeal to you, brothers, to watch out for those who cause divisions and create obstacles contrary to the doctrine that you have been taught; avoid them.

ROMANS 16:17

Heresies and errors ought not to be tolerated. People ought not to connive at, or comply with, those ways and opinions which they are convinced are false, erroneous, contrary to sound doctrine. This is especially so if they are credibly supposed to shake any fundamentals of the common faith. Rather, with all their strength and abilities, in all lawful ways, upon every just call, people ought to oppose, suppress, and overthrow them—to root them up and cast them out, that they may not, as noxious weeds and tares, overgrow and choke the good corn, amongst which they are covertly scattered.

All predictions of 'false Christs, false prophets, false teachers to come', are to be avoided. Heed all cautions to 'try spirits, avoid heretics, beware of seducers, keep close to the truth received, avoid endless disputes, strife of words, old fables, languishing about unprofitable questions'. There are many descriptions of heresies—they are 'pernicious, damnable, diseases, works of the flesh', and the like. These are all encouragements to us to apply all expedient means for the removal of these stumbling-blocks.

Let the Scriptures be searched, and all ways embraced which the gospel holds forth for the discovering, convincing, silencing, reproving, confuting of errors and persons erring, by admonitions, reproofs, mighty Scripture convictions, and evidencing of the truth. Let this be done with fervent prayers to Almighty God, the God of truth, that he would give us one heart and one way. If these weapons of our warfare do not prevail, we must let them know that one day their disobedience will be revenged with being cut off, and 'cast out as unprofitable branches, fit to be cast into the fire'.

JANUARY 28

Godly Ministers

True instruction was in his mouth, and no wrong was found on his lips. He walked with me in peace and uprightness, and he turned many from iniquity.

MALACHI 2:6

That an exemplary life was ever required in the dispensers of holy things, both under the Old Testament and New, is apparent. The glorious vestments of the old ministering priests, the soundness and integrity of their person, without imperfection or blemish, with many other ornaments—these pointed forwards to Jesus Christ, yet did not obscurely set out the purity and holiness required in the priests themselves. In the New Testament, the shining of their light in all good works is eminently required (Matt. 5:16), and this not only that no offence be taken at the ways of God, and his worship administered by them, but also that those who are outside the church may be convinced (1 Tim. 3:7), and the churches directed in the practice of all the will and mind of God by them revealed.

A pastor's life should be vocal; sermons must be practised as well as preached. Though Noah's workmen built the ark, yet they themselves were drowned. God will not accept of the tongue where the devil has the soul. Jesus himself did 'do and teach' (Acts 1:1). If pastors teach uprightly and walk crookedly, more will fall down in the night because of their lives than they built in the day by their doctrine.

Now, as to the completing of the exemplary life of a minister, it is required that the principle of it be that of the life of Christ in him (Gal. 2:20), that when he has taught others he be not himself 'a cast-away' (1 Cor. 9:27).

JANUARY 29

Pastoral Loyalty

Therefore I endure everything for the sake of the elect, that they also may obtain the salvation that is in Christ Jesus with eternal glory.

2 TIMOTHY 2:10

People must adhere to their pastors and abide by them in all trials and persecutions for the word. A common cause should be carried on by common assistance. That which concerns all should be supported by all. When persecution arises for the word's sake, generally it begins with the leaders. The common way to scatter the sheep is by smiting the shepherds (Zech. 13:7-8). It is for the church's sake they are reviled and persecuted (Col. 1:24) and, therefore, it is the church's duty to share with them and help to bear their burden.

All the fault in scattering congregations has not been in ministers; the people did not stand by them in their trial. The Lord lay it not to their charge! The captain is betrayed and forced to mean conditions with his enemy who, going on with the assurance of being followed by his soldiers, finds, on looking back, that they have all run away when danger arose. In England, usually, no sooner had persecution laid hold of a minister, but the people willingly received another, perhaps a wolf, instead of a shepherd. Should a wife forsake her husband because he is come into trouble for her sake?

Whilst a pastor lives, if they suffer for the truth, the church cannot desert them, nor cease the performance of all required duties, without horrid contempt of the ordinances of Jesus Christ. This is a burden that is commonly laid on the shoulders of ministers, that for no cause whatsoever they must leave their charge, when those that laid it on them often freely leave them and their ministry without any cause at all.

JANUARY 30

Unity and Divisions

In the last time there will be scoffers, following their own ungodly passions. It is these who cause divisions, worldly people, devoid of the Spirit.

JUDE 18-19

Unity is the main aim and most proper fruit of love; neither is there any thing or duty of the saints in the gospel pressed with more earnestness and vehemency of exhortation than this. Purely *spiritual* unity we have by participation in the same Spirit of grace, and fellowship in the same Christ—one head to all. This we have with all the saints in the world, in whatever condition they are; yes, even with those that are departed, sitting down in the kingdom of heaven with Abraham, Isaac, and Jacob.

If the preservation of unity ought to be our aim, then certainly the causes and causers of division ought to be avoided. From such turn away. There is a generation whose tongues seem to be controlled by the devil; James calls it, 'set on fire by hell' (James 3:6). As though they were the mere offspring of serpents, they delight in nothing but in the fire of contention; disputing, quarrelling, backbiting, and endless strivings are what they live on. Note such people, and avoid them. Generally, they are people of private interests, fleshly ends, high conceits, and proud spirits.

Christians must choose the good, and refuse the evil. In order to exercise this duty aright, they must get their senses exercised in the word, 'to discern good and evil' (Heb. 5:14). They must especially get from the Scripture a 'form of sound words' (2 Tim. 1:13), of the main truths of the gospel and fundamental articles of religion, so that when they hear the opposite, they may turn away from the one who brings it, and not bid them 'God-speed' (2 John 10).

JANUARY 31

Spiritual Equality

My brothers, show no partiality as you hold the faith in our glorious Lord Jesus Christ.

JAMES 2:1

In church affairs we must make no difference between people, but condescend to the meanest persons and services for the use of the brethren. Where the Lord has not distinguished, neither should we. In Jesus Christ there is neither rich nor poor, high nor low, but a new creature. Generally, 'God hath chosen the poor of this world to confound the mighty' (1 Cor. 1:27).

Experience shows us that not many great, not many wise, not many mighty after the flesh, are partakers of the heavenly calling. Not that the gospel of Christ in any way opposes or takes away those many differences and distinctions among the sons of men caused by power, authority, earthly blessings, or age, according to the institution and appointment of God, with all that respect, reverence, duty, obedience, and subjection due to persons in those distinctions. It only declares that in things purely spiritual, these outward things are of no value or esteem. People in the church are considered as saints, and not as great or rich. All are equal, all are naked, before God.

We are brethren in the same family, servants of the same Master, employed about the same work, animated by the same precious faith, enjoying the same purchased privileges, expecting the same reward and eternal abode. Let the greatest, then, account it their greatest honour to perform the meanest necessary service to the meanest of the saints. A community in all spiritual advantages should give equality in spiritual affairs. Not the one who is richest, not the one who is poorest, but the one who is humblest, is accepted before the Lord.

FEBRUARY

This month, we will be reading from Owen's works published in the tumultuous years of 1648–49. As a Parliamentary army laid siege to Royalist forces occupying Colchester during the civil war, General Fairfax made his headquarters in Coggeshall, where Owen was now pastor. Owen acted as chaplain to the famous and victorious soldier, and when the siege was over, he preached two sermons at thanksgiving services for the victory, on Habakkuk 3:1-9, called 'Eben-ezer: a Memorial of the Deliverance of Essex, County, and Committee'.

That same year, Owen also put pen to paper in defence of the doctrine of definite atonement or particular redemption in a book called *The Death of Death in the Death of Christ*. This has remained one of his most popular—and also controversial—works ever since.

In January 1649, the civil wars were finally brought to a dramatic end as King Charles I himself was convicted of treason and beheaded. Parliament invited Owen to be their preacher as they assembled for the first time without a monarch. What does one preach the day after the execution of a king? When publishing the infamous sermon, Owen also added a discourse on toleration.

Later that same year, Owen addressed the honourable members of Parliament again, along with senior army officers, on Hebrews 12:27, in a sermon for revolutionary times aptly entitled 'The Shaking and Translating of Heaven and Earth'. After this, Oliver Cromwell insisted that Owen accompany him on his fateful campaign to Ireland (along with Owen's younger brother who was in the army). Here then, we begin to see Owen moving out of the local sphere, and more and more into the national spotlight, during a period of significant upheaval and uncertainty.

FEBRUARY 1

Desperate Prayer

Hear my cry, O God, listen to my prayer; from the end of the earth I call to you when my heart is faint. Lead me to the rock that is higher than I, for you have been my refuge, a strong tower against the enemy.

PSALM 61:1-3

Prayer is the believer's constant, sure retreat in an evil time, in a time of trouble. It is the righteous person's wings to the 'name of the Lord', a 'strong tower' (Prov. 18:10), a Christian soldier's sure reserve in the day of battle. If all other forces are overthrown, here they will stand by it, and no power under heaven can prevail upon them to give one step backward. Hence, that title of Psalm 102, 'A prayer of the afflicted, when he is overwhelmed.' It is the overwhelmed believer's refuge and employment. When they 'faint with anguish', this fetches them to life again. In our greatest distresses let neither unbelief nor self-contrivances jostle us out of this way to the rock of our salvation.

A messenger has done only half their business if they deliver their errand but do not return an answer. Those who bring God's message of threats to his people, must return his people's message of entreaties unto him. Some think they have fairly discharged their duty when they have revealed the will of God to people, without labouring to reveal the condition and desires of people unto God. Those who are more frequent in the pulpit *to* their people than they are in private prayer *for* their people, are but sorry watchmen. Where there is a burden upon the people, there must be a prayer for the people. Woe to them who have denounced desolations, and not poured out supplications! Such people delight in the evil which the prophet Jeremiah puts far from him: 'I have not desired the day of distress' (Jer. 17:16).

FEBRUARY 2

Wind in the Sails

For the moment all discipline seems painful, rather than pleasant, but later it yields the peaceful fruit of righteousness to those who have been trained by it.

HEBREWS 12:11

We must fill all our sails towards God at once, and *exercise all our affections*. I have heard that a full wind behind the ship does not drive her forward so fast as a side wind which seems almost so much against her as with her. The reason, they say, is because a full wind only fills some of her sails, which keep it from the rest, which are empty. But a side wind fills all her sails, and sets her speedily forward. Whichever way we go in this world, our affections are our sails; and as they are spread and filled, so we pass on, swifter or slower, to wherever we are steering.

Now, if the Lord should give us a full wind, and a continual gale of mercies, it would only fill some of our sails, some of our affections—joy, delight, and the like. But when he gives us a side wind—something which seems almost as much against us as for us—then he fills all our sails, takes up all our affections, making his works wide and broad enough to engage everyone. Then we are carried freely and fully towards the haven where we would be.

A song upon Shigionoth (Hab. 3:1) leaves not one string of our affections untuned. It is a song that reaches every line of our hearts, to be framed by the grace and Spirit of God. Hope, fear, reverence, with humility and repentance, have a share in this; as well as joy, delight, and love, with thankfulness. Changing situations take up all our affections, with all our graces; for they are gracious affections, exercised and seasoned with grace, of which we speak.

FEBRUARY 3

Wait for the Lord

I wait for the LORD, my soul waits, and in his word I hope.

PSALM 130:5

They say some people can administer a poison that works imperceptibly over seven years to kill someone. But the great Physician of his church knows how to give his sin-sick people potions that shall work by degrees, and at such an appointed season take away all their iniquity. God will not continue his course of medicine to them one day beyond the recovery of their health. This is all the fruit of their afflictions, to take away their iniquities (Isa. 27:9), and when that is done, who shall keep bound what God would loosen? When sin is taken away from within, trouble must depart from without.

In every distress learn to wait with patience for this appointed time. 'The one who believes will not be in haste' (Isa. 28:16). 'If it is slow, wait for it; it will surely come; it will not delay' (Hab. 2:3). He who is infinitely good has appointed the time, and therefore it is best. He who is infinitely wise has determined the season, and therefore it is most suitable. He who is infinitely powerful has set it down, and therefore it shall be accomplished. Wait for it believing; wait for it praying; wait for it contending.

Waiting is not a lazy hope, a sluggish expectation. When Daniel knew the time had come, he prayed more earnestly (Dan. 9:2-3). You will say, perhaps, 'Why did he need to pray for it, when he knew the time was accomplished?' I answer: there was even more need then. Prayer helps the promise to bring forth. Because a woman's time is come, therefore shall she have no midwife? No, that's exactly when we provide her with one.

FEBRUARY 4

Stores of Mercy

Mary treasured up all these things, pondering them in her heart.

LUKE 2:19

All promises being made to every believer, and all mercies being the fruit of these promises, they must all belong to every believer. See what use you make of past mercies, deliverances, blessings, and promises. Carry them about with you by faith, that you may use them when you need to. Take a store of mercies along with you in every trial. Use them, or they will grow rusty, and not pass in heaven. Forget not your perils. Do not scatter away your treasure. Be rich in a heap of mercies—faith will make you so.

The love, the comfort, the benefit, of all former and future blessings are yours, if you know how to use them. Oh, how have we lost our mercies in every hedge and ditch! Have none of us skill to lay up the last eminent deliverance against a rainy day?

Learn how to make the poorest and most afflicted condition comfortable and full of joy. Stock your home, your sick-bed, by faith, with all sorts of mercies. They are the richest furniture in the world. Gather up what is already cast out, and fetch the rest from heaven. Bring the first-fruits of glory into your heart. See the Jews called, the residue of opposers subdued, the gospel exalted, Christ enthroned, all your sins pardoned, corruption conquered, glory enjoyed. Roll yourself in those golden streams every day. Let faith fetch in new and old, ancient mercies to support you, everlasting mercies for your consolation. Those who have faith, have all things.

FEBRUARY 5

Creation Bows

The earth quaked, the heavens poured down rain, before God, the One of Sinai.

PSALM 68:8

God often in the Scripture sets forth his power and majesty by the trembling of heaven and the shaking of the earth, the vanishing of mountains and the bowing of perpetual hills—the professed humble subjection of the most eminent parts of the creation. The sea shall fly, as afraid; the rocks, as weak, rend and crumble; the heavens shall be darkened; the mountains skip like rams, and the little hills like young sheep (Ps. 114:4).

The almighty Creator holds the whole frame of the building in his own hand, and makes what portion he pleases, and when he pleases, to tremble and vanish before him. Though many things are not capable of sense and reason, yet he will make them do such things as sense and reason should prompt the whole subjected creation to do—to teach those who are endued with sense and reason what their duty is.

See hence the stoutness of sinful hearts—more stubborn than the mountains, more flinty than the rocks, more senseless than the great deep. Friend, are you stronger than the mountain of Horeb? Yet that trembled at the presence of this mighty God, whom it never had provoked. Are your lusts like the streams of Jordan? Yet they ran back from his chariots of salvation. Are your corruptions more firmly seated on your soul than the mountains on their bases? Yet the mountains leaped like frighted sheep before that God against whom they had not sinned. And will you, a small handful of sinful dust, that has ten thousand times provoked the eyes of his glory, not tremble before him, coming on his horses and chariots of salvation—his mighty works and powerful word?

FEBRUARY 6

He Gives His Word

Into your hand I commit my spirit; you have redeemed me,
O LORD, faithful God.

PSALM 31:5

God has done everything 'as he promised' (Josh. 22:4; 2 Sam. 7:21). He brought out his people of old with a mighty hand, with temptations, signs, and wonders, and a stretched-out arm; and all because he would keep the oath which he had sworn, and the engagement which he had made to their fathers (Deut. 7:8). Whatever obstacles may have lain in the way, he has done it, and he will do it.

Take just one instance. It was the purpose of his heart to bring his elect home to himself, from their forlorn condition. This he engaged himself to do, assuring Adam of a recovery from the misery he was involved in by Satan's prevailing. This, surely, is no easy work. If the Lord will have it done, he must lay out all his attributes in the demonstration of them to the uttermost. His wisdom and power must bow their shoulders, as it were. His engaged love must be carried along through so many secret, mysterious marvels, as the angels themselves 'desire to look into' (1 Pet. 1:12) and shall forever adore. The effecting of it required that which man could not do, and God could not suffer; yet his wisdom will find out a way, that one who is both God and man shall both do it and suffer it. To make good his engagement to his elect, he spared not his only Son.

Now, this is a precedent for God's actions in all his other promises. Whatever it costs him, he will spare nothing to make them good to the uttermost.

FEBRUARY 7

If God so clothes the grass, which is alive in the field today, and tomorrow is thrown into the oven, how much more will he clothe you, O you of little faith!

LUKE 12:28

You that have received such great mercy, we that have seen it, and all who have heard the doctrine confirmed, let us learn to live by faith. Live above all things that are seen; subject them to the cross of Christ. Measure your condition by your interest in God's all-sufficiency. Do not in distress calculate what such and such things can effect, but what God has promised. Reckon upon that, for it shall come to pass. If you could only get this one thing by all your sufferings and dangers, to trust the Lord to the utmost extent of his promises, it would prove a blessed captivity. All carnal fears would then be conquered, all sinful compliances with wicked people removed.

Be exhorted to great thankfulness, you that have been made partakers of great deliverances. In great distresses, nature itself prompts the sons of men to make great promises. Do not come up short on any of your engagements. There is no greater revelation of a hypocritical frame, than to flatter the Lord in trouble, but then to decline upon deliverance, in cold blood. The Lord of heaven give you strength to make good all your resolutions, in all godliness and honesty, following hard after God in every known way of his.

Consider, if there is so much sweetness in a temporal deliverance, oh! what excellency is there in that eternal redemption which we have in the blood of Jesus! If we rejoice in being delivered from those who could have killed the body, what unspeakable rejoicing is there in that mercy by which we are freed from the wrath to come!

FEBRUARY 8

Salvation of Sinners

The saying is trustworthy and deserving of full acceptance, that Christ Jesus came into the world to save sinners.

1 TIMOTHY 1:15

Do you wish to know the *end* for which, and the *intention* with which, Christ came into the world? Let us ask Jesus himself (who knew his own mind, as also all the secrets of his Father's heart), and he will tell us that the 'Son of man came to save that which was lost,' (Luke 19:10)—to recover and save poor lost sinners. That was his intent and design.

Now, if you will ask who these sinners are towards whom he has this gracious intent and purpose, he himself tells you that he came to 'give his life a ransom for *many*' (Matt. 20:28). In other places the *many* are called *us*, believers, distinguished from the world: for he 'gave himself for *our* sins, that he might deliver *us* from this present evil *world*, according to the will of God and our Father' (Gal. 1:4). That was the will and intention of God, that he should give himself for *us*, that we might be saved, being separated from the world. 'He loved the church, and gave himself for it' (Eph. 5:25); 'He gave himself for us, that he might redeem us from all iniquity, and purify unto himself a peculiar people, zealous of good works' (Titus 2:14).

Thus clear, then, and apparent, is the intention and design of Christ and his Father in this great work—namely, to save us, to deliver us from the evil world, to purge and wash us, to make us holy, zealous, fruitful in good works, to render us acceptable, and to bring us unto God; for through him 'we have access into the grace wherein we stand' (Rom. 5:2).

FEBRUARY 9

Particular Redemption

Father, I desire that they also, whom you have given me, may be with me where I am, to see my glory.

JOHN 17:24

The death of Jesus Christ has achieved eternal redemption for all those that are concerned in it, consisting in grace here and glory hereafter. But there is a spreading persuasion that he died to redeem *all and every one*,—not only for *many*, his *church*, the *elect* of God, but for everyone. Now, the masters of this opinion do see full well and easily, that if *that* be the *end* of the death of Christ, then either, first, God and Christ failed in their proposed end, and did not accomplish that which they intended. This seems to us blasphemously injurious to the wisdom, power, and perfection of God, as likewise derogatory to the worth and value of the death of Christ. Second, if Christ died to redeem more than the church, then all people, all the posterity of Adam, must be saved, purged, sanctified, and glorified. But this, surely, they will not maintain, because the Scripture and the woeful experience of millions will not allow it.

Therefore, the only way to cast a tolerable colour upon their persuasion, is that they must and do deny that God or his Son had any such absolute aim or end in the death or blood-shedding of Jesus Christ as we before recounted; but that God intended nothing, neither was anything effected by Christ. They must say that no benefit arises to anyone immediately by his death but what is common to all and every soul, though never so cursedly unbelieving here and eternally damned hereafter—until the faith of some, *not* procured for them by Christ (for if it were, why don't they all have it?), distinguishes them from others.

FEBRUARY 10

Trinity in Action

I have come down from heaven, not to do my own will but the will of him who sent me.

JOHN 6:38

The agent in, and chief author of this great work of our redemption is the whole blessed Trinity. For all the outward works of the Deity are undivided and belong equally to each person, their distinct manner of subsistence and order being observed. It is true, there were various human instrumental causes in the passion of Christ, but the work cannot in any sense be ascribed unto them; for the issue of their endeavours was contrary to their own intentions, and in the close they did nothing but what the 'hand and counsel of God had before determined should be done' (Acts 4:28). They were in no way able to accomplish what they aimed at, for Christ himself laid down his life, and none was able to take it from him (John 10:17-18).

In the several persons of the holy Trinity, the joint author of the whole work, the Scripture proposes distinct acts or operations peculiarly assigned to them. According to our weak manner of apprehension, we will consider these severally and apart, beginning with those that are ascribed to the Father.

There are two particular acts in this work of our redemption by the blood of Jesus, which may be properly assigned to the person of the Father: First, the sending of his Son into the world for this employment. Secondly, a laying of the punishment due to our sin upon him. The Father loves the world, and sends his Son to die: He 'sent his Son into the world that the world through him might be saved' (John 3:17). Our Saviour describes himself as 'he whom the Father has sent' (John 10:36).

FEBRUARY 11

Our Saviour's Confidence

*The Lord GOD helps me; therefore I have not been disgraced;
therefore I set my face like a flint, and I know that I shall not
be put to shame.*

ISAIAH 50:7

The Father enters into a covenant and compact with his Son
concerning the work to be undertaken. There are two parts of this.
First, his promise to protect and assist him in the accomplishment
and perfect fulfilling of the whole business. The Father engaged
himself, that for his part, upon his Son's undertaking this great
work of redemption, he would not lack any assistance in trials,
strength against oppositions, encouragement against temptations,
and strong consolation in the midst of terrors. Christ then undertakes this heavy burden, so full of misery and trouble.

Hence arose that confidence of our Saviour in his greatest and
utmost trials. He was assured, by virtue of his Father's engagement
in this covenant, upon a treaty with him about the redemption
of mankind, that he would never leave him nor forsake him.
With what confidence, blessed Saviour, you underwent all this
shame and sorrow! With this assurance he was brought as a 'lamb
to the slaughter, and as a sheep before her shearers is dumb, so
he opened not his mouth' (Isa. 53:7). For 'when he was reviled,
he did not revile in return; when he suffered, he threatened not;
but committed himself to him that judges justly' (1 Pet. 2:23). So
the ground of our Saviour's confidence and assurance in this great
undertaking, and a strong motive to exercise his graces received in
the utmost endurance, was this engagement of his Father upon
this compact of assistance and protection.

This, then, our Saviour certainly aimed at, as being the
promise upon which he undertook the work,—the gathering of
the sons of God together, their being brought to God, and their
passing to eternal salvation.

FEBRUARY 12

All we like sheep have gone astray; we have turned—every one—to his own way; and the LORD has laid on him, the iniquity of us all.

ISAIAH 53:6

Laying upon Christ the punishment of sins is everywhere ascribed to the Father. 'He was stricken by God'; indeed, 'the Lord laid upon him the iniquity of us all' and 'it pleased the LORD to bruise him' (Isa. 53:4, 6, 10). Surely it was a close and strong trial, and that immediately from his Father, he now underwent; for how meekly and cheerfully did he submit, without any regret or trouble of spirit, to all the cruelty and violence offered to his body. He cries, 'My God, my God, why have you forsaken me?'

His sufferings were far from consisting in mere corporal afflictions. It was no more nor less than the curse of the law of God which he underwent for us, for he freed us from the curse 'by being made a curse' (Gal. 3:13), which contained all the punishment that was due to sin, either in the severity of God's justice, or according to the demand of that law which required obedience. In dying for us, Christ not only aimed at our good, but also directly died in our stead.

The punishment due to our sin and the chastisement of our peace was upon him—the pains of hell, in their nature and being, in their weight and pressure, which the justice of God will inevitably inflict to eternity upon sinners. Yet it seems strange to me that some say Christ underwent the pains of hell in the place of those who lay in the pains of hell before he underwent those pains, and shall continue in them to eternity. We affirm, rather, that Christ underwent the pains of hell for all the sins of all the elect in the world.

FEBRUARY 13

Christ's Prayers

Christ Jesus is the one who died—more than that, who was raised—who is at the right hand of God, who indeed is interceding for us.

ROMANS 8:34

Christ intercedes for all and every one of those for whom he gave himself up. He did not suffer for them, and then refuse to intercede for them; he did not do the greater, and omit the less. The price of our redemption is more precious in the eyes of God and his Son than that it should, as it were, be cast away on perishing souls, without any care taken of what becomes of them afterward.

Christ refused to pray for the world, in opposition to his elect. 'I pray for them,' says he. 'I pray not for the world, but for those you have given me' (John 17:9). There was no foundation for such an interceding for them, because he was not a sacrifice of propitiation for them. If he should intercede for all, all should undoubtedly be saved for 'he is able to save to the uttermost those who come to God through him, since he always lives to intercede for them' (Heb. 7:25).

This intercession is not a humble, dejected supplication, but an authoritative presenting himself before the throne of his Father, sprinkled with his own blood, saying, 'Father, I will that those whom you have given me should be with me where I am' (John 17:24). So that for whomsoever he suffered, he appears for them in heaven with his satisfaction and merit. So we may draw near with the full assurance of faith, for by one offering he has perfected forever those that are sanctified (Heb. 10:14).

FEBRUARY 14

The Spirit of Jesus

He was declared to be the Son of God in power according to the Spirit of holiness by his resurrection from the dead, Jesus Christ our Lord.

ROMANS 1:4

The Holy Spirit evidently concurred, in his own distinct operation, to all the grand parts of this work. First, in the *incarnation* of the Son, including his plenary assistance in the course of his life whilst he dwelt amongst us. For his mother was found 'to have conceived in her womb of the Holy Spirit' (Matt. 1:18). If you ask, with Mary, 'How that could be?', the angel answers, 'The Holy Spirit shall come upon you, and the power of the Most High shall overshadow you: therefore the holy one to be born shall be called the Son of God' (Luke 1:35). It was an overshadowing power in the Spirit: so called by an allusion taken from fowls that cover their eggs, that by their warmth, young may be hatched; for this conception was by the sole power of the Spirit. As this child was conceived by the power of the Spirit, so he was also filled with the Spirit, and 'became strong in Spirit' (Luke 1:80), until he was thoroughly furnished and fitted for his great undertaking with the gifts and graces of the Spirit.

Secondly, in his *passion*, we know how 'by the Eternal Spirit he offered himself without spot to God' (Heb. 9:14). The willing offering of himself through that Spirit was the eternal fire under this sacrifice, which made it acceptable unto God. Thirdly, in his *resurrection*; of which the apostle writes, 'But if the Spirit of him that raised up Jesus from the dead dwell in you, he that raised up Christ from the dead shall also quicken your mortal bodies by his Spirit that dwells in you' (Rom. 8:11).

FEBRUARY 15

Treasures of Wrath

I also will walk contrary to you and I myself will strike you sevenfold for your sins.

LEVITICUS 26:24

God's treasures of wrath against a sinful people have various consequences for the accomplishment of the appointed end. When God walks contrary to a people, it is not always in one path; he has seven ways to do it, and will do it seven times (Lev. 26:24). He strikes not always with one weapon, nor in one place. As he has various kinds of grace (1 Pet. 4:10)—love and compassion of every variety suited to our manifold poverties; so there is wrath 'stored up' or 'treasured' (Rom. 2:5), suiting itself in its flowings out to the provocations of stubborn sinners.

The first emblem of God's wrath against man was a 'flaming sword turning every way' (Gen. 3:24). Not only in one or two, but in all their paths, he meets them with his flaming sword. As a wild beast in a net (Isa. 51:20), so are sinners under inexorable judgments; the more they strive, the more they are enwrapped and entangled; they shuffle themselves from under one calamity, and fall into another: 'As if a man fled from a lion, only to meet a bear, or went into the house and rested his hand on the wall, only to be bitten by a snake' (Amos 5:19).

'Take this plague away!' says Pharaoh (Exod. 10:17). If he can escape from under this pressure, he thinks he shall be free; but when he fled from the lion, still the bear met him; and when he went into the house, the serpent bit him. And as the flaming sword turns every way, so God can put it into everything.

FEBRUARY 16

The Devil's Wages

Indeed, all who desire to live a godly life in Christ Jesus will be persecuted.

2 TIMOTHY 3:12

The instruments of God's greatest works and glory are often the chief objects of a professing people's cursing and opposition. There is nothing new under the sun: the reward which God's labourers may reap in this generation may be the same as always. Men who, under God, deliver a kingdom, may in turn experience the kingdom's curses for their pains.

When Moses had brought the people of Israel out of slavery, by that wonderful and unparalleled deliverance, he was forced to appear with the Lord for the destruction of Korah and his associates, who would have seduced the congregation to its utter ruin. At length, he received this reward for all his pains—all the congregation gathered themselves against him and Aaron, laying murder and sedition to their charge, telling them they had 'killed the people of the LORD' (Num. 16:41-42)—a goodly reward for all their travails.

If God's works do not please the lusts, prejudices, and interests of men, they will labour to give his instruments the devil's wages. Let not upright hearts sink because they meet with thankless men. To do good and suffer evil is to be a Christian. A person may have the blessing of God and the curse of a professing people at the same time. When we are condemned by people, we are acquitted by God as Tertullian says (*Apology* 50:16). Human condemnation and God's absolution often come to the same people, for the same things. If you labour to do the work of the Lord, do not think it strange if human curses are your rewards and detestation your wages.

FEBRUARY 17

False Expectations

*He had no form or majesty that we should look at him, and
no beauty that we should desire him.*
                                          ISAIAH 53:2

Faith can be weak when God's ways seem unfathomable to
us. Whilst people see the paths in which the Lord walks, they
can follow him through some difficulties; but when that is hid
from them, they are ready to faint and give up. God is pleased
sometimes to make darkness his covering and his secret place
(Ps. 18:11).

God's righteousness, his kindness, is like a great mountain
that is easy to be seen; no one can overlook it, unless they wilfully
shut their eyes. But his judgments are like the great deep. Who
can look into the bottom of the sea, or know what is done in the
depths of it? God's works are often so strange to us that, when
they have come to light, many have rejected and opposed them
because they are so surprising.

It is evident from the gospel that the people of the Jews were
full of expectation and longing for the great work of the coming
of the Messiah; yet when he came, because he did not match their
pre-imaginations, they rejected him, as having neither beauty
nor majesty to attract us to him (Isa. 53:2). And the prophet
Amos tells many who desired the day of the Lord, that that day
would be darkness to them, and not light (Amos 5:18, 20). So,
in every generation, many who desire the accomplishment of
God's work are shaken off from any share in it, by finding it
displeasing to their reason and expectations.

FEBRUARY 18

Hell on Earth

They are darkened in their understanding, alienated from the life of God because of the ignorance that is in them, due to their hardness of heart.

EPHESIANS 4:18

God gives helpers and deliverers to a sinful people; yet because of their provocations, some or all of them shall not taste of the deliverance to be procured by them. He sustains their lives in being, so they might have opportunity to know his mind and their own peace; yet he gives them a power to contend with their helpers. Being so exasperated and provoked, the Lord, who is free in all his dispensations, refuses to make out to them that healing grace by which they might be kept from a sinful opposition. Indeed, being justly provoked, and resolved that they should not taste of the plenty to come, he makes them foolish and giddy in their reasonings and counsels. He blinds them in their understandings, that they shall not be able to discern plain and evident things, tending to their own good, but in all their ways shall err like a drunken man in his vomit. He leaves them to contend for their own ruin.

The methods of sinful people's working in such opposition would take too long for me to declare. What prejudices are erected, what lusts pursued, what corrupt interests acted on and followed! How self is honoured, what false pretences coined, how God is slighted! Nothing is more loathsome and abominable than looking into the hell of these times. Let it suffice, that sinful self, sinful lusts, sinful prejudices, sinful blindness, sinful carnal fears, sinful corrupt interests, sinful fleshly reasonings, sinful passions, and vile affections, do all concur in such a work, are all woven up together in such a web.

FEBRUARY 19

As for a person who stirs up division, after warning him once and then twice, have nothing more to do with him.

TITUS 3:10

All Christians, almost, are heretics to some enjoying authority. For three hundred years, the church had no assistance from any magistrate against heretics; and yet, in all that space, there was not one long-lived or far-spreading heresy, compared to those that followed. As the disease is spiritual, so was the remedy which in those days was applied, and the Lord Jesus Christ made it effectual.

The expressions of the most ancient Christians concerning heretics are sharp and cutting; their avoiding of them, being admonished, was precise and severe; their confutations of them were laborious and diligent; their church censures and ejections were piercing and sharp. Communion amongst the churches was close, exact, and carefully preserved, so that a stubborn heretic was thrust out of Christian society. But there is not a syllable in their writings about corporeal punishment to be inflicted on them. Until Augustine was changed from his first resolution and persuasion, this doctrine had but poor footing in antiquity.

Some say that these Christians would have been of another mind had they enjoyed Christian magistrates. But that is so unworthy of them, that it would be wrong for me to try and defend such an idea. The spiritual sense of their sharp expressions is clear. John, they say, would not abide in a bath where Cerinthus the heretic, infected with Judaism and paganism, was; saying, 'Let us depart, lest the building fall on us where Cerinthus is!'

FEBRUARY 20

When he sits on the throne of his kingdom, he shall write for himself in a book a copy of this law. And it shall be with him, and he shall read in it all the days of his life, that he may learn to fear the LORD his God.

DEUTERONOMY 17:18-19

Magistrates, even as such, are bound to know the mind and will of God in the things which concern his honour and worship, as all people in general are. They are bound, I say, to know it. This obligation lies upon all creatures capable of knowing the Creator, according to the light which they have of him, and the means of revelation which they enjoy. They are supposed to have that most sovereign and supreme of all outward teachings, the word of God, with such other helps as are revealed by it, and appointed in it; so as they are bound to know the will of God in everything that concerns them. If they fail in this and come short of the truth, it is their sin—the defect being not in the manner of the revelation, but in the corruption of their darkened minds.

Now, that they are to make this inquiry in reference to his calling, is evident from the case of David in 2 Samuel 23:3, 'to rule over people in righteousness one must rule in the fear of God'. This fear is only taught by the word. Without a right knowledge of God and his mind, there can be no true fear of him. That command, also, for the Jewish magistrate to study it day and night, and to have the book of the law continually before him, because it was the rule of that civil polity of which he was under God the head and preserver, by analogy confirms this truth (see Deut. 17:18-19).

FEBRUARY 21

Protect the Word

All authority in heaven and earth has been given to me. Go therefore and make disciples of all nations.

MATTHEW 28:18-19

It belongs to the duty of the supreme magistrate, the governor or shepherd of the people in any nation to take care that the truth of the gospel be preached to all the people of that nation. God will quickly reject them from their power who, knowing their Master's will, are negligent in this.

As they are to declare it, so they are to protect it from all violence whatever. Jesus Christ is the great king of nations, as well as the holy king of saints. His gospel has a right to be preached in every nation, and to every creature under heaven. Whoever forbids or hinders the free passage of it, is not only sinful and impious towards God, but also injurious towards people. The right to preach and receive the gospel is superior to all other earthly privileges. The magistrate is to protect it, that under them we 'may lead a quiet and peaceable life, in all godliness and honesty' (1 Tim. 2:2).

For this cause, they to whom the sword is committed may with the sword lawfully defend the truth, as the undoubted right and privilege of those who do enjoy it, and of which they cannot be deprived without the greatest injury. It is the duty of the magistrate to protect and defend the gospel against all or any persons that, by force or violence, shall seek to hinder the progress or stop the passage of it, under any pretence. A neglect of this will be attended with the anger of the Lord, and the kindling of his wrath.

FEBRUARY 22

Perseverance

This phrase, 'Yet once more', indicates the removal of things that are shaken—that is, things that have been made—in order that the things that cannot be shaken may remain.

HEBREWS 12:27

The main design of the apostle in this Scripture to the Hebrews, is to prevail with his countrymen who had undertaken the profession of the gospel, to abide constantly and faithfully in it, without any apostasy into, or mixture with Judaism (which they and God had forsaken). In such backsliders, the soul of the Lord has no pleasure (Heb. 10:38).

Whoever undertakes this task, in any age, shall find it exceedingly weighty and difficult. It is to persuade Christians to hold out and continue in the glory of their profession to the end, that with patience doing the will of God they might receive the promise—especially if there are 'lions in the way' (Prov. 26:13) and they face opposition or persecution. Of all that deformity which has come upon us by the Fall, there is no defect more evident than instability of mind and inconstancy in embracing that which is spiritually good. Mankind being turned from its unchangeable rest, seeks to quiet and satiate its soul with restless movings towards changeable things.

He who works all our works *for* us and *in* us (Isa. 26:12), works them also *by* us (1 Thess. 1:3). Therefore, that which he will give, he persuades us to have, that his bounty and our duty may be manifest in the same thing. Of this nature is perseverance in the faith of Christ: by him it is promised, and therefore is a grace; so to us it is prescribed, and thereby is a duty.

FEBRUARY 23

Shaken!

*At that time his voice shook the earth, but now he has promised,
'Yet once more will I shake not only earth but also heavens.'*

HEBREWS 12:26

What are the things that are shaken? As the apostle here applies a part of the prophecy of Haggai (Hag. 2:6), so that prophecy, even in the next words, gives light into the meaning of the apostle. Look what heaven and earth the prophet speaks of. The Spirit of God in the Scripture is his own best interpreter. See, then, the order of the words as they lie in the prophet, 'I will shake heaven and earth: I will shake all nations.' God, then, shakes heaven and earth when he shakes all nations; that is, he shakes the heaven and earth *of the nations*.

The heavens of the nations, what are they?—even their political heights and glory, those forms of government which they have framed for themselves and their own interest, with the grandeur and lustre of their dominions. The nations' earth is the multitudes of their people, their strength and power, whereby their heavens, or political heights, are supported. It is, then, neither the material heavens and earth, nor yet Mosaical ordinances, but the political heights and splendour, the popular multitudes and strength, of the nations of the earth, that are thus to be shaken.

In the denunciations of the judgments of God through all the prophets, heaven, sun, moon, stars, and the like appearing beauties and glories of the heavens, are taken for governments, governors, dominions in political states.

The Lord Jesus Christ, by his mighty power, will so far shake and translate the political heights, governments, and strength of the nations, as shall serve for the full bringing in of his own peaceable kingdom—the nations so shaken becoming thereby a quiet habitation for the people of the Most High.

FEBRUARY 24

Unshaken!

The things that cannot be shaken may remain.

HEBREWS 12:27

What are 'the things that cannot be shaken'? They are called 'a kingdom that cannot be moved' (v. 28), a kingdom subject to none of those shakings and alterations which have tossed other dominions to and fro. Now this may be considered as purely internal and spiritual; which is the rule of his Spirit in the hearts of all his saints. This 'does not come in a way that you can observe', but is within us (Luke 17:20-21). It consists in 'righteousness, peace, and joy in the Holy Spirit' (Rom. 14:17). It may also be considered as external, and appearing in gospel administrations. So is Christ described as a king in the midst of their kingdom (Rev. 1:14-17).

The things that cannot be shaken are these:

First, the growth of righteousness, peace, and joy in the saints, being filled with light and love from the special presence of Christ; with a wonderful increase of the number of them, multitudes of the elect are going to be born in those days. The remnant of the Jews and fullness of the Gentiles will meet in one fold, and righteousness dwells there (2 Pet. 3:13).

Secondly, the administration of gospel ordinances, in power and purity, according to the appointment of the Lord Jesus, and acceptable to him.

Thirdly, the glorious and visible manifestation of those administrations in the eyes of all the world, in peace and quietness—none making afraid or hurting in the whole mountain of the Lord (Isa. 65:25).

FEBRUARY 25

Vengeance

O Sovereign Lord, holy and true, how long before you will judge and avenge our blood on those who dwell on the earth?

REVELATION 6:10

The kings of the earth have given their power to Antichrist, endeavouring to the utmost to keep the kingdom of Christ out of the world. What has been their main business for seven hundred years and upwards? How have they earned the titles 'Eldest Son of the Church', 'The Catholic and Most Christian King', 'Defender of the Faith', and the like? Has it not been by the blood of saints? Are there not, in every one of these kingdoms, the slain and the banished ones of Christ to answer for?

In particular, has not the blood of the saints of Jesus, Wickliffites and Lollards, cried from the ground for vengeance upon the English nation for a long season? Did not their bodies lie in the streets of France, under the names of Waldenses, Albigenses, and poor men of Lyons? Has not Germany and the annexed territories her Huss and Hussites to answer for? Is not Spain's inquisition enough to ruin a world, much more a kingdom? Have not all these, and all the kingdoms round about, washed their hands and garments in the blood of thousands of Protestants? And do not the kings of all these nations as yet stand up in the place of their ancestors with the same implacable enmity to the power of the gospel?

For the present, the government of the nations is purely framed for the interest of Antichrist. No kind of government in Europe, or line of governors, is so ancient but that the beast is as old as they, and had a great influence on their constitution or establishment, to provide that it might be for his own interest.

FEBRUARY 26

Signs

You hypocrites! You know how to interpret the appearance of earth and sky, but why do you not know how to interpret the present time?

LUKE 12:56

Our Saviour gives a sure testimony to the Pharisees' hypocrisy in Luke 12:54-56. They were wise in earthly things, and had drawn out experiences, by long observation, of what was likely to come to pass regarding the weather; but despite all their pretences, and possession of Moses' chair, despite mighty signs and the accomplishment of prophecies all pointing to the instant establishment of the kingdom of God in the coming of the Messiah, they could not discern them at all. Instead, they come to him and cry 'If you are the Christ, give us a sign!' Heaven and earth were full of signs round about them.

People who will not receive God's signs imagine that they would be wonderfully proficient if only they might have signs of their own fancying. The rich glutton thought that if his way of teaching might have been set up by people rising from the dead, there would have been a world of converts, more than were made by preaching the word of God (Luke 16:29-30). People suppose that if God from heaven should provide some obvious sign, oh, how abundantly should they then be satisfied!

The truth is, the same lust and corruption that makes them disbelieve God's signs, moves them to look for signs of their own. For this very thing, then, were the Pharisees branded as hypocrites. I pray God none such be found in our day.

FEBRUARY 27

Sinful Cares

*The cares of the world and the deceitfulness of riches choke the
word, and it proves unfruitful.*

MATTHEW 13:22

Many are taken up with sinful cares—anxious and dubious
thoughts about such things as, perhaps, the Lord intends utterly
to destroy, or, at least, render useless. Wouldn't it have been the
greatest folly in the world for Noah and his sons, when the flood
was approaching to sweep away the creatures from the face of
the earth, to have been overly concerned about flocks and herds
that were speedily to be destroyed? Even today, many people's
thoughts devour them about things which, if they knew the
season, would be contemptible to them.

Would you labour for honour, if you knew that God was
at this time labouring to lay all the 'honour of the earth in the
dust?' (Isa. 23:9) Could you set your heart on the increase of
riches, if you understood that God intends instantly to make
'silver as common as stones, and cedars as plentiful as sycamores'
(1 Kings 10:27)? Would our spirits sink for fear of this or that
persecutor or oppressor, if it was revealed to us that in a short
time 'nothing shall hurt or destroy in the whole mountain of the
Lord'? (Isa. 65:25) Would we tremble at the force and power
of this or that growing monarchy giving its power to the Beast,
if God revealed to us that he was going to shake it until it was
changed? Certain it is, that the root of all the sinful cares which
are sometimes ready to devour the hearts of God's people, is this
unacquainted-ness with the work and mind of the Lord.

FEBRUARY 28

False Christs

The kingdom of God is not a matter of eating and drinking, but of righteousness and peace and joy in the Holy Spirit.

ROMANS 14:17

Give the Lord Jesus a throne in your hearts, or it will not at all be to your advantage that he has a throne and kingdom in the world. Perhaps you will see the plenty of it, but not taste one morsel. Take first that which does not come in a way you can observe, that which is within you, which is 'righteousness, and peace, and joy in the Holy Spirit'. Take it in its power, and you will be the better enabled to observe it coming in its glory. 'Seek first this kingdom of God, and its righteousness, and all these things shall be added to you.'

Oh, that it were the will of God to put an end to all that pretended holiness, hypocritical humiliation, and self-interested religion, that have been among us. We have flattered God with our lips, whilst our hearts have been far from him! Oh, that it might be the glory of this assembly, above all the assemblies of the world, that every ruler in it might be a sincere subject in the kingdom of the Lord Jesus! Oh, that it might suffice that we have had in our Parliament, and among our ministers, so much of the form and so little of the power of godliness. We have called *the world* Christ, and *lusts* Christ, and *self* Christ, working indeed for them, when we pretended it was all for Christ! Oh, that I could nourish this one contention, that you might strive to excel in setting up the Lord Jesus in your hearts!

FEBRUARY 29

Christ's Interest

Yet a little while, and the coming one will come and will not delay.

HEBREWS 10:37

Wait upon your King, the Lord Christ, to know his mind. If you lay any stone in the whole building that advances itself against his sceptre, he will shake all again. Dig you never so deep, build you never so high, it shall be shaken. Nay, it is not enough that there is no opposition—he has given light enough to have all things framed for his own advantage. The time is come, yea, the full time is come, that it should be so; and he expects it from you. Say not, in the first place, this or that suits the interest of England; but look to what suits the interest of Christ, and assure yourselves that the true interest of any nation is wrapped up in that.

Be encouraged under all those perplexities and troubles which you are, or may be, wrapped in. Lift up the hands that hang down, and let the feeble knees be strengthened: 'In just a little while, the one who is coming shall come, and he will not delay' (Heb. 10:37). The more you are for Christ, the more enemies you shall be sure to have, but the Lamb shall overcome. He is come to revenge the blood of his slain upon this generation, and to free the remnant from the jaws of the terrible. He is our rock, and his work is perfect. What he has begun, faster or slower, he will surely accomplish.

It is a thing of the utmost imaginable indifference whether any of us in particular behold these things here below or not. If we do not, we shall for the present have rest with him, and stand in our lot at the end of the days. But for the work itself, 'the decree has gone forth', and it shall not be recalled. Receive strength and refreshment in the Lord.

MARCH

This month, we will be reading Owen's works from the years 1650–1652. This was a tumultuous and bloody time, as the English fought against Irish and Scottish forces to establish and secure their revolution.

Of the Death of Christ, the Price he Paid, and the Purchase he Made was written in Dublin whilst Owen was busy attending to the affairs of Trinity College, there on the orders of Oliver Cromwell. It interacts with Richard Baxter's complaints about his previous book on the death of Christ.

'The Steadfastness of Promises, and the Sinfulness of Staggering' was a sermon given to Parliament after Owen's return from Ireland, urging the House to continue its urgent work of gospel reformation and not hold back. 'The Branch of the Lord, the Beauty of Sion: or, the Glory of the Church in its Relation unto Christ' was a sermon given in Berwick as Cromwell's army marched North to defeat the Scots at the Battle of Dunbar.

Another sermon, called 'The Advantage of the Kingdom of Christ in the Shaking of the World', was given on a day of thanksgiving for victory against the Scots under King Charles II in the Battle of Worcester, whilst 'The Labouring Saints Dismission to Rest' was preached at the funeral of the Lord Deputy of Ireland, General Henry Ireton. Finally, Owen also preached to Parliament in October 1652 on 'Christ's Kingdom and the Magistrate's Power'.

In 1652, he also published a primer on how to teach children to read English, and a catechism to instruct them in the Christian religion. Along with a number of others, he also contributed to some 'humble proposals' to Parliament 'for the furtherance and propagation of the gospel in this nation', and wrote an introduction to Henry Whitfield's book *Strength out of Weakness; or A Glorious Manifestation of the Further Progress of the Gospel among the Indians in New England.*

MARCH 1

Punished for Us

Christ redeemed us from the curse of the law by becoming a curse for us—for it is written, 'Cursed is everyone who is hanged on a tree.'

GALATIANS 3:13

All the punishment due to us was contained in the curse and sanction of the law. This was undergone by the Lord Christ, for 'he has redeemed us from the curse of the law, being made a curse for us' (Gal. 3:13).

The Scripture has expressly revealed the translation of punishment in respect of the subjects suffering it. But it has not spoken one word of the change of the kind of punishment, but rather the contrary is affirmed: 'He did not spare his own Son, but gave him up for us all' (Rom. 8:32).

Where God condemns sin, there he condemns it in that very punishment which is due to the sinner for it. The condemning of sin is the infliction of punishment due to sin. The whole penalty of sin is death (Gen. 2:17). This Christ underwent for us: Hebrews 2:9 says 'He tasted death'. And to die for another is to undergo that death which that other should have undergone (see 2 Sam. 18:33). In the meeting of our iniquities upon Christ (Isa. 53:6), and his being thereby made sin for us (2 Cor. 5:21), lay the very punishment of our sin, as threatened to us, upon him. It was no less than the weight of the wrath of God and the whole punishment due to sin that he wrestled under.

MARCH 2

The Gift of Faith

To those who have obtained a faith of equal standing with ours by the righteousness of our God and Saviour Jesus Christ: May grace and peace be multiplied to you in the knowledge of God and of Jesus our Lord.

2 PETER 1:1-2

The meritorious cause of our deliverance is the death of Christ. The fruits of the death of Christ are to be communicated to us on a condition, but that condition is among those fruits, and is itself to be absolutely communicated unconditionally. So all the fruits of the death of Christ are as absolutely procured for them for whom he died, as if no condition had been prescribed. Faith, which is this condition, is itself procured by the death of Christ for them for whom he died.

The Lord Jesus, by the satisfaction and merit of his death and offering (made for all his elect, and them only) has actually and absolutely purchased and procured for them all spiritual blessings of grace and glory. These are made out to them, and bestowed on them, in God's way and time, without dependence on any condition to be performed by them which has not already been absolutely procured for them by it. By this, they come to have a right to the good things purchased by him, and in due time they possess them, according to God's way, method, and appointment.

MARCH 3

Only by Grace

All have sinned and fall short of the glory of God.

ROMANS 3:23

In the first chapters of this epistle to the Romans, the apostle Paul, from Scripture and the constant practice of all sorts of people of all ages, Jews and Gentiles, wise and barbarians, proves all the world, and every individual in it, to 'have sinned and fallen short of the glory of God'. And not only so, but he also shows that it was utterly impossible that, by their own strength, or by virtue of any assistance communicated, or privileges enjoyed, they should ever attain to a righteousness of their own that might be acceptable unto God.

Paul then concludes that discourse with these two positive assertions: First, that for what is past, 'every mouth must be stopped, and the whole world be held accountable to God' (Rom. 3:19). Secondly, for the future: though they should labour to amend their ways, and improve their assistances and privileges to a better advantage than formerly, 'yet by the deeds of the law shall no human being be justified in the sight of God' (Rom. 3:20).

Now, it being the main drift of the apostle, in this epistle, and in his whole employment, to manifest that God has not shut up all the sons of men hopeless and remediless under this condition, he immediately reveals and opens the rich supply which God, in free grace, has made and provided for the delivery of his own from this calamitous state, even by the righteousness of faith in Christ. This he then unfolds, asserts, proves, and vindicates from objections, to the end of the third chapter.

MARCH 4

Shaky Faith

Abraham believed God and he counted it to him as righteousness.

GENESIS 15:6

That this was Abraham's condition appears from verse 2 of that chapter; where God having told him that he was his shield, and his exceeding great reward, he replies, 'O Lord God, what will you give me, for I continue childless?' (Gen. 15:2) As if he should have said, 'Lord God, you told me when I was in Haran, now nineteen years ago, that in me and my seed "all the families of the earth should be blessed"' (Gen. 12:3). You said that the blessed, blessing seed, should be of me: but now I wax old, all appearances grow up against the direct accomplishment of that word; and it was that which, above all, in following you, I aimed at. If I am disappointed in this, what shall I do? And what will it benefit me to have a multitude of earthly enjoyments, and leave them in the end to my servant?'

I cannot but observe, that this sighing, mournful complaint of Abraham, has much infirmity, and something of diffidence mixed with it. He shakes in the very bottom of his soul, that improbabilities were growing up, as he thought, to impossibilities against him in the way of promise.

Yet hence also mark these two things: First, that he does not fret in himself, and keep up his burning thoughts in his breast, but sweetly breathes out the burden of his soul into the bosom of his God. 'Lord God,' says he, 'what will you give me, for I continue childless?' It is of sincere faith, to unload our unbelief in the bosom of our God. Secondly, that the Lord overlooks the weakness and causeless wailings of his, takes them at the best, and then gives his witness to them.

MARCH 5

Staggering

No unbelief made him waver concerning the promise of God,
but he grew strong in his faith as he gave glory to God.

ROMANS 4:20

To stagger at the promise, is to take into consideration the promise itself, and alongside that, all the difficulties that lie in the way for the accomplishment of it, and then so to dispute it in your thoughts, as not fully to cast it off.

For instance, the soul considers the promise of free grace in the blood of Jesus, looks upon it, weighs as well as it is able the truth of God, who makes the promise; but at the same time, takes into its thoughts one's own unworthiness, sinfulness, unbelief, hypocrisy, and the like.

The promise draws the soul upward, and the weight of its unbelief sinks it downward. Sometimes the promise attracts so powerfully, you would think the heart quite drawn up into it; and sometimes again unbelief presses down, that you would think it gone forever. But neither prevails utterly, the poor creature wavers between both. This is to stagger.

Like a man travelling a journey, and meeting with two paths that promise both fairly, and he knows not which is his proper way. He guesses, and guesses, and at length cries, 'Well, I know not which of these ways I should go; but this is certain, if I make a mistake, I am undone. I'll go in neither, but here I'll sit down, and not move one step in either of them, until someone comes who can give me direction.' The soul very frequently sits down in this hesitation, and refuses to step one step forward, till God comes mightily and leads out the spirit to the promise, or the devil turns it aside to unbelief.

MARCH 6

Truth Confirmed

Sanctify them in the truth; your word is truth.

JOHN 17:17

Is there truth in God's promises? If there is the least occasion in the world to suspect the truth of the promises or the veracity of the promiser, then our staggering at them may arise from that, and not from our own unbelief. On this ground it is that all human faith, which is based merely on the testimony of a human, is at best but a probable opinion. For everyone is a liar, and possibly may lie in that very thing they are engaged to us in. But the author of the promises of which we speak, is truth itself—the God of truth, who has taken this as his special attribute, to distinguish him from all others. His word is said not only to be true, but 'truth' (John 17:17).

But yet farther, that it may be evident that there can be no occasion for staggering, this God of truth, whose word is truth, has in his infinite wisdom condescended to our weakness, and used all possible means to cause us to apprehend the truth of his promises. The Lord might have left us in the dark, to gather his mind and will towards us from obscure expressions. People in misery are glad to lay hold of the least word that drops from him that can relieve them, and to take courage from it. But, to shut up all objections, and to stop forever the mouth of unbelief, he has not only spoken plainly, but has condescended to use all the ways of confirming the truth of what he says and speaks that ever were in use among the sons of men.

MARCH 7

Sure Covenant

So when God desired to show more convincingly to the heirs of the promise the unchangeable character of his purpose, he guaranteed it with an oath.

HEBREWS 6:17

When a person says the same thing again and again, it is a sign that they speak the truth, or, at least, that they would be thought so to do. If an honest person clearly, fully, plainly, often engages themselves to us in the same thing, we count it a vile jealousy not to believe the real truth of their intentions. Now, the Lord in his promises often speaks the same things—he speaks once and twice. There is not anything that he has promised us but he has done it again and again. For instance, he says, 'I will be merciful to your sins'; I pray believe me for, 'I will pardon your iniquities'; yes, it shall be so, 'I will blot out your transgressions as a cloud.'

The second way of confirming any truth is by an oath. Though we fear the truth of some people in their assertions, yet when once they come to swear anything in justice and judgment, there are very few so knowingly profligate, and past all sense of God, but that their statements do gain credit and pass for truth. That nothing may be wanting to win our belief to the promises of God, he has taken this course also.

That all doubtings and staggerings may be excluded, he has wrapped them all up in a covenant, and brought himself into a federal engagement, that upon every occasion, and at every temptation, we may draw out his hand and seal, and say to Satan and our own false hearts: 'See here, behold God engaged in covenant, to make good the word in which he has caused me to put my trust. And this is his nature, that he is a God-keeping covenant.' So having his promise *redoubled*, and confirmed by an *oath*, all sealed and made sure by an unchangeable *covenant*, what more can we require to assure us of the truth?

MARCH 8

Carnal Policy

My kingdom is not of this world.

JOHN 18:36

The power of religion has totally been devoured by that lean, hungry, never-to-be-satisfied beast of carnal policy. Conformity to Christ in gospel graces is looked on as a mean, contemptible thing. Some have fallen to downright atheism, or to wretched formality in the things of God. What now lies at the bottom of all this? When God does not answer Saul, he goes to the devil. When the promise will not support us, we go to carnal policy.

If people begin once to stagger at the promise, and to conclude, in their fears, that it will not receive accomplishment, that the fountain will be dry, they cannot but think it high time to dig cisterns for themselves. Oh, let not the things of God be mixed any more with carnal reasonings! His truths are all eternal and unchangeable. Give them at once the sovereignty of your souls, and have not the least thought of making them bend to serve your own ends, though good and righteous.

How is it that Jesus Christ is in Ireland only as a *lion*, staining all his garments with the blood of his enemies; and none hold him out as a *lamb*, sprinkled with his own blood to his friends? Is it the sovereignty and interest of England that is alone to be there transacted? I could heartily rejoice, that the Irish might enjoy Ireland so long as the moon endures, as long as Jesus Christ might possess the Irish.

Is this to deal fairly with the Lord Jesus—call him out to the *battle*, and then keep away his *crown*? God has been faithful in doing great things for you; be faithful in this one: do your utmost for the preaching of the gospel in Ireland.

MARCH 9

Troubles

See to it that no one fails to obtain the grace of God; that no 'root of bitterness' springs up and causes trouble.

HEBREWS 12:15

Until you know how to believe for your own souls, you will scarcely know how to believe for a nation. In our staggerings, our doubtings, our disputes, we are apt to assign this or that reason for them; when the sole reason, indeed, is our unbelief. 'Were it not for such and such a reason, I could believe'—that is, were there no need of faith. That is, faith must remove the mountains that lie in the way, and then all will be plain.

It is not the greatness of sin, nor continuance in sin, nor backsliding into sin, that is the true cause of your staggering. It is solely your unbelief, that 'root of bitterness' which springs up and troubles you. It is not the distance of the earth from the sun, nor the sun's withdrawing itself, that makes a dark and gloomy day; but the interposition of clouds. Neither is your soul beyond the reach of the promise, nor does God withdraw himself; but the vapours of your carnal, unbelieving heart do cloud you.

It is said of one place, 'Christ could do no great work there' (Mark 6:5). Why so? For lack of power in him? Not at all; but merely for lack of faith in them. People complain, that were it not for various things, they could believe; when it is their unbelief that casts those problems in the way. As if someone should cast nails and sharp stones in their own way, and say, 'Truly, I could run, were it not for those nails and stones'—when they continue to cast them there. You could believe, were it not for these doubts and difficulties, these staggering perplexities; when, alas! they are all from your unbelief.

MARCH 10

Gentiles Called

For my house shall be called a house of prayer for all peoples.

ISAIAH 56:7

In Isaiah 56:3-8, you have promises and predictions of calling in Gentiles and strangers to the church of God. Any objections or hindrances laid in their way by ceremonial constitutions are all to be removed in the cross of Christ (Eph. 2:13-16; Col. 2:14). This makes way for the accomplishment of that signal promise which is given in Isaiah 2:2, 'It shall come to pass in the latter days that the mountain of the house of the LORD shall be established as the highest of the mountains… and all the nations shall flow to it.'

In verse 7 you have a description of the services performed by the Gentiles upon their coming: 'their burnt offerings and their sacrifices will be accepted on my altar', which is similar to that eminent prediction of the solemn worship of the called Gentiles in Malachi 1:11, 'For from the rising of the sun to its setting my name will be great among the nations, and in every place incense will be offered to my name, and a pure offering. For my name will be great among the nations, says the LORD of hosts.' The spiritual services of the saints of the Gentiles are in each place set forth by those ceremonial ordinances of incense, altar, and sacrifice, as were then most acceptable, from the Lord's own appointment.

So, then, observe:

I. Christ's church of saints, of believers, is God's house.

II. The church of Christ under the gospel is to be gathered out of all nations.

III. There are established ordinances and appointed worship for the church of Christ under the gospel.

MARCH 11

Holy Church

Worship the LORD in the splendour of holiness; tremble before him, all the earth!

PSALM 96:9

The comeliness and beauty that is in a sanctified soul is above all the glory of the world. This is that which the psalmist calls 'The beauty of holiness' (Ps. 96:9). The glory of the ordinances of the gospel is their vigour and purity. There is nothing so glorious as our King on his throne, Christ in his court, this house reigning in the administration of his ordinances. The apostle exalts the glory of gospel administrations exceedingly above the old tabernacle and temple worship,—which yet was exceeding pompous and glorious. 'For if what was being brought to an end came with glory, much more will what is permanent have glory' (2 Cor. 3:11).

Let people think as meanly as they please of the spiritual service of God amongst his people, all glory that ever yet appeared in the world was but a bubble to it. All that God ever instituted before came exceedingly short of it. He who knows the haughty from afar, delights in it (Ps. 138:6).

It is glorious in respect of the exaltation it has above and the triumph over all its opposers. To see a house, a palace, hung round about with ensigns, spoils, and banners taken from the enemies that have come against it, is a glorious thing. Thus is this house of God decked. Never any arose, or shall arise, against this house, and go forth unto final prosperity. Let the people of the world take heed how they burden themselves with the foundation-stone of this house—it will assuredly break them all in pieces.

MARCH 12

The Ark

God put forward Christ as a propitiation by his blood, to be received by faith.

ROMANS 3:25

Christ is the *ark* of this house. The ark in the tabernacle, and afterwards in the temple, was the most holy thing in the most holy place. There was nothing in it but the two tablets of stone written with the finger of God: before it was Aaron's rod that budded, with a pot full of manna; over it was the mercy-seat, being a plate of gold as long and as broad as the ark, covering it, being shadowed with the cherubims of glory. Now all this glorious fabric signified that, unless the law with its condemning power was hidden in the ark, and covered with the mercy-seat, no person could stand before the Lord.

The Law was the old covenant of works, and was renewed to them chiefly to be subservient to the gospel and, partly, with its carnal administration, to be the tenure of the Israelites' holding the land of Canaan. This being in the ark, it was said to contain the covenant, and is frequently called 'The ark of the covenant'. Jesus Christ is the ark of this spiritual house. When the temple was opened in heaven, there was seen in the temple the ark of God's testament (Rev. 11:19)—Jesus Christ, made conspicuous to all, who lay much hidden under the Old Testament. God is said to set forth Christ to be 'a propitiation', or mercy-seat (Rom. 3:25); for by that very term is the mercy-seat expressed (Heb. 9:5). He is, then, the ark and the mercy-seat covering it.

Christ is the ark of this house, as containing in himself the new covenant; it is made with him originally, established in him irreversibly, made out through him in all the grace of it faithfully.

MARCH 13

Conquest

Do you not know that your body is a temple of the Holy Spirit within you, whom you have from God? You are not your own, for you were bought with a price.

1 CORINTHIANS 6:19-20

'Do you not know,' says the apostle, 'that you are the temple of the Spirit of Christ?' Well, and how did we come to be so? 'You were bought with a price' (1 Cor. 6:19-20). Those who affirm that he also purchased the unclean sties of the devil, know not what they say.

Unto *purchase* he must also add *conquest*. An unjust usurper had taken possession of this house, and kept it in bondage. Satan had seized on it, and brought it, through the wrath of God, under his power. He, then, must be conquered, that the Lord Christ may have complete possession of his own house. 'For this purpose,' then, 'was the Son of God revealed, that he might destroy the works of the devil' (1 John 3:8). And how does he do it? He overpowers him and destroys him, in that 'through death he destroyed him that had the power of death; that is, the devil' (Heb. 2:14). And he plundered him, having overcome him. He bound the strong man, and then plundered his goods (Matt. 12:29). All that darkness, unbelief, sin, and hardness, that he had stuffed this house with, Christ spoils and scatters them all away.

And to make his conquest complete, Christ triumphs over his enemy, and, like a mighty conqueror, makes an open show of him, to his everlasting shame (Col. 2:15), 'He disarmed the rulers and authorities and put them to open shame, by triumphing over them in his cross'; and by this means he strengthens his title to his inheritance.

MARCH 14

Christ Is Near

The Lord is at hand; do not be anxious about anything, but in everything by prayer and supplication with thanksgiving let your requests be made known to God.

Philippians 4:5-6

The house of God, which seems so often to be near to destruction, is yet preserved from ruin. Often it is brought into a condition that all that look on say, 'Now it is gone forever.' But still it recovers, and gets up again. The Lord Christ looks on all the while: he knows how far things may proceed, as a trial. When it comes to that pass that, if pressures and troubles should continue, the house will be overborne indeed, then he puts in, rebukes the winds and waves, and makes all things still again.

A father, who looks upon his child in a difficult and dangerous business, knows that he can relieve them when he pleases, but would willingly see them try their strength and cunning. He leaves them alone until perhaps the child thinks themselves quite lost, and wonders why their father does not help them. But when the condition comes to be such that, without help, they will be lost indeed, instantly the father puts in his hand and saves them. So deals the Lord Jesus with his house. He often lets it strive and wrestle with great oppositions, to draw out and exercise all the graces of it; but yet all this while he looks on, and when danger is near indeed, he is not far off.

MARCH 15

Providence Ignored

Great are the works of the LORD, studied by all who delight in them.

PSALM 111:2

All the works of God's providence—which are great, and studied by all who have pleasure in them (Ps. 111:2)—have such a stamp and impress of his own image on them, his wisdom, goodness, power, love, that they declare their author, and reveal from heaven his kindness and wrath towards the children of men. Yet such are the prejudices, lusts, inordinacy of affections, and interest of many, that it has always been a long and difficult task to convince them of his presence in them, when it has been most uncontrollably evident. The Egyptians will wrestle with many a plague, by thinking the 'magicians' can do so (Exod. 7:11-12).

Indeed, often (especially when judicial blindness has come upon them) though they cannot but see his arm awakened as of old and made bare, they will not rest in his sovereign disposal of things, but rise up against the works of his vengeance and holiness. Like wild beasts that are pursued, when all ways of escape and turning are shut up, they fly in the face of him that follows them. They repent not of their evil deeds, but bite their tongues for anger, and blaspheme the God of heaven (Rev. 16:10-11). Such is the power of deceivable lusts, that many will admire at the blindness of others in former generations who considered not the works of God (such as the Jews in the wilderness), when they themselves are under actual contempt of no less glorious dispensations; like the Pharisees, who bewailed the folly of their fathers in persecuting the prophets, when they themselves were endeavouring to kill the Son of God (Matt. 23:29-30).

MARCH 16

God's Aim

And he shall stand and shepherd his flock in the strength of the Lord, in the majesty of the name of the Lord his God. And they shall dwell secure, for now he shall be great to the ends of the earth.

MICAH 5:4

In the midst of all the tumults and conflicts of the nations, that which the Lord takes peculiarly as his own design, into his own management, is the carrying on of the kingdom of the Lord Jesus.

You are about your work, says the Lord—I also am about mine. You have your branches and cedars—I also have one to plant, that shall flourish. 'In the days of those kings the God of heaven will set up a kingdom that shall never be destroyed' (Dan. 2:44). There is not a persecuting Pharaoh, but God raises him up for his own purpose (Exod. 9:16). But yet, in respect of the kingdom of his Son, he speaks of them as if he had nothing to do with them. In their days I will do my own work—advance the kingdom of the Lord Christ.

There are great and mighty works in hand in this nation; tyrants are punished, the jaws of oppressors are broken and, we hope, governors set up that may be 'just, ruling in the fear of God, that they may be as the light of the morning' (2 Sam. 23:3-4). The hand of the Lord has been wonderfully exalted in all these things. But yet, if we rest in them, and they are not be brought into an immediate subserviency to the kingdom of the Lord Jesus, the Lord will quickly distinguish between them and his own peculiar design. The carrying on of the interest of Christ is his peculiar aim. May he, of his goodness, make it ours also!

MARCH 17

Unexpectedly Weak

The LORD sees not as man sees: man looks on the outward appearance, but the LORD looks on the heart.

1 SAMUEL 16:7

The actings of God's providence, in carrying on the interest of Christ, are and shall be exceedingly unsuited to the reasonings and expectations of most people. He has a glorious work here to be accomplished. Of whom should he now make use? Surely the 'high tree', the 'green tree' will be employed. If one is to be anointed in the family of Jesse, will it not be goodly Eliab (1 Sam. 16:6)? If the king will honour any, who should it be but I, says Haman (Esther 6:6)? But all on the contrary, the low, dry tree is taken: David from the flock, and Mordecai from the gate. The thoughts of God are not as our thoughts, neither does he look on outward appearances.

The Jews had high expectations for the coming of the Messiah. Upon every considerable appearance, they cry, 'Is this he?' And what did they expect? Outward glory, beauty, deliverance, carnal power, and dominion. God at length comes to do his work, and brings forth a poor man, that had nowhere to lay his head, who had 'no form or majesty that we should look at him, and no beauty that we should desire him' (Isa. 53:2). He was persecuted, despised, crucified—quite another thing than what they looked for. Thus lays he the foundation of the gospel in the person of his Son, by frustrating the expectations of most people.

Then, contrary to all the wisdom of the flesh, he takes a few ignorant, weak, unlearned fishermen, despised upon all accounts, and commits this great work to them; and accordingly, out they go, friendless, helpless, harbourless, unto their great employment.

MARCH 18

Praying People

In your majesty ride out victoriously for the cause of truth and meekness and righteousness.

PSALM 45:4

Believe the promises, close with them, exercise faith upon them, and you will believe the beast unto destruction, antichrist into the pit, and Magog to ruin. Believe that the enemies of Christ shall be made his footstool, that the nations shall be his inheritance, that he shall reign gloriously in beauty, that he shall smite in pieces the heads of diverse nations—live in the faith of these things. It will give you the sweetness of them before they come, and it will hasten their coming beyond the endeavours of thousands, even millions of armed men.

Meet him with your supplications. Cry out to him. This will make you be the armies of heaven, that follow him in his great undertakings (Rev. 19:14). It is his praying people who are his conquering armies that follow him. Shoot not two or three arrows, and so give over; but never leave shooting until the enemies of the Lord are all destroyed. Seeing it is his gospel whose advancement the Lord Jesus aims at in all these dispensations, and whose quarrel alone he prosecutes (whatever people may do), help the advancement of that gospel of his. Formerly, it was oppressed by the height and tyranny of the tower of Babel, and for the present, it is exceedingly denied and encumbered by the rubbish of it being in some measure cast down. But be still and know that he is God (Ps. 46:10). Be silent before him, for he is risen out of his holy habitation. Say, God has done great things for these; who has hardened himself against him and prospered?

MARCH 19

Walking and Worship

*Take my yoke upon you, and learn from me, for I am gentle
and lowly in heart, and you will find rest for your souls.*

MATTHEW 11:29

Inquire diligently into God's mind and will, that you may know
his paths, and be acquainted with his statutes. I dare say, no
temptation in the world presses with more colour and violence
upon people under mercies, than that temptation to a neglect of
walking and holding communion with God in his ordinances.
The devil thinks thus to avenge himself on the Lord Jesus—
his own yoke being broken, he thinks to prevail to the casting
away of his. Christ has a yoke, though it is gentle and easy
(Matt. 11:29).

You that do *enjoy holy ordinances*, labour to have holy hearts
answerable to them. You have heavenly institutions, so labour
to have heavenly conversations. If we are like the world in our
walking, it is no great matter if we are like the world in our
worship. It is sad, walking contrary to God in his own paths.
Show out the power and efficacy of all gospel institutions in a
frame of spirit, course of life, and evenness of spiritual temper,
all your days.

Keep up the power of *private worship*, both personal and
family. Look what the roots are in the family; such will the fruit
be in the church and commonwealth. If your spirits are not well
manured there, you will be utterly barren elsewhere. That is
done most clearly to God which is done within doors.

MARCH 20

Heavenly Wisdom

Who is wise and understanding among you? By his good conduct let him show his works in the meekness of wisdom.

JAMES 3:13

There is a manifold wisdom which God imparts to people. There is *spiritual* wisdom, that, by the way of eminency, is said to be 'from above' (James 3:17). This is nothing but the gracious acquaintance of the soul with the hidden wisdom of God in Christ (1 Cor. 2:7). And there is a *civil* wisdom, or a sound ability of mind for the management of the human affairs, in subordination to the providence and righteousness of God. Though both of these were in Daniel, yet it is in respect of the latter that his wisdom is so peculiarly extolled.

There are sundry things that distinguish this wisdom from that policy which God abhors—which is 'earthly, unspiritual, demonic' (James 3:15)—though it is the great darling of the people of the world. One is a gracious discerning of the mind of God, according to his appearance in the affairs in which people are employed. 'The voice of the Lord cries to the city—and it is sound wisdom to fear your name' (Micah 6:9). It is the wisdom of a person, to see the name of God, to be acquainted with his will, his mind, his aim in things, when his providential voice cries to the city. All the works of God have their voice, their instruction: those of signal providences speak aloud; they cry to the city. Here is the wisdom of a person: they are a person of substance, a substantial person, who can see their name in such dispensations.

MARCH

MARCH 21

Appointed Time

Well done, good and faithful servant. You have been faithful over a little; I will set you over much. Enter into the joy of your master.

MATTHEW 25:21

People are placed by God in their stations; they have their appointed season, and are then dismissed from their watch. Some keep guard in the winter, a time of storms and temptations, trials and great pressures; others in the sunshine, the summer of a more flourishing estate and condition. Yet all endure some hardship, and have their appointed season for their dismissal. Often, this dismissal is in the midst of their work for which they seem to be most eminently qualified.

The three most eminent works of God, in the days of old, were his giving his people the law, and settling them in the land of Canaan; his recovering them from the Babylonian captivity; and his proclamation of the gospel to them. In these three works, he employed three most eminent persons: Moses in the first, Daniel in the second, and John the Baptist in the third. And none of them saw the work accomplished in which they were so eminently employed. Moses died the year before the people entered Canaan; Daniel, some few years before the foundation of the temple; and John the Baptist in the first year of the baptism of our Saviour, when the gospel which he began to preach was to be published in its beauty and glory. They all had only their appointed seasons.

I do not know of any great work that the Lord carried out, where the same people both began it and ended it. He gave them all their seasons, that *his* power and wisdom might the more evidently appear.

MARCH 22

Redeem the Time

Whatever your hand finds to do, do it with your might, for there is no work or thought or knowledge or wisdom in Sheol, to which you are going.

ECCLESIASTES 9:10

Daniel lies down in the dust in rest and peace. And why so? The spirit of prophecy is poured out on Haggai and Zechariah; they must also carry on this work, and bear my name before my people, says the Lord. Consider this as an exhortation to all who are employed in the work of God, especially such as with eminent abilities are engaged in eminent employments. You have but your allotted season for your work. Be wise, then, to redeem the time that is in your hands.

This is the praise of a person: that they do the will of God before they fall asleep; that they faithfully serve their generation, until they are no more. Whatever, then, you find to do, do it with all your strength; for there is neither wisdom nor power in the grave, to which you are going (Eccles. 9:10).

Compare yourselves with the saints of God, who were faithful in their generations, and are now fallen asleep. What a deal of work did Josiah do in a short season! What a light did John set up in a few years! It is said of Caesar, that he was ashamed of his own sloth, when he found that Alexander had conquered the eastern world at the age in which he had done nothing. Provoke one another by examples.

MARCH 23

Using Power

Work, for I am with you, declares the LORD of hosts.

HAGGAI 2:4

Be diligent to finish your work, and let it not too long hang upon your hands. Your appointed season may come before you bring it to the close. So search out work for God. You who are entrusted with power, trifle not away your season. Is there no oppressed person that with diligence you might relieve? Is there no poor distressed widow or orphan whose righteous requests you might expedite and despatch? Are there no stout offenders against God and people that might be chastised? Are there no slack and slow counties and cities in the execution of justice, that might be quickened by your example? Are there no places destitute of the gospel that might be furnished and supplied by your industry and wisdom?

Can you not find out something of this or the like nature to be despatched with vigour and diligence? Indeed, do not innumerable examples of each kind lie upon your hands? And is not your non-performance of them such a sacrifice as God is not well pleased with? Your time is limited and appointed; you know not how soon you may be overtaken with it; and would it not be desirable unto you, that you had done these things? Will it be bitterness in the end, that you so laid out your endeavours?

But remember: All people have but their seasons in any work; only God abides in it for ever. Let him be eyed as the principal and only abiding agent in any great undertaking.

MARCH 24

Enjoy Serving

Serve not by the way of eye-service, as people-pleasers, but as bondservants of Christ, doing the will of God from the heart.

EPHESIANS 6:6

You who are engaged in the work of God, seek for a reward of your service in the service itself. Few of you may live to see that beauty and glory which perhaps you aim at as the end of all your great undertakings for God. God will proceed at his own pace, and calls on us to go along with him.

Those whose minds are so fixed on, and swallowed up with, some end (though good) which they have proposed to themselves, do seldom see good days and are serene in their own souls. They have bitterness, wrath, and trouble all their days—are still pressing to the end proposed, and commonly are dismissed from their station before it be attained. There is a sweetness, there are wages to be found in the work of God itself.

People who have learned to hold communion with God in every work he calls them to, though they never see the main harvest they aim at in general, will rest satisfied, and submit to the Lord's limitation of their time. Seeing God often dismisses his choicest servants before they see or taste of the main fruits of their endeavours, I see not upon what account consolation can be had in following the Lord in difficult dispensations, but only in that reward which every duty brings along with it, by communion with God in its performance. Make, then, this your aim, that in sincerity of heart you do the work of God in your generation. Find his presence with you, his Spirit guiding you, his love accepting you in the Lord Christ; and, whenever you receive your dismissal, it will be rest and peace.

MARCH 25

Eternal Rest

*Blessed are the dead who die in the Lord from now on.
'Blessed indeed,' says the Spirit, 'that they may rest from their
labours, for their deeds follow them!'*

REVELATION 14:13

This, in general, is the first thing that the dismissed saints are at
rest from: they sin no more; they wound the Lord Jesus no more;
they trouble their own souls no more; they grieve the Spirit no
more; they dishonour the gospel no more. They are troubled no
more with Satan's temptations without, no more with their own
corruption within, but lie down in a constant enjoyment of one
everlasting victory over sin.

The Spirit says, 'They rest from their labours' (Rev. 14:13)—
those labours which make them faint and weary, their
contending with sin to the uttermost. They are no more cold in
communion; they have not one thought that wanders off from
God to eternity. They lose him no more, but always lie down in
his bosom, without the least possibility of disturbance. Even the
very remembrance of sin is sweet unto them, when they see God
infinitely exalted and admired in the pardoning of it.

The saints are either *doing* for God or *suffering* for God; some
both do and suffer great things for him. In either of them, there
is pain, weariness, travail, labour, trouble, sorrow, and anxiety of
spirit; neither is there any eminent doing or working for God
but is carried on with much suffering to the outward man. But
many spend their days deliciously, with so much contentment to
the flesh that it is impossible they should have any foretaste and
sweet relish of their rest that is to come.

MARCH 26

Daniel's Anxiety

As for me, Daniel, my spirit within me was anxious, and the visions of my head alarmed me.

DANIEL 7:15

Daniel was a man highly favoured of God above all in his generation; so richly furnished with gifts and graces that he is once and again brought forth as an example, by God himself, on account of his eminence in wisdom and piety. Yet all this does not preserve him from falling into this perplexed condition of being grieved in his spirit.

The principal work of all the holy prophets who have been since the world began, was to preach, set forth, and declare the Lord Jesus Christ, the Messiah who was for to come. Some particulars about his person, righteousness, and kingdom, were in a special manner committed to each of them respectively: his passion and righteousness to Isaiah; the covenant of grace in him to Jeremiah; and to this Daniel, most eminently, the great works of the providence of God in the shaking and overturning of kingdoms and nations in a subserviency to his kingdom. With the revelation of this, for the consolation of the church in all ages, did the Lord honour him of whom we speak.

For the present, he describes himself in a somewhat perplexed condition. His spirit (mind and soul) was grieved, sick, troubled, or disquieted in the midst of his body. Like David, when he argued with his soul about it—'Why are you so sad, my soul? And why are you so disquieted within me?' (Ps. 43:5)—he knew not what to say, what to do. He was filled with sad thoughts, sad apprehensions of what was to come to pass, and what might be the issue of the things that had been revealed unto him.

MARCH 27

Christ's Kingdom

God exalted Jesus at his right hand as Leader and Saviour, to give repentance to Israel and forgiveness of sins.

ACTS 5:31

People have had various thoughts about the kingdom of Christ in all ages. That the Messiah was to be a King, a Prince, a Ruler—that he was to have a kingdom, and that the government was to be on his shoulder—is evident from the Old Testament. That all this was and is accomplished in Jesus of Nazareth, whom God exalted, made a Prince and a Saviour, is no less evident in the New. But about the nature of this kingdom, its rise and manner of government, there have been, and are, many contests.

The Jews, to this very day, expect it as a thing carnal and temporal, visible, outwardly glorious, in which they shall bear rule over the nations at their will; and of some such thing it may be supposed the apostles themselves were not without thoughts, until they had conversed with the Lord after the resurrection (Luke 9:46; Acts 1:6). Neither are all amongst us free from such thoughts at this day.

Those who with any simplicity profess the name of Christ, do generally agree that first, and principally, Christ's kingdom is *internal and spiritual*, in and over the souls of people, over spirits both good and bad. Towards his elect, who are given unto him of his Father, he converts, rules, and preserves them, under and through a great variety of dispensations, internal and external, until he brings them unto himself. He takes possession of their hearts by his power, dwelling in them by his Spirit, making them kings in his kingdom, and bringing them infallibly into glory. Oh, that this rule, this kingdom of his, might be carried on in our hearts!

MARCH 28

Quiet Kingdom

The kingdom of God is not coming in ways that can be observed, nor will they say, 'Look, here it is!' or 'There!' for behold, the kingdom of God is in the midst of you.

LUKE 17:20-21

Jesus will rule in the universal judgment, which the Father has committed to him—rewarding, crowning, receiving some to himself; judging, condemning, casting others into utter darkness (John 5:22-27; Acts 2:36; Rom. 14:9; Acts 17:31). And of this universal, righteous judgment, he gives many warnings to the world, by pouring forth sundry vials of his wrath upon great Nimrods and oppressors (Ps. 110:6; Micah 4:3; Rev. 19:11-13).

But now, whether the Lord Christ shall bear an outward, visible, glorious rule, setting up a kingdom like those of the world, to be ruled by strength and power; and if so, when or how it shall be brought in; into whose hands the administration of it shall be committed, and upon what account; whether he will personally walk in it or not; whether it shall be clearly distinct from the rule he now bears in the world, or only differentiated by more glorious degrees and manifestations of his power—endless and irreconcilable are the contests about such things among those who profess his name.

This we find, by woeful experience: all who, from the spirituality of the rule of Christ, and delight in that, have degenerated into carnal apprehensions of the beauty and glory of it, have, for the most part, been given up to carnal actings, suited to such apprehensions. They have been so dazzled with gazing after temporal glory, that the kingdom which comes not by observation has been vile in their eyes.

MARCH 29

Perplexity

As for me, Daniel, my spirit within me was anxious, and the visions of my head alarmed me. I approached one of those who stood there and asked him the truth concerning all this. So he told me and made known to me the interpretation of the things.

DANIEL 7:15-16

When considering God's marvellous actings in the world, in order to the carrying on of the gospel and the interest of the Lord Jesus Christ, the hearts of his saints are often filled with perplexity and trouble. They do not know what will happen, nor sometimes what they should do. Daniel received a vision of the things which, in part, we live under: and if they filled his heart with astonishment, is it any wonder if they come close to us, and fill us with anxious, perplexing thoughts, upon whom the things themselves are fallen?

The only way to deliver and extricate our spirits from under such perplexities and entanglements, is to draw near to God in Christ, to discover his will. So did Daniel here; he went to one of those who ministered before the Lord, to be acquainted with his will. Otherwise, thoughts and contrivances will but farther perplex you. Like people in the swamp, whilst they pluck one leg out, the other sticks faster in, whilst you relieve yourselves in one thing, you will be more hampered in another. The great healing of all is in God.

When God makes known the interpretations of things, it will quiet your spirits, in your walking before him, and actings with him. This is what brought the spirit of Daniel into a settlement.

MARCH 30

Ask for Wisdom

If any of you lacks wisdom, let him ask God, who gives generously to all without reproach, and it will be given him.

JAMES 1:5

It is too manifest that many of our piercing and perplexing thoughts come from the tumult and disorder of our own lusts. The only way to extricate and deliver our spirits from under perplexities and entanglements, is to draw nigh to God in Christ for the discovery of his will. So did Daniel in Daniel 7.

I fear this is too much neglected. You take counsel with your own hearts, you advise one another and listen to people with a reputation for wisdom. All this only increases your trouble—you do but more and more entangle and disquiet your own spirits. God stands by and says, 'I am wise also', and little notice is taken of him. We think we are grown wise ourselves, and do not remember we never prospered but only when we went unto God, and told him plainly we knew not what to do.

Public fastings are neglected, despised, spoken against. Private meetings are used to show ourselves wise in the debate of things, with a form of godly words; and sometimes for strife, tumult, division, disorder. When we do sometimes wait upon God, do not many seem to ask amiss, to spend it on their lusts (James 4:3), not waiting on him poor, hungry, empty, to know his will, to receive direction from him; but rather going full, fixed, resolved, settled on thoughts, perhaps prejudices, of our own, almost taking it upon us to prescribe unto the Almighty, and to impose our poor, low, carnal thoughts upon his wisdom and care of his church?

MARCH 31

Zeal for Truth

Because you are lukewarm, and neither hot nor cold, I will spit you out of my mouth.

REVELATION 3:16

Labour to be fully persuaded in your own minds, that you are not carried up and down with every wind of doctrine, and tempted to hearken after every spirit, as though you had received no truth as it is in Jesus. It is a sad condition, when people have no zeal for truth, nor against that which is opposite to it, whatever they seem to profess. Indeed, having not taken in any truth, in the power and principle of it, they are filled with sad thoughts, wholly at a loss whether there is any truth or not. This is an unhappy frame indeed—the proper condition of those whom God will spew out of his mouth (Rev. 3:16).

Know that error and falsehood have no right or title, either from God or people, to any privilege, protection, advantage, liberty, or any good thing you are entrusted with. To give to a lie what is due to truth, is to deal treacherously with him by whom you are employed. All the tenderness and forbearance to such persons as are infected with such abominations is solely upon a civil account, and that plea which they have for tranquillity whilst they neither directly nor morally are a disturbance to others.

If people's consciences are seared, and they have given themselves up to a reprobate mind, to do those things that are not appropriate, there is no doubt but they ought to suffer such things as are assigned and appointed to such practices. 'Though they know God's righteous decree that those who practise such things deserve to die, they not only do them but give approval to those who practise them' (Rom. 1:32).

APRIL

This month, we will taste some of Owen's work during the time he first became Dean of Christ Church, Oxford and Vice Chancellor of the University of Oxford (1653-1656). We will be reading from more weighty scholarly works, as well as his sermons from this period.

His *Diatriba de Justitia Divina* or 'Dissertation on Divine Justice' (1653) is an academic work first written in Latin, in which Owen sought to establish the necessity of the atonement. In 1654, Owen also published a substantial tome devoted to *The Doctrine of the Saints' Perseverance*, which was particularly aimed against a popular Arminian Congregationalist preacher in London called John Goodwin.

In 1655, Owen wrote a large and detailed volume against the anti-Trinitarian group known as the Socinians, called *Vindiciae Evangelicae, or The Mystery of the Gospel Vindicated*. Written at the request of the Council of State, this particularly unravels the errors of the English heretic, John Biddle, on the Trinity and the cross.

Finally, we will dig into two sermons given during these years. In September 1656, Owen preached a sermon called 'God's Work in Founding Zion, and his People's Duty Thereupon' at Westminster Abbey, to Cromwell and Parliament. This looks at how the reformation of the church should be continued, during a time when the Protestant English navy was busy battling their greatest maritime foe, Spain, but there was peace and freedom at home. In October that same year, he preached again to members of Parliament at St Margaret's, Westminster, on 'God's Presence with a People, the Spring of their Prosperity'. During this period, Owen also wrote prefaces to books by William Twisse on the doctrine of election, George Kendall on the perseverance of the saints, William Eyre on justification, and Lewis Du Moulin against Amyraut.

APRIL 1

Peace and Polemics

If possible, so far as it depends on you, live peaceably with all.

ROMANS 12:18

Even Christian authors have their polemics; and these, alas, are too much fitted to excite, increase, and promote bloody strife; such is the blindness, nay, the madness of most people. My hope is, that the Lord and Judge of all will find me intently occupied in preaching Christ and him crucified, in season and out of season, and wrestling in prayer with God our gracious Father, for the salvation of the little flock of his well-beloved Son. Not as if it were in our power to keep free from controversies, for he who declared himself to have been sent, according to his own and the Father's counsel, not to destroy but to save the lives of people (that is, spiritually and eternally), predicted that from the innate malice of people perversely opposing themselves to heavenly truth—not love, not tranquillity and peace, but strife, hatred, war, and the sword, would ensue upon the promulgation of that truth.

Peace, indeed, he bequeathed to his own; but it was that divine peace which dwells in the bosom of the Father, and in the inmost recesses of their own souls. In truth, whilst his disciples live mingled with other people, and are exposed to national disturbances, how can they but share, like a small boat attached to a ship, in the same tempest and agitation with the rest? But since we have it in command, 'If possible, so far as it depends on you, live peaceably with all' (Rom. 12:18), that contention is alone pleasing which is in defence of truth; and it is pleasing only because for the truth we are bound to contend.

APRIL 2

Wise Theology

The wisdom from above is first pure, then peaceable, gentle, open to reason, full of mercy and good fruits, impartial and sincere.

JAMES 3:17

I hold myself bound, in conscience and in honour, not even to imagine that I have attained a proper knowledge of any one article of truth, much less to publish it, unless through the Holy Spirit I have had such a taste of it, in its spiritual sense, that I may be able from the heart to say, 'I have believed, and therefore have I spoken' (Ps. 116:10). Those who, in the investigation of truth, make it their chief care to have their mind and will rendered subject to the faith, and obedient to the 'Father of lights'—they alone attain to true wisdom.

It has, then, been my principal object, whilst I, a poor worm, contemplated the majesty and glory of him concerning whose perfections I was treating—to attend and obey, with all humility and reverence, what the great God the Lord has spoken in his word; not at all doubting but that, whatever way he should incline my heart, by the power of his Spirit and truth, I should be enabled, in a dependence on his aid, to bear the contradictions of a false knowledge, and all human and philosophical arguments.

I have adopted the opinion which I defend from no regard to the arguments of either one or another learned man, and much less from any slavish attachment to authority, example, or prejudices of tradition. Theology is the 'wisdom from above' a habit of grace and spiritual gifts, the manifestation of the Spirit, reporting what is conducive to happiness. It is not a science to be learned from the precepts of people, or from the rules of arts, or method of other sciences.

APRIL 3

Evangelical Truth

I ask that the God of our Lord Jesus Christ, the Father of glory, may give you the Spirit of wisdom and of revelation in the knowledge of him.

EPHESIANS 1:17

There can be no doubt but that many points of doctrine still remain, on which the labours of the godly and learned may be usefully employed. Many reverend and learned divines, both of the present and former age—from the time, at least, when God granted to our fathers that glorious regeneration, or time of reformation, of a purer religion and of sound learning, after a long reign of darkness—have composed from the sacred writings a synopsis, or methodical body of doctrine or heavenly truth, and published their compositions under various titles. Other theological writings, catechetical, dogmatical, exegetical, casuistical, and polemical, have increased to such a mass that the 'world can hardly contain the books that have been written'.

Yet such is the nature of divine truth, so deep and inexhaustible the fountain of the sacred Scriptures, whence we draw it, so innumerable the salutary remedies and antidotes proposed in these to dispel all the poisons and temptations with which the adversary can ever attack either the minds of the pious or the peace of the church and the true doctrine, that serious and thinking people can entertain no doubt but that we perform a service praise-worthy and profitable to the church of Christ, when, under the direction of 'the Spirit of wisdom and revelation' (Eph. 1:17) we bring forward, explain, and defend the most important and necessary articles of evangelical truth.

APRIL 4

Holy Eyes

For you are not a God who delights in wickedness; evil may not dwell with you.

PSALM 5:4

Habakkuk ascribes to God such an immortal hatred of sin that he cannot look upon it: 'You who are of purer eyes than to see evil and cannot look at wrong' (Hab. 1:13). With a wrathful aversion of his countenance, he abominates and dooms it to punishment. The Holy Spirit gives us a reason, namely, the purity of God's eyes. There is no one who can doubt that the prophet here intended the holiness of God. The incomprehensible, infinite, and most perfect holiness or purity of God is the cause of why he hates and detests all sin.

Of the same import is the admonition of Joshua in his address to the people of Israel, 'You are not able to serve the LORD' (that is, he will not accept a false and hypocritical worship from you), 'for he is a holy God. He is a jealous God; he will not forgive your transgressions or your sins' (Josh. 24:19). God, then, will not forgive transgressions—that is, he will most certainly punish them—because he is most holy.

Moreover, it is manifest that God meant this holiness in that promulgation of his glorious name, or of the essential properties of his divine nature, made face to face to Moses in Exodus 34:5-7, 'The LORD, The LORD… who will by no means clear the guilty.' He leads us to the contemplation of that excellence essentially inherent in his nature, which induces him to such an act. But those who deny this hatred of sin and sinners, and the disposition to punish them, to be perpetually, immutably, and habitually inherent in God, I am afraid have never strictly weighed in their thoughts the divine purity and holiness.

APRIL 5

God's Anger

He let loose on them his burning anger, wrath, indignation, and distress.

PSALM 78:49

God assumes no affection of our nature so often to himself in Scripture as anger; and that, too, in words which for the most part, in the Old Testament, denote the greatest commotion of mind. Wrath, fury, the heat of great anger, indignation, hot anger, smoking anger, wrathful anger, anger appearing in the countenance, inflaming the nostrils, rousing the heart, flaming and consuming, are often assigned to him, and in words, too, which among the Hebrews express the parts of the body affected by such commotions.

But since with God, beyond all doubt, 'there is no variation or shadow due to change' (James 1:17), it will be worthwhile strictly to examine what he means by this description of his most holy and unchangeable nature, so well accommodated to our weak capacities. With him there is no commotion of the blood, and likewise those troublesome affections of sorrow and pain are entirely excluded, so we must consider what this anger of God means.

First, it is manifest that by 'the anger of God', the *effects of anger* are denoted. So when Ephesians 5:6 says 'because of these things the wrath of God comes upon the sons of disobedience', it means God will most assuredly punish them. Hence the frequent mention of 'the wrath to come' that is, the last and everlasting punishment. Thus, that great and terrible day, 'on which he will judge the world in righteousness by a man whom he has appointed' (Acts 17:31) is called 'the day of his wrath' (Rom. 2:5) because it is the day of the revelation of the righteous judgment of God.

APRIL 6

Wrath Revealed

The wrath of God is revealed from heaven against all ungodliness and unrighteousness of men, who by their unrighteousness suppress the truth.

ROMANS 1:18

God hates sin, as contrary to himself, and therefore it is impossible for a sinner with safety to appear before him. But if God hates sin, he does it either from *his nature*, or because he so *wills* it. But it cannot be because he wills it, for in that case he might not will it; a supposition most absurd. But if God hates sin by nature, then by nature he is just, and vindicatory justice is natural to him.

The apostle testifies that a revelation of God's wrath is made from heaven. Even the most abandoned cannot but observe punishments of various kinds wreaking havoc everywhere in the world, and innumerable evils brooding, as it were, over the very texture of the universe. But because they wish for and desire nothing more ardently than either that there were no God, or that he paid no regard to human affairs, they either really ascribe, or pretend to ascribe, all these things to chance, fortune, the revolutions of the stars and their influence, or, finally, to natural causes.

In order to free people's minds from this pernicious deceit of atheism, the apostle affirms that all these things come to pass 'from heaven', that is, under the direction of God, or by a divine power and providence punishing sins and wickedness, and manifesting the justice of God. Thus, by that punishment inflicted on Sodom and Gomorrah from heaven, he has set up an example, to every future age, for all those who should afterwards persevere in the like impieties.

APRIL 7

Preservation

*We know that for those who love God all things work together
for good, for those who are called according to his purpose.*

ROMANS 8:28

It is one part of my aim and intention in handling the doctrine
of the perseverance of the saints, that no sound persons may
be shaken, because unhealthy ones are shattered—that those
may not tremble who are built on the rock, because those
are cast down who are built on the sand. I shall little dabble
in the waters of strife. One Scripture, in its own plainness and
simplicity, will be of more use for the end I aim at than twenty
academic arguments, pressed with never so much accurateness
and subtlety.

God has promised to make 'all things work together for
good for those who love him' (Rom. 8:28). In his infinite love
and wisdom, he is pleased to exercise them with great variety,
both within and without, in reference to themselves and others,
for the accomplishing towards them all the good pleasure of his
goodness. He wishes them to continue in that holy, humble,
dependent frame, which is needful for the receiving from him
of those gracious supplies without which it is impossible they
should be preserved.

To this end are they often exposed to winnowings of fierce
winds. Not that God is delighted with their fears and jealousies,
but with the trial and exercise of their graces unto which he calls
them.

APRIL 8

The Saints

He has delivered us from the domain of darkness and transferred us to the kingdom of his beloved Son, in whom we have redemption, the forgiveness of sins.

COLOSSIANS 1:13-14

The saints, or believers, may be briefly described thus:

1. That whereas 'by nature children of wrath, like the rest of mankind' and 'dead in trespasses and sins' (Eph. 2:1-3), that faith and holiness which they are in due time invested with, by which they are made believers and saints, is an effect and fruit of, and flows from, God's eternal purpose concerning their salvation or election.

2. They obtain this precious faith by God giving to them that Holy Spirit of his by whom he raised Jesus from the dead, to raise them from their death in sin, to quicken them unto newness of life, enduing them with a new life, with a spiritual, gracious, supernatural habit, spreading itself upon their whole souls, making them new creatures throughout.

3. The holy and blessed Spirit, who effectually and powerfully works this change in them, is bestowed upon them as a fruit of the purchase and intercession of Jesus Christ, to dwell in them and abide with them for ever.

4. By all this, they are really changed from death to life, from darkness to light, from universal, habitual uncleanness to holiness, from a state of enmity, stubbornness, and rebellion, into a state of love, obedience, and delight. Whereas they were children of wrath, under the curse and condemning power of the law, they are now, upon the score of him who was made a curse for them and is made righteousness to them, accepted, justified, adopted, and admitted into that family of heaven and earth which is called after the name of God.

APRIL 9

Chastisement

*For my name's sake I defer my anger; for the sake of my praise
I restrain it for you, that I may not cut you off.*

ISAIAH 48:9

What shall we suppose are the thoughts of Jesus Christ towards a withering member, a dying brother, a perishing child, a wandering sheep? Sin procures, by the way of merit, the taking away of the Spirit and removal of the habit graciously bestowed. Believers deserve by sin that God should take his Spirit from them, and the grace that he has bestowed on them: they do so indeed; it cannot be denied. But will the Lord deal so with them? Will he judge his house with such fire and vengeance? Is that the way of a father with his children?

Until God has taken away his Spirit and grace, although they are rebellious children, yet they are his children still. And is this the way of a tender father, to cut the throats of his children when it is in his power to mend them? The casting of a wicked man into hell is not a punishment to be compared to this; the loss of God's presence is the worst of hell. So infinitely must their needs be more sensible of it who have once enjoyed it than those who were strangers to it from the womb!

Certainly, the Lord bears another testimony concerning his kindness to his sons and daughters than that we should entertain such dismal thoughts of him. He chastises his children, indeed, but he does not kill them; he corrects them with rods, but his kindness he takes not from them.

APRIL 10

The Enemy Within

*Now if I do what I do not want, it is no longer I who do it,
but sin that dwells within me.*

ROMANS 7:20

One of the many enemies that fight against the welfare of our souls is indwelling sin, whose power and policy, strength and prevalence, nearness and treachery, the Scripture exceedingly sets out, and the saints daily feel.

Concerning its nearness to us, it is indeed *in us*; and that not as a thing different from us, but it cleaves to all the faculties of our souls. It is an enemy born with us, bred up with us, carried about in our bosoms, by nature our familiar friend, our guide and counsellor, as dear to us as our right eye, as useful as our right hand, our wisdom, and our strength.

The apostle Paul calls it the 'sin that dwells within us' (Rom. 7:17, 20). It has in us, in the faculties of our souls, its abode and station. It does not pass by and away, but there it dwells, so that it never goes from home, is never out of the way when we have anything to do. That is why in Romans 7:21, he calls it the 'evil that lies close at hand'. When we go about anything that is good, or have opportunity for or temptation unto any thing that is evil, it is never absent, but is ready to pluck us back or to put us on, according as it serves its ends. It is such an inmate that we can never be quit of its company; and so intimate unto us that it puts itself forth in every acting of the mind, will, or any other faculty of the soul. Though people would fain shake it off, yet when they would do good, this evil will be present with them.

APRIL 11

Spreading Sin

If your eye is bad, your whole body will be full of darkness.
If then the light in you is darkness, how great is the darkness!

MATTHEW 6:23

Sin is not restricted into a corner of the soul; it is spread over the whole, all the faculties, affections, and passions. That which is born of the flesh is flesh; it is all flesh, and nothing but flesh. It is darkness in the understanding, keeping us, at best, that we know but in part, and are still dull and slow of heart to believe. Naturally, we are all darkness, nothing but darkness; and though the Lord shines into our mind, to give us in some measure the knowledge of his glory in the face of Jesus Christ, yet we are still very dark; and it is a hard work to bring in a little light upon the soul.

Especially this is seen in particular practical things; though in general we have very clear light, yet when we come to particular acts of obedience, how often does our light grow dim and fail us, causing us to judge amiss of that which is before us, by the rising of that natural darkness which is in us! It is perverseness, stubbornness, obstinacy in the *will*, that carries it with violence to disobedience and sin. It is sensuality upon the *affections*, bending them to the things of the world, alienating them from God. It is slipperiness in the *memory*, making us like leaking vessels, so that the things that we hear of the gospel do suddenly slip out, whereas other things abide firm in its cells and chambers. It is senselessness and error in the *conscience*, staving it off from the performance of that duty which, in the name and authority of God, it is to accomplish. And, in all these, there is daily enticing and seducing of the heart to folly, conceiving and bringing forth sin.

APRIL 12

Unchanging Love

For I the LORD do not change; therefore you, O children of Jacob, are not consumed.

MALACHI 3:6

The Lord manifests the unchangeableness of his love towards those whom he has once graciously accepted in Christ. In Malachi 3:6, the 'children of Jacob' are the children of the faith of Jacob, the Israel of God, not all the seed of Jacob according to the flesh. In this prophecy, the Holy Spirit makes an eminent distinction between these two (Mal. 3:16-18, 4:1-3). The beginning of this chapter contains a most evident and clear prediction and prophecy of the bringing in of the kingdom of Christ in the gospel.

Very many of those who looked and waited for that coming of his are cut off and cast out, as persons that have neither lot nor portion in the mercy that came with it. Though they said within themselves that they had Abraham as their father, and were the children and posterity of Jacob, yet to those who are only the carnal seed, and do also walk in the ways of the flesh, he threatens a sore revenge and swift destruction, when others shall be invested with all the eminent mercies which the Lord Christ brings along with him (Mal. 3:5).

To the true children of Jacob, he reveals the foundation of their preservation to the end, even the unchangeableness of his own nature and being, to which his love for them is conformed. He plainly intimates that unless he and his everlasting deity are subject and liable to alteration and change (which to even imagine, would be to cast him down from his excellency), it could not be that they should be cast off for ever and consumed.

APRIL 13

Covenant Blessings

Jesus is the guarantor of a better covenant.

HEBREWS 7:22

This, then, is wrapped up in the promise of the covenant to the elect, with whom it is established: God will be a God to them forever, and that to bless them with all the blessings which he communicates in and by the Lord Jesus Christ, the promised seed. The continuance of his favour to the end is to us unquestionably a spiritual blessing; and if so, it is in Christ, and shall certainly be enjoyed by them to whom God is a God in covenant.

Many, in times of spiritual difficulties and pressures, have closed with this engagement of God in the covenant, and have had experience of its bearing them through all perplexities and entanglements, when the waves of temptation were ready to go over their souls. When David viewed all the difficulties he had passed through, he concluded that, 'God has made with me an everlasting covenant, ordered in all things and sure: this is all my salvation, and all my desire' (2 Sam. 23:5). The covenant from which he had his sure mercies—not changeable, not alterable, not liable to failings, as the temporal prosperity of his house was—was what he rejoiced in.

Are we, in the covenant of grace, left to our own hearts, ways, and walkings? Is it not different to that which has been abolished? Is it not the great distinguishing character of it that all the promises of it are stable, and shall certainly be accomplished in Jesus Christ? 'For all the promises of God find their Yes in him. That is why it is through him that we utter our Amen to God for his glory' (2 Cor. 1:20).

APRIL 14

Sure Covenant

For the LORD of hosts has purposed, and who will annul it?

ISAIAH 14:27

The immutability of the covenant which God ratified in the blood of Christ is easily demonstrated. When two enter into covenant and agreement, no one can undertake that their covenant shall be firm and stable if it equally depends upon both parties. Indeed, both may perhaps be changeable, and so actually changed before the accomplishing of the thing engaged about.

However, though the one should be faithful, yet the other may fail, and so the covenant is broken. Thus it was with God and Adam. It could not be undertaken that their covenant should be kept inviolable, because though God continues faithful, yet Adam might prove (as indeed he did) faithless; and so the covenant was annulled, as to any power of knitting together God and man. Thus it is with the covenant between husband and wife; the one party cannot undertake that the whole covenant shall be observed, because the other may prove treacherous.

In the covenant in Christ, the case is otherwise. God himself has undertaken the whole, both for his continuing with us and our continuing with him. Though there are sundry persons in covenant, yet there is but one who undertakes for all, and that is God himself. It does not depend upon the will of another, but on him only who is faithful, who cannot lie, who cannot deceive, who will make all his engagements good to the utmost. Blessed be his name that he has not laid the foundation of a covenant in the blood of his dear Son, and then left it to us and our frail wills to carry it on, that it should be in our power to make void the great work of his mercy!

APRIL

APRIL 15

Free Grace

If the inheritance comes by the law, it no longer comes by promise; but God gave it to Abraham by a promise.

GALATIANS 3:18

Gospel promises are:

1. The free and gracious dispensations, and,

2. revelations of God's good-will and love,

3. to sinners,

4. through Christ,

5. in a covenant of grace;

6. in which, upon his truth and faithfulness, he engages himself to be their God, to give his Son to them and for them, and his Holy Spirit to abide with them, with all things that are either required in them or are necessary for them to make them accepted before him, and to bring them to an enjoyment of him.

All the promises of the gospel are but one, and every one of them comprehends and tenders the same love, the same Christ, the same Spirit, which are in them all. They are *free* and *gracious* as to the rise and fountain of them. They are given to us merely through the goodwill and pleasure of God. That which is of *promise* is everywhere opposed to that which is of *doubt*, or that which is any way *deserved* or procured by us. 'If the inheritance comes by the law' (which includes all that is desirable in us, acceptable, and deserving), 'it no longer comes by promise,'— that is, free, and of mere grace.

Jesus Christ is himself in the promise. He is the great original, matter, and subject of the promises, and the giving of him was doubtless of free grace and mercy.

APRIL 16

Peculiar Promise

I will be with you. I will not leave you or forsake you.

JOSHUA 1:5

This promise in Joshua 1:5, it is true, is originally a grant to one single person entering upon a peculiar employment. But the Holy Spirit has eminently taught the saints of God to plead and improve it in all generations for their own advantage. That is not only upon the account of the general rule of the establishment of all promises in Jesus Christ to the glory of God—'all the promises of God find their Yes in him' (2 Cor. 1:20); but also because God himself applies it to them, whenever they stand in need of the faithfulness of God in it: 'Keep your life free from love of money, and be content with what you have, for he has said, "I will never leave you nor forsake you,"' (Heb. 13:5).

The apostle lays down an exhortation in the beginning of Hebrews 13:5 against the inordinate desire of the things of the world, that are laboured after upon the account of this present life. To give power and efficacy to his exhortation, he says that all such desires are altogether needless, upon consideration of his all-sufficiency who has promised never to forsake us. He proves this by quoting this promise given to Joshua, giving us a rule for the application of all the promises of the Old Testament which were made to the church and people of God. Some labour much to rob believers of the consolation intended for them in the evangelical promises of the Old Testament, though made in general to the church, because they were made to the Jews, and do not concern us. But to every believer God also says 'I will never leave you, nor forsake you.'

APRIL 17

The Helper's Support

The Helper, the Holy Spirit, whom the Father will send in my name, he will teach you all things and bring to your remembrance all that I have said to you.

JOHN 14:26

There are two special ways whereby the Spirit communicates support to the saints when they are ready to sink, and that upon two accounts: first, of consolation; and then of strength.

The first he does by bringing to mind the things that Jesus Christ has left in store for their support. Our Saviour Christ, informing his disciples how they should be upheld in their tribulations, tells them that the Comforter, which should dwell with them and be in them (John 14:16-17) should bring to remembrance what he had told them (v. 26). Christ had said many things, things gracious and heavenly, to his disciples. He had given them many rich and precious promises to uphold their hearts in their greatest perplexities. But knowing full well how ready they were to forget and to let slip the things that were spoken (Heb. 2:1), and how coldly his promises would come in to their assistance when retained only in their natural faculties and made use of by their own strength, he tells them that this work he commits to the charge of another, who will do it to the purpose.

And this he does every day. How often, when the spirits of the saints are ready to faint within them—when straits and perplexities are round about them, that they know not what to do, nor where to go for help or support,—the Spirit that dwells in them brings to mind some seasonable, suitable promise of Christ, that bears them up quite above their difficulties and distractions. This opens such a new spring of life and consolation to their souls that they who but now stooped, yea were almost bowed to the ground, do stand upright, and feel no weight or burden at all!

APRIL 18

God Doesn't Guess

This Jesus, delivered up according to the definite plan and foreknowledge of God, you crucified and killed by the hands of lawless men.

ACTS 2:23

God, by the free actions of men (some of which he foretells) fulfils his own counsel as to judgments and mercies, rewards and punishments. They may be things of the greatest import in the world, and in their accomplishment as much of the wisdom, power, righteousness, and mercy of God is manifest, as in any of the works of his providence whatsoever. The selling of Joseph, the crucifying of his Son, the destruction of antichrist, are far too important that God should only conjecture at their happening.

Taking away God's foreknowledge of things contingent would render his providence useless as to the government of the world. To what end should any rely upon him, seek for him, commit themselves to his care through the course of their lives, when he knows not what will or may befall them the next day? How shall he judge or rule the world who every moment is surprised with new emergencies which he did not foresee, which must necessitate him to make new determinations?

APRIL 19

Equality with God

Who, though he was in the form of God, did not count equality with God a thing to be grasped, but emptied himself, by taking the form of a servant.

PHILIPPIANS 2:6-7

The intention and design of the apostle in this place is evidently to exhort believers to self-denial, mutual love, and condescension one to another. He proposes to them the example of Jesus Christ; and lets them know that he, being 'in the form of God', and 'equal with God' did yet, in his love to us, 'make himself of no reputation'. He laid aside and eclipsed his glory, in this, that 'he took the form of a servant,' being made man, that in that form and nature he might be 'obedient unto death' for us and on our behalf.

He that was 'in the form of God', and 'equal with God', and took on the nature and 'form of a servant',—he is God by nature, and was incarnate or made flesh. Between that which is finite and that which is infinite, that which is eternal and that which is temporal, the creature and the Creator, God by nature and him who by nature is not God—it is utterly impossible there should be any equality. God having so often avouched his infinite distance from all creatures, his refusal to give his glory to any of them, his inequality with them all, it must have been the highest robbery that ever any could be guilty of, for Christ to make himself equal to God if he were not God.

To work great works by the power of God argues no equality with him, or else all the prophets and apostles who worked miracles were also equal to God. The infinite inequality of nature between the Creator and the most glorious creature will not allow that it be said they are equal to him. Nor is it said that Christ was equal to God in respect of the works he did, but, absolutely, 'He thought it not robbery to be equal with God.'

APRIL 20

God the Spirit

The grace of the Lord Jesus Christ and the love of God and the fellowship of the Holy Spirit be with you all.

2 CORINTHIANS 13:14

The Spirit created, formed, and adorned this world, and is therefore God. 'The builder of all things is God' (Heb. 3:4). 'By the word of the LORD the heavens were made, and by the breath of his mouth all their host' (Ps. 33:6). 'By his wind the heavens were made fair' (Job 26:13). 'The Spirit of God has made me, and the breath of the Almighty gives me life' (Job 33:4; Ps. 104:30). He that makes the heavens and garnishes them, he who makes mankind and gives them life, is God.

And so, that which is ascribed to God absolutely in one place, is in another ascribed to the Spirit absolutely. What it is affirmed that God does, will do, or did, is affirmed of the Spirit (Acts 1:16, 28:25). What is said of God is affirmed of the Spirit (Isa. 63:10, Acts 7:51). Innumerable other instances of the same kind might be added.

He regenerates us (John 3:5). From him is our illumination (Eph. 1:17) And he foretells 'things to come' (John 16:13, 1 Tim. 4:1) which is a property of God, by which he will be known from all false gods (Isa. 41:22-23 etc.). And he is in some of these places expressly called God, as also 1 Corinthians 12:5, 6, compared with verse 11, and he is immense, who dwells in all believers. He dwells in us, as God dwells in a temple (Rom. 8:9, 1 Cor. 3:16), thereby sanctifying us, comforting us, and helping our infirmities; mortifying our sins, creating in us Christian graces; yea, he is the author of all grace.

He is the object of divine worship, we being baptised into his name, as that of the Father and Son (Matt. 28:19). And grace is prayed for from him as from Father and Son (2 Cor. 13:14).

APRIL 21

Covenant of Grace

In the LORD all the offspring of Israel shall be justified and shall glory.

ISAIAH 45:25

The covenant of works was, 'Do this, and live.' By perfect obedience you shall have life. Mercy and pardon of sins were utter strangers to that covenant, and therefore, by it, the Holy Spirit tells us that no one could be saved.

The church of old had the promises of Christ (Rom. 9:4, Gen. 3:15, 12:3). They were justified by faith (Gen. 15:6, Rom. 4, Gal. 3). They obtained mercy for their sins, and were justified in the Lord (Isa. 45:24-25). They had the Spirit for conversion, regeneration, and sanctification (Ezek. 11:19, 36:26). They expected and obtained salvation by Jesus Christ—things as remote from the covenant of works as the east is from the west.

It is true, the administration of the covenant of grace which they lived under was dark, legal, and low, in comparison with that which we now are admitted to since the coming of Christ in the flesh. But the covenant in which they walked with God and that in which we find acceptance is the same, and the justification of Abraham their father is the pattern of ours (Rom. 4:4-5).

APRIL 22

Worship Jesus Christ

To him who sits on the throne and to the Lamb be blessing and honour and glory and might forever and ever!

REVELATION 5:13

Jesus Christ the mediator, being God and man, is to be worshipped with divine, religious worship, even as the Father. By 'worshipped with divine worship' I mean believed in, hoped in, trusted in, invoked as God, as an independent fountain of all good, and a sovereign disposer of all our present and everlasting concerns. By doing this we acknowledge in him, and ascribe to him, all divine perfections—omnipotence, omniscience, infinite goodness, omnipresence, and the like.

In Revelation, we have the most solemn representation of the divine, spiritual worship of the church, both the church militant on the earth and the church triumphant in the heavens. By both is the worship mentioned given to the Mediator. 'To him' (to Jesus Christ) 'who loves us, and has freed us from our sins by his blood, be glory and dominion forever and ever, Amen' (Rev. 1:5-6). So again, the same church, represented by four living creatures and twenty-four elders, falls down before the Lamb:

'Worthy is the Lamb who was slain, to receive power and wealth and wisdom and might and honour and glory and blessing!' (Rev. 5:12). And in verse 13, joint worship is given to him who sits upon the throne and to the Lamb by the whole creation. Now, the Lamb is neither Christ in respect of the divine nature nor Christ in respect of the human nature, but it is Christ the mediator. Christ was mediator in respect of both natures. It is, then, the person of the mediator, God and man, who is the 'Lamb of God who takes away the sin of the world' (John 1:29) to whom all this honour and worship is ascribed.

APRIL

APRIL 23

The Purpose of Punishment

The LORD has laid on him the iniquity of us all.

ISAIAH 53:6

Consider the ends of punishment, and see which of them is applicable to the transaction between God and Christ.

1. Was it for his *own correction?* No, says the prophet: 'he had done no violence, and there was no deceit in his mouth' (Isa. 53:9). He was perfectly innocent, so that he had no need of any chastisement for his amendment. And so signally, in sundry places, where mention is made of the death of Christ, his own spotless innocence is often pleaded.

2. Neither was it for his *instruction*, that he might be wise and instructed in the will of God. For at the very beginning of the prophecy, Isaiah says he shall 'act wisely and be exalted' (Isa. 52:13). He was faithful before in all things. And though he experimentally learned obedience by his sufferings (Heb. 5:8), yet habitually to the utmost he was prepared to do the will of God, before the afflictions here principally intended.

3. Neither was he punished for *example*, to be made an example to others that they might not offend. For what can offenders learn from the punishment of one who never offended? 'He was cut off, but not for himself' (Dan. 9:26 KJV). And the end assigned, verse 11, which is not the instruction only, but the justification and salvation of others, will not allow this end: 'He shall make many to be accounted righteous, and he shall bear their iniquities' (Isa. 53:11). He set us an example in his obedience, but he was not punished for an example.

It appears, then, from all that has been said, that our iniquities that were laid on Christ were the punishment due to our iniquity.

APRIL 24

Lingering Death

Look to Jesus, the founder and perfecter of our faith, who for the joy that was set before him endured the cross, despising the shame.

HEBREWS 12:2

The death of the cross was ignominious and shameful—the death of slaves, malefactors, robbers, pests of the earth and burdens of human society, like those crucified with him. Hence he is said to be 'obedient to death, the death of the cross' (Phil. 2:8), that shameful and ignominious death. And when he 'endured the cross', he 'despised the shame' (Heb. 12:2). To be brought forth and scourged as a malefactor amongst malefactors in the eye of the world, made a scorn and a byword, men wagging their heads and making mouths at him in derision, when he was full of torture, bleeding to death, is no small aggravation of it. Hence the most frequent expression of his death is by the cross, or crucifying.

It was a lingering death. Sudden death, though violent, is an escape from torture. Christ's death was torture. From his agony in the garden, when he began to die (all the powers of hell being then let loose upon him), until the giving up of his spirit, it was from the evening of one day to the evening of another. From his scourging by Pilate, after which he was under continual pain and suffering in his soul and in his body, to his death, it was six hours. And all this while he was under exquisite tortures.

He also suffered invisible spiritual suffering in the attempts of the devil. Christ looked on him at a distance, in his approach to set upon him. 'The ruler of this world is coming' (John 14:30). He saw him coming, with all his malice, fury, and violence, to set upon him, to ruin him if it were possible. And that he had a close combat with him on the cross is evident from the conquest that Christ there made of him (Col. 2:15), which was not done without wounds and blood; when he broke the serpent's head, the serpent bruised his heel (Gen. 3:15).

APRIL 25

By No Works

We know that a person is not justified by works of the law but through faith in Jesus Christ.

GALATIANS 2:16

Paul is very troublesome to all the Pharisees of this age. They therefore turn themselves a thousand ways to escape the authority of the word and truth of God, by him fully declared and vindicated against their forefathers. They labour to fortify themselves with distinctions, which, as they suppose, but falsely, their predecessors were ignorant of. Paul denies all works, all works whatsoever, to have any share in our justification before God, as the matter of our righteousness or the cause of our justification.

1. He excludes all *works of the law*, as is confessed. The works of the law are the works that the law requires. Now, there is no work whatever that is good or acceptable to God but it is required by the law; so that in excluding works of the law, he excludes all works whatever.

2. He expressly excludes all *works done by virtue of grace* and *after calling*, which, if any, should be exempted from being works of the law. These Paul excludes expressly 'By grace you are saved … not of works' (Eph. 2:8-10) What works? Those which 'we are created for in Christ Jesus'.

3. All *works that are works* are excluded expressly, and set in opposition to grace in this business: 'if it is by grace, it is no longer on the basis of works; otherwise grace would no longer be grace' (Rom. 11:6).

4. All *works are excluded that take off from the absolute freedom of the justification of sinners* by the redemption that is in Christ (Rom. 3:20-28). Now, this is not peculiar to any one sort of works, or to any one work more than to another.

APRIL 26

The Promised Seed

Now the promises were made to Abraham and to his offspring. It does not say, 'And to offsprings', referring to many, but referring to one, 'And to your offspring', who is Christ.

GALATIANS 3:16

There is a twofold knowledge of Christ the mediator: First, in general, knowledge of a mediator, the Messiah promised; which was the knowledge of the saints under the Old Testament. Second, particular knowledge, that Jesus of Nazareth was that Messiah; which also was and is known to the saints under the New Testament.

An explicit knowledge of the way and manner of salvation, which was to be wrought, accomplished, and brought about by the Messiah, the promised seed, Jesus Christ, it was much more evidently and clearly given after the resurrection and the ascension of Christ than before, the Spirit of revelation being then poured out in a more abundant manner than before.

Before Christ's coming into the world, the saints of the Old Testament did pray, and were appointed of God to pray, in the name of Jesus Christ, inasmuch as, in all their addresses unto God, they leaned on him, as promised to them, through whom they were to receive the blessing and to be blessed, believing that they should be accepted on his account. This was virtually prayer to God in the name of Christ, or through him. This is evident from the tenor of the covenant in which they walked with God, in which they were called to look to the Seed of the woman, to expect the blessing in the Seed of Abraham, speaking of the Seed as of one and not of many (Gal. 3:16).

If they had any promise of him, if any covenant in him, if any types representing him, if any light of him, if any longing after him, if any benefit by him or fruit of his mediation, all their worship of God was in him and through him.

APRIL 27

Preserved in Zion

The LORD has founded Zion, and in her the afflicted of his people find refuge.

ISAIAH 14:32

The great design of God, in his mighty works and dispensations in the world, is the establishment of his people, and their proper interest, in their several generations.

It is not for this or that *form of government*, or civil administration of human affairs that God has wrought his mighty works amongst us. It is not for these or those *governors*, much less for the advantage of one or another sort of people, for the enthroning of any one or another persuasion, gainful or helpful to some, few or more. But it is that *Zion may be founded*, and the general interest of all the sons and daughters of Zion be preserved. And so far as anything is subservient to that, so far, and no farther is it accepted with him. And whatever sets itself up against it, on whatsoever account, shall be broken in pieces.

What answer, then, should we give to inquirers? 'The LORD has founded Zion.' This is that, and that alone, which we should insist upon, and take notice of, as the *peculiar* work of God amongst us. Let the reports of other nations be what they will—let them acquaint the messengers of one another with their glory, triumphs, enlarging of their empires and dominions—when it is inquired what he has done in England, let us say, 'He has founded Zion.'

'*In her the afflicted of his people find refuge*'—the poor preserved remnant are carried through the fiery trial, and preserved to see some comfortable issue of God's dealing with them, though yet wrestling with difficulties and perplexities.

APRIL 28

Providence and Prejudice

How unsearchable are his judgments and how inscrutable his ways!

ROMANS 11:33

In many works of his power and righteousness, God will have us bow our souls to the law of his providence, and his sovereignty, wisdom, and goodness in it, when his footsteps are in the deep, and his paths are not known. This is the most reasonable thing in the world.

It is chiefly from ourselves and our own follies that we come short of such an acquaintance with the works of God as to be able to give an answer to everyone that shall demand an account of them. When David was staggered at the works of God, he gives this reason of it, 'I was brutish and ignorant; I was like a beast toward you' (Ps. 73:22). That thoughtfulness and wisdom which keeps us in darkness, is our folly.

There are sundry things that are apt to cloud our apprehensions as to the mind of God in his dealing with his people. These include *self-fulness* of our own private apprehensions and designs. You seldom see someone take up an opinion, but they instantly lay more weight upon it than upon all religion besides. If that is not enthroned, be it a matter of never so small importance, they scarce care what becomes of all other truths. When people have fixed to themselves that this or that particular must be the product of God's providential dispensations, that alone fills their aims and desires, and leaves no room for any other apprehension.

Fear, hope, wrath, anger, discontentment, with a rabble of the like mind-darkening affections, are the attendants of such a frame. He who knows anything of the power of prejudices in diverting minds from passing a right judgment, and the efficacy of disordered affections for the creating and confirming of such prejudices, will discern the power of this darkening disturbance.

APRIL 29

Lacking Reformation?

You then who teach others, do you not teach yourself?

Take heed lest that evil be still abiding upon any of our spirits, that we should be crying out and calling for reformation without a due consideration of what it is, and how it is to be brought about. I wish one of many of them who have prayed for it, and complained for lack of it, had endeavoured to carry it on as they might. Would you have a reformation? Be more humble, more holy, more zealous. Delight more in the ways, worship, ordinances of God. Reform your persons in your lives, relations, families, parishes, as to gospel obedience, and you will see a glorious reformation indeed.

God has now, for sundry years, tried us, whether indeed we love reformation or no. Have any provoked us or compelled us to defile the worship of God with ceremonies or superstitions, and our own consciences? Have we been imposed on in the ways of God by people ignorant of them? Has not God said to us, 'You that have prayed under persecution for reformation, you that have fought in the high places of the field for reformation, you that have covenanted and sworn for reformation—go now, reform yourselves!'

If, after all this, we still cry out, 'Give us a reformation!' and don't complain of our own negligence, folly, hatred of personal reformation, to be the only cause of that lack, it is easy to judge what we would have, if we had our desires.

APRIL 30

Seek the Lord

If you seek him, he will be found by you, but if you forsake him, he will cast you off forever.

1 Chronicles 28:9

Would you be with God? Take direction from him by Christ in all your undertakings; so do in *deed*, and not in *word* or *profession* only.

1st. Captivate all your desires to his glory. Set your hearts on nothing, but with this express reserve, 'if it is consistent with and expedient unto the glory of Christ and his kingdom'. Lay all your aims and designs at his feet always, becoming as weaned children before him.

2nd. Bear before him a *real sense* of your own weakness and folly, that in his pity and compassion he may relieve you.

3rd. Keep your *hearts* in that integrity, that you may always press and urge him with his own interest in all your affairs. This is a thing that none but upright hearts can do uprightly.

4th. Actually inquire by *faith and prayer*, what is his will and mind. Do it privately, publicly; do it every day, and in days set apart for that purpose. He will assuredly be found of you.

If, instead of these things, you bear yourselves up on the wings of your own wisdom and contrivances, though you may seem for a season to have attained a fair pitch and flight, you will be entangled, and brought down in the midst of your course with shame and sorrow: for the Lord will not be with you.

This month, we will be reading some of the works Owen wrote during the high point of his career in Oxford, during the last few years of the English republic.

Of the Mortification of Sin in Believers is a treatise, based on Romans 8:13, on a subject of perennial interest to keen Christians. In 1657, Owen finally published *Of Communion with God the Father, Son, and Holy Spirit*, after repeated requests from friends. This is a unique work on the distinct relationship of believers with each of the three persons of the Trinity.

Two further books from 1657, *Of Schism*, and *A Review of the True Nature of Schism*, were attempts to defend Congregationalism from the accusations of other parties in the church. What is the true nature of the fellowship churches are meant to have with each other?

Owen returned in 1658 to practical spirituality with *Of Temptation, the Nature and Power of It*, based on some discourses delivered in Oxford. *Of the Divine Original, Authority, Self-evidencing Light, and Power of the Scriptures* was published that same year and he also wrote a Latin treatise against the 'fanatical' Quakers on the same themes, called *Pro Sacra Scripturis*.

Finally, we will hear again from Owen the preacher in 'The Glory and Interest of Nations Professing the Gospel', which was preached at a private fast to the House of Commons in 1659.

During this period, Owen also wrote prefaces to books by George Kendall and William Guild, reviewed the suspect biblical annotations of Dutch Arminian scholar, Hugo Grotius, and helped to draft *A Declaration of the Faith and Order Owned and Practised in the Congregational Churches in England*, also known as the Savoy Declaration (1659), as well as continuing to write about the power of the state in issues of religion.

MAY 1

Mortification of Sin

If by the Spirit you put to death the deeds of the body, you will live.

ROMANS 8:13

The choicest believers, who are assuredly freed from the condemning power of sin, ought yet to make it their business all their days to mortify the indwelling power of sin.

The principal *efficient cause* of the performance of this duty is the Spirit: 'If *by the Spirit* ...' All other ways of mortification are vain, all helps leave us helpless; it must be done by the Spirit. People, as the apostle intimates in Romans 9:30-32, may attempt this work on other principles, by other means. But, he says, 'This is the work of the Spirit; by him alone is it to be wrought, and by no other power is it to be brought about.' Mortification from a self-strength, carried on by ways of self-invention, unto the end of a self-righteousness, is the soul and substance of all false religion in the world.

To kill a person, or any other living thing, is to take away the principle of all their strength, vigour, and power, so that they cannot act. So it is in this case. Indwelling sin is compared to a person, a living person, called 'the old man', with his faculties, and properties, his wisdom, craft, subtlety, strength. This, says the apostle, must be killed, put to death, mortified, that is, have its power, life, vigour, and strength to produce its effects, taken away by the Spirit. The 'old man' is said to be 'crucified with Christ' (Rom. 6:6), and ourselves to be 'dead' with him. But the whole work is by degrees to be carried on towards perfection all our days.

The vigour, and power, and comfort of our spiritual life depends on the mortification of the deeds of the flesh.

MAY 2

Kill or Be Killed

Put to death therefore what is earthly in you.

COLOSSIANS 3:5

The choicest believers, who are assuredly freed from the condemning power of sin, ought yet to make it their business all their days to mortify the indwelling power of sin.

In Colossians 3, the apostle speaks to those who are 'raised with Christ' (v. 1), who 'died' with him (v. 3), who will 'appear with him in glory' (v. 4). Do you mortify? Do you make it your daily work? Be always at it whilst you live. Cease not a day from this work. Be killing sin or it will be killing you.

Your being dead with Christ virtually, your being quickened with him, will not excuse you from this work. And our Saviour tells us how his Father deals with every branch in him that bears fruit, every true and living branch. 'He prunes it, that it may bring forth more fruit' (John 15:2). He prunes it, and that not for a day or two, but whilst it is a branch in this world. And the apostle tells you what was his practice: 'I discipline my body and keep it under control' (1 Cor. 9:27). And if this was the work and business of Paul, who was so incomparably exalted in grace, revelations, enjoyments, privileges, consolations, above the ordinary measure of believers, on what may we possibly base an exemption from this work and duty whilst we are in this world?

When sin lets us alone, we may let sin alone; but as sin is never less quiet than when it seems to be most quiet, and its waters are for the most part deep when they are still, so ought our contrivances against it to be vigorous at all times and in all conditions, even where there is least suspicion.

MAY 3

Sinning without Bitterness

Christ gave himself for us to redeem us from all lawlessness and to purify for himself a people for his own possession who are zealous for good works.
TITUS 2:14

Various evils certainly attend every un-mortified professor. Let them pretend what they will, they have *slight thoughts of sin*; at least, of sins of daily infirmity. The root of an un-mortified course is the digestion of sin without bitterness in the heart. When someone is able, without bitterness, to swallow and digest daily sins, they are at the very brink of turning the grace of God into lasciviousness, and being hardened by the deceitfulness of sin.

Neither is there a greater evidence of a false and rotten heart in the world. To use the blood of Christ—which is given to *cleanse* us (1 John 1:7); the exaltation of Christ, which is to give us *repentance* (Acts 5:31); the doctrine of grace, which teaches us to *deny all ungodliness* (Titus 2:11-12)—to countenance sin, is a rebellion that, in the issue, will break the bones.

At this door have gone out from us most of the professors that have apostatised in the days we live in. For a while, they were most of them under convictions; these kept to their duties, and brought them to profession; so they 'escaped the pollutions that are in the world, through the knowledge of our Lord Jesus Christ' (2 Pet. 2:20). But having got an acquaintance with the doctrine of the gospel, and being weary of duty, for which they had no principle, they began to countenance themselves in manifold neglects from the doctrine of grace. Now, when once this evil had laid hold of them, they speedily tumbled into perdition.

MAY 4

God's Way Not Ours

In vain do they worship me, teaching as doctrines the commandments of men.

MARK 7:7

God only is sufficient for this work. All ways and means without him are as a thing of nought. He works in us as he pleases.

In vain do people seek other remedies; they shall not be healed by them. What several ways have been prescribed for this, to have sin mortified, is known. Now, the reasons why some can never, with all their endeavours, truly mortify any one sin, amongst others, are:

1. Because many of the ways and means they use and insist upon for this end were never appointed of God for that purpose. Now, there is nothing in religion that has any efficacy for achieving an end, except from God's appointment of it to that purpose. Such as these are rough garments, vows, penances, disciplines, the course of monastical life, and the like; concerning all of which God will say, 'Who has required these things at your hand?' (Isa. 1:12) and, 'in vain do they worship me, teaching as doctrines the commandments of men' (Mark 7:7). Of the same nature are sundry self-vexations insisted on by others.

2. Because those things that are appointed of God as means are not used by them in their due place and order, such as are praying, fasting, watching, meditation, and the like. These have their use in the business in hand; but whereas they are all to be looked on as streams, they look on them as the fountain. Whereas they effect and accomplish the end as means only, subordinate to the Spirit and faith, they look on them to do it by virtue of the work wrought. If they fast so much, and pray so much, and keep their hours and times, the work is done. So they are always mortifying, but never come to any sound mortification.

This is the general mistake of people ignorant of the gospel about this thing.

MAY 5

It is God who works in you, both to will and to work for his good pleasure.

PHILIPPIANS 2:13

He does not so work our mortification in us as not to keep it still an act of our *obedience*. The Holy Spirit works in us and upon us, as we are fit to be wrought in and upon; that is, so as to preserve our own liberty and free obedience. He works upon our understandings, wills, consciences, and affections, agreeably to their own natures he works *in us* and *with us*, not *against us* or *without us*. He works such that his assistance is an encouragement as to the facilitating of the work, and no occasion of neglect as to the work itself.

I might here bewail the endless, foolish labour of poor souls, who, being convinced of sin, and not able to stand against the power of their convictions, do set themselves, by innumerable perplexing ways and duties, to keep down sin. But, being strangers to the Spirit of God, it is all in vain. They combat without victory, have war without peace, and are in slavery all their days. They spend their strength for that which is not bread, and their labour for that which profits not.

This is the saddest warfare that any poor creature can be engaged in. A soul under the power of conviction from the law is pressed to fight against sin, but has no strength for the combat. They cannot but fight, and they can never conquer. The *law* drives them on, and sin beats them back.

And if the case be so sad with them who do labour and strive, and yet enter not into the kingdom, what is their condition who despise all this; who are perpetually under the power and dominion of sin, and love to have it so; and are troubled at nothing, but that they cannot make sufficient provision for the flesh, to fulfil the lusts of it?

MAY 6

Un-mortified Sin

There is no health in my bones because of my sin.

PSALM 38:3

Every un-mortified sin will certainly do two things:—1. It will *weaken* the soul, and deprive it of its vigour. 2. It will *darken* the soul, and deprive it of its comfort and peace.

1. It *weakens* the soul, and deprives it of its strength. When David had, for a while, harboured an un-mortified lust in his heart, it broke all his bones, and left him no spiritual strength; hence he complained that he was sick, weak, wounded, faint. 'There is', he says, 'no soundness in my flesh' (Ps. 38:3), 'I am feeble and crushed' (v. 8). An un-mortified lust will drink up the spirit, and all the vigour of the soul, and weaken it for all duties. For:

1st. It *un-tunes* and un-frames the heart itself, by entangling its affections. It diverts the heart from the spiritual frame that is required for vigorous communion with God. It lays hold on the affections, rendering its object beloved and desirable, so expelling the love of the Father (1 John 2:15, 3:17); so, that the soul cannot say uprightly and truly to God, 'You are my portion', having something else that it loves. Fear, desire, hope, which are the choice affections of the soul, that should be full of God, will be one way or other entangled with it.

2nd. It fills the *thoughts* with contrivances about it. Thoughts are the great purveyors of the soul to bring in provision to satisfy its affections; if sin remains un-mortified in the heart, they must ever and anon be making provision for the flesh, to fulfil the lusts of it. They must glaze, adorn, and dress the objects of the flesh, and bring them home to give satisfaction; and this they are able to do, in the service of a defiled imagination, beyond all expression.

MAY 7

Studying Sin

I know my transgressions, and my sin is ever before me.

Psalm 51:3

To know that we have an enemy to deal with, to take notice of it, to consider it as an enemy indeed, and one that is to be destroyed by all means possible, is required for mortification. The contest is vigorous and hazardous—it is about the things of eternity. When, therefore, people have slight and transient thoughts of their lusts, it is no great sign that they are mortified. This is everyone's 'knowing the affliction of their own heart' (1 Kings 8:38), without which no other work can be done. It is to be feared that very many have little knowledge of the main enemy that they carry about with them in their bosoms. This makes them ready to justify themselves, and to be impatient of reproof or admonition, not knowing that they are in any danger (2 Chron. 16:10).

To labour to be acquainted with the ways, wiles, methods, advantages, and occasions of its *success*, is the beginning of this warfare. So do men deal with enemies. They inquire out their counsels and designs, ponder their ends, consider how and by what means they have formerly prevailed, that they may be prevented. In this consists the greatest skill in conduct. Take this away, and all waging of war, in which is the greatest improvement of human wisdom and industry, would be brutish. So do they deal with lust who mortify it indeed. Not only when it is actually vexing, enticing, and seducing, but in their retirements they consider, 'This is our enemy; this is his way and progress, these are his advantages, thus has he prevailed, and thus he will do, if not prevented.' And, indeed, one of the choicest and most eminent parts of practically spiritual wisdom consists in finding out the subtleties, policies, and depths of any indwelling sin.

MAY 8

Communion with God

God is light, and in him is no darkness at all.

1 JOHN 1:5

By nature, since the entrance of sin, no one has any communion with God. He is *Light*, we *darkness*; and what communion has light with darkness? He is *life*, we are *dead*,—he is *love*, and we are *enmity*; and what agreement can there be between us? People in such a condition have neither Christ, nor hope, nor God in the world (Eph. 2:12), 'being alienated from the life of God through the ignorance that is in them' (Eph. 4:18).

Now, two cannot walk together, unless they be agreed (Amos 3:3). Whilst there is this distance between God and man, there is no walking together for them in any fellowship or communion. Our first interest in God was so lost by sin, that there was left to us (in ourselves) no possibility of a recovery. As we had deprived ourselves of all power for a return, so God had not revealed any way of access to himself; or that he could, under any consideration, be approached by sinners in peace.

The manifestation of grace and pardoning mercy, which is the only door of entrance into any such communion, is not committed to any but to him alone *in* whom it is, *by* whom that grace and mercy was purchased, *through* whom it is dispensed, who reveals it from the bosom of the Father. Hence, this communion and fellowship with God is not in express terms mentioned in the Old Testament. The thing itself is found there; but the clear light of it, and the boldness of faith in it, is discovered in the gospel, and by the Spirit administered in it. By that Spirit we have this liberty (2 Cor. 3:18).

MAY 9

Distinct Communion

Now there are varieties of gifts, but the same Spirit; and there are varieties of service, but the same Lord; and there are varieties of activities, but it is the same God who empowers them all in everyone.

1 CORINTHIANS 12:4-6

The saints have distinct communion with the Father, and the Son, and the Holy Spirit (that is, distinctly with the Father, and distinctly with the Son, and distinctly with the Holy Spirit).

The Father, the word, and the Holy Spirit bear witness to the sonship of Christ, and the salvation of believers in his blood (1 John 5:7). Now, how do they bear witness to it? Even as three, as three distinct witnesses. When God witnesses concerning our salvation, surely it is incumbent on us to receive his testimony. The Father bears witness, the Son bears witness, and the Holy Spirit bears witness; for they are three distinct witnesses. So, then, are we to receive their several testimonies: and in doing so we have communion with them severally; for in this giving and receiving of testimony consists no small part of our fellowship with God.

In 1 Corinthians 12:4-6, the apostle, speaking of the distribution of gifts and graces unto the saints, ascribes them distinctly, in respect of the fountain of their communication, to the distinct persons. So graces and gifts are bestowed, and so are they received. And not only in the emanation of grace from God, but also in all our approaches to God, is the same distinction observed. 'For through Christ we have access by one Spirit to the Father' (Eph. 2:18)—the persons being here considered as engaged *distinctly* unto the accomplishment of the counsel of the will of God revealed in the gospel.

MAY 10

The Father's Love

But when the goodness and loving kindness of God our Saviour appeared, he saved us.

TITUS 3:4-5

I come now to declare how, peculiarly and eminently, the saints have communion with the Father. And this is love—free, undeserved, and eternal love. This the Father peculiarly fixes upon the saints; this they are immediately to eye in him, to receive of him, and to make such returns for it as he is delighted with. This is the great discovery of the gospel: for whereas the Father, as the fountain of the Deity, is not known any other way but as full of wrath, anger, and indignation against sin, nor can the sons of men have any other thoughts of him (Rom. 1:18)—here he is now revealed peculiarly as love, as full of love to us; the manifestation of which is the peculiar work of the gospel (Titus 3:4).

'God is love' (1 John 4:8). That the name of God is here taken personally, and for the person of the Father, not essentially, is evident from verse 9, where he is distinguished from his only begotten Son whom he sends into the world. Now, says John, 'The Father is love.' In verse 10, he says 'he loved us, and sent his Son to be the propitiation for our sins.' And that love is peculiarly to be eyed in him, the Holy Spirit plainly declares, in making it prior to the sending of Christ, and all mercies and benefits by him received.

So in that distribution made by the apostle in his solemn parting benediction (2 Cor. 13:14): 'The grace of the Lord Jesus Christ, the love of God, and the fellowship of the Holy Spirit, be with you all.' Ascribing sundry things to the distinct persons, it is *love* that he peculiarly assigns to the Father. Let us look on him by faith, as one that has had thoughts of kindness towards us from everlasting.

MAY 11

Everything in Christ

Blessed are those who hunger and thirst for righteousness, for they shall be satisfied.

MATTHEW 5:6

The fellowship we have with the second person of the Trinity, is with him as Mediator. Christ is that tree of life, which has brought forth all things that are needful for life eternal. In him is that righteousness which we hunger after. In him is that water of life, and whoever drinks of it shall thirst no more (John 4:14). Oh, how sweet are the fruits of Christ's mediation to the faith of his saints! The one who can find no relief in mercy, pardon, grace, acceptance with God, holiness, sanctification, etc., is an utter stranger to these things. Also, they have shades for refreshment and shelter—shelter from wrath without, and refreshment because of weariness from within.

Consider his excellency to endear, from his complete suitableness to all the wants of the souls of mankind. There is no one who has any lack in reference to the things of God, but Christ will be to them that which they want. I speak of those who are given to him by his Father. Are they *dead*? Christ is *life*. Are they *weak*? Christ is the *power* of God, and the *wisdom* of God. Have they the *sense of guilt* upon them? Christ is complete *righteousness*,—'The Lord our Righteousness' (Jer. 23:6). Many poor creatures are aware of their wants, but know not where their remedy lies. Indeed, whether it be life or light, power or joy, all is wrapped up in him.

MAY 12

Sin's Seriousness

He did not spare his own Son but gave him up for us all.

ROMANS 8:32

To see a *slave* beaten and corrected, it argues a fault committed; but yet perhaps the demerit of it was not very great. The correction of a son argues a great provocation; that of an only son, the greatest imaginable. Never was sin seen to be more abominably sinful and full of provocation, than when the burden of it was upon the shoulders of the Son of God.

God having made his Son—the Son of his love, his only begotten, full of grace and truth—sin for us, to manifest his indignation against it, and how utterly impossible it is that he should let the least sin go unpunished; he lays hand on him, and spares him not. Is it not most clear from the blood of the cross of Christ, that such is the demerit of sin, that it is altogether impossible that God should pass by any, the least, unpunished? If he would have done it for any, he would have done it in reference to his only Son; but he spared him not.

God is not at all delighted with, nor desirous of the blood, the tears, the cries, the inexpressible torments and sufferings, of the Son of his love. For he delights not in the anguish of any (Lamentations 3:33), much less the Son of his bosom. Only, he required that his law be fulfilled, his justice satisfied, his wrath atoned for sin; and nothing less than all this would bring it about. If the debt of sin might have been paid back at a cheaper rate, it would never have been paid by the price of the blood of Christ. If one drop less than was shed, one pang less than was laid on, would have done it, those other drops would not have been shed, nor those other pangs laid on. God did not crucify the dearly-beloved of his soul for nought.

MAY 13

The Holy Spirit

The heavenly Father will give the Holy Spirit to those who ask him!

LUKE 11:13

The presence of the Holy Spirit with believers as a comforter, sent by Christ for those ends and purposes for which he is promised, is better and more profitable for believers than any *corporeal* presence of Christ can be, now he has fulfilled the one sacrifice for sin which he was to offer.

The Holy Spirit is promised under a twofold consideration: 1. As a *Spirit of sanctification* to the elect, to convert them and make them believers. 2. As a *Spirit of consolation* to believers, to give them the privileges of the death and purchase of Christ.

On this account, we are to pray to the Father and the Son to give the Spirit to us. 'Your heavenly Father will give the Holy Spirit to those who ask him' (Luke 11:13). Now the Holy Spirit, being God, is no less to be invoked, prayed to, and called on, than the Father and Son.

Hence is that great weight, in particular, laid upon our *not grieving the Spirit* (Eph. 4:30), because he comes to us in the name, with the love, and upon the condescension, of the whole blessed Trinity.

The mystery of the Father and the Son, and the matter of commission and delegation were not under the Old Testament so clearly discovered: 'until the Spirit is poured upon us from on high, and the wilderness becomes a fruitful field, and the fruitful field is deemed a forest' (Isa. 32:15)—that is, till the Gentiles be called, and the Jews rejected.

MAY 14

The Gift of the Spirit

To each is given the manifestation of the Spirit for the common good.

1 CORINTHIANS 12:7

Take a view, then, of the state and condition of those who, professing to believe the gospel of Jesus Christ, do yet treat with contempt and despise his Spirit, as to all his operations, gifts, graces, and dispensations to his churches and saints.

Whilst Christ was in the world with his disciples, he made them no greater promise, neither in respect of their own good nor of carrying on the work which he had committed to them, than this of giving them the Holy Spirit. He instructed them to pray to the Father for him, as that which is needful for them, as bread for children (Luke 11:13). He promises him to them, as a well of water springing up in them, for their refreshment, strengthening, and consolation unto everlasting life (John 7:37-39), as also to carry on and accomplish the whole work of the ministry to them committed (John 16:8-11).

Upon his ascension, this is laid as the foundation of that glorious communication of gifts and graces in his plentiful effusion (Eph. 4:8-12)—namely, that he had received of the Father the promise of the Holy Spirit (Acts 2:33), and in such an eminent manner as thereby to make the greatest and most glorious difference between the administration of the new covenant and old.

The whole work of the ministry especially relates to the Holy Spirit. He calls men to that work, and they are separated unto him (Acts 13:2). He furnishes them with gifts and abilities for that employment (1 Cor. 12:7-10). So that the whole religion we profess, without this administration of the Spirit, is nothing; nor is there any fruit without it of the resurrection of Christ from the dead.

MAY 15

I appeal to you, brothers, by the name of our Lord Jesus Christ, that all of you agree, and that there be no divisions among you.

1 CORINTHIANS 1:10

The divisions mentioned are entirely in one church, amongst the members of one particular society. No mention is there in the least of one church divided against another, or separated from another or others, whether all true or some true, some false or but pretended. Whatever the crime be, it lies wholly within the verge of one church, that met together for the worship of God and administration of the ordinances of the gospel.

There is no mention of any particular man's, or any number of men's, separation from the holy assemblies of the whole church. Nor does the apostle lay any such thing to their charge, but plainly declares that they continued all in the joint celebration of that worship and performance together of those duties which were required of them in their assemblies. Only, they had groundless, causeless differences amongst themselves.

All the divisions of one church from another, or others, the separation of any one or more persons from any church or churches, are things of another nature, made good or evil by their circumstances. They are not at all that which the Scripture knows and calls by the name of schism. And therefore, there was no such thing or name as schism, in such a sense, known in the Judaical church, though in the former it abounded. All the different sects to the last still communicated in the same carnal ordinances; and those who utterly deserted them were apostates, not schismatics. So were the body of the Samaritans; they worshipped they knew not what, nor was salvation among them (John 4:22).

MAY 16

Unity and Schism

Be eager to maintain the unity of the Spirit in the bond of peace.

EPHESIANS 4:3

The schism described by the apostle in 1 Corinthians consists in causeless differences and contentions amongst the members of a particular church, contrary to that exercise of love, prudence, and forbearance, which are required of them to be exercised amongst themselves, and towards one another. The one who is guilty of this sin of schism is a schismatic—that is, the one who raises, or entertains, or persists in such differences. Nor are these terms used by the divine writers in any other sense.

For anyone to fall under this guilt, it is required:

1. That they be members of or belong to some one church, which is so by the institution and appointment of Jesus Christ. And we shall see that there is more required for this than the bare being a believer or a Christian.

2. That they either raise or entertain, and persist in causeless differences with others of that church, more or less, to the interruption of that exercise of love, in all the fruits of it, which ought to be amongst them, and the disturbance of the due performance of the duties required of the church in the worship of God.

3. That these differences be occasioned by and do belong to some things with reference to the worship of God.

This is that crime which the apostle rebukes, blames, condemns, under the name of schism, and tells the Corinthians that were guilty of it that they showed themselves to be carnal, or to have indulged to the flesh, and the corrupt principle of self, and their own wills, which should have been subdued to the obedience of the gospel.

MAY 17

Love One Another

Be kind to one another, tenderhearted, forgiving one another,
as God in Christ forgave you.

EPHESIANS 4:32

Schism is evidently a despising of the authority of Jesus Christ, the great sovereign Lord and Head of the church. How often has he commanded us to forbear one another, to forgive one another, to have peace among ourselves, that we may be known to be his disciples, to bear with them that are in anything contrary-minded to ourselves! Let that which at any time is the cause of such hateful divisions be brought to the rule of love and forbearance in the latitude of it, as prescribed to us by Christ. Such differences, though arising on real miscarriages and faults of some, because they might otherwise be handled and healed, and ought to be so, cannot be persisted in without the contempt of the immediate authority of Jesus Christ.

If it was considered that he 'stands in the congregation of the mighty' (Ps. 82:1), that he dwells in the church in glory, 'as in Sinai, in the holy place' (Ps. 68:17-18), walking 'in the midst of the lampstands' (Rev. 1:13), with his eyes upon us as 'a flame of fire' (Rev. 1:14)—then his presence and authority would, perhaps, be more prevalent with some than they seem to be.

MAY 18

Taught by God

But you have been anointed by the Holy One, and you all have knowledge.

1 JOHN 2:20

All who are united to Christ by the inhabitation of the same Spirit in him and them, are by it, from and according to the word, 'taught of God' (Isa. 54:13; John 6:45). They are so taught, every one of them, as to come to Christ (John 6:47), that is, by believing, by faith. They are so taught of God as that they shall certainly have that measure of knowledge and faith which is needful to bring them to Christ, and to God by him.

And this they have by the anointing or Spirit which they have received (1 John 2:20, 27), accompanying the word, by virtue of God's covenant with them (Isa. 59:21). And by this are all the members of the church catholic—however divided in their visible profession by any differences among themselves, or distinguished by the several measures of gifts and graces they have received—brought to the perfection aimed at, to the 'unity of the faith and of the knowledge of the Son of God, to mature manhood, to the measure of the stature of the fullness of Christ' (Eph. 4:13).

MAY 19

Fundamentals

One Lord, one faith, one baptism.

To preserve the unity of the church, it is required that all those grand and necessary truths of the gospel (without the knowledge of which no one can be saved by Jesus Christ) be so far believed as to be outwardly and visibly professed. There is a measure of saving truths, the explicit knowledge of which in people enjoying the use of reason within and the means of grace without, is of indispensable necessity to salvation. Without this, it is impossible that any soul, in an ordinary way, should have communion with God in Christ, not having sufficient light for converse with him, according to the tenor of the covenant of grace. These are commonly called fundamentals, or first principles, which are justly argued by many to be clear, perspicuous, and few.

Let someone profess ten thousand times that they believe all the saving truths of the gospel, and, by the course of a wicked and profane life evidence to all that they believe none of them— shall their protestation be admitted? Profession of the knowledge of God, contradicted by a course of wickedness, is not to be admitted as a thing giving any privilege whatever.

The belief and profession of all the necessary saving truths of the gospel, without the manifestation of an internal principle of the mind inconsistent with the belief of them (or adding of other things in profession that are destructive to the truths so professed) is the bond of the unity of the visible professing church of Christ. Where this is found, though otherwise accompanied with many failings, sins, and errors, the unity of the faith is so far preserved as that they are thereby rendered members of the visible church of Christ, and are by him so esteemed.

MAY 20

Separation

Go out from their midst, and be separate from them, says the Lord.

2 CORINTHIANS 6:17

Where any church is overborne by a multitude of wicked and profane people, so that it cannot reform itself, or will not, according to the mind of Christ, a believer is so far at liberty that they may desert the communion of that society without the least guilt of schism.

The church of Corinth was undoubtedly a true church. We confess the abuses and evils mentioned had crept into the church, and do thence grant that many abuses may do so into any of the best of the churches of God. Nor did it ever enter into the heart of anyone to think that so soon as any disorders fall out or abuses creep into it, it is instantly the duty of any to fly out of a church, like Paul's mariners out of the ship when the storm grew hazardous (Acts 27:30). It is the duty of all the members of such a church, untainted with the evils and corruptions of it, upon many accounts, to attempt and labour the remedy of those disorders, and rejection of those abuses to the uttermost. This is what Paul advised the Corinthians to do. In obedience to which, they were recovered.

Yet, had the church of Corinth continued in the condition before described—that notorious, scandalous sins had gone unpunished, unreproved, drunkenness continued and practised in the assemblies, people abiding by the denial of the resurrection, so overturning the whole gospel, and the church refusing to do her duty and exercise her authority to cast all those disorderly persons, upon their obstinacy, out of her communion—it would have been the duty of every saint of God in that church to have withdrawn from it, to come out from among them, and not to have been partaker of their sins, unless they were willing to partake of their plague also, which on such an apostasy would certainly ensue.

MAY 21

Revealing Tests

God left Hezekiah to himself, in order to test him and to know all that was in his heart.

2 CHRONICLES 32:31

God does not tempt us, to lead us into evil (James 1:13). But he does test us to show what is in us, either our grace or our corruption.

Grace and corruption lie deep in the heart. People often deceive themselves in the search after the one or the other of them. When we give vent to the soul, to try what grace is there, corruption comes out; and when we search for corruption, grace appears. So is the soul kept in uncertainty; we fail in our trials.

God comes with a gauge that goes to the bottom. He sends his instruments of trial into the inmost parts of the soul, and lets us see what is in us, of what metal we are constituted.

Thus, he tempted Abraham to show him his *faith*. Abraham did not know what faith he had (I mean, what power and vigour was in his faith) until God drew it out by that great trial and temptation (Gen. 22:1-2). When God says he knew it, he made Abraham know it. In the same way, he tried Hezekiah to discover his *pride*; God left him that he might see what was in his heart (2 Chron. 32:31). He did not know that he had such a proud heart, so apt to be lifted up, as he appeared to have, until God tried him, and so let out his filth, and poured it out before his face.

It is God alone who keeps us from all sin. Until we are tempted, we think we live on our own strength: 'though all people do this or that, we will not!' When the trial comes, we quickly see, by standing or falling, where our preservation comes from.

MAY 22

Temptation

Lead us not into temptation, but deliver us from evil.

MATTHEW 6:13

To *enter* into temptation, is not merely to *be tempted*. It is impossible that we should be so freed from temptation as not to be at all tempted. Whilst Satan continues in his power and malice, whilst the world and lust are in being, we shall be tempted. 'Christ', says someone, 'was made like us, that he might be tempted; and we are tempted that we may be made like Christ.'

We have no promise that we shall not be tempted at all; nor are we to pray for an absolute freedom from temptations, because we have no such promise of being heard in that. The direction we have for our prayers is, 'Lead us not into temptation' (Matt. 6:13). It is 'entering *into* temptation' that we are to pray against. We may be tempted, yet not enter into temptation.

Something more is intended by this expression than the ordinary work of Satan and our own lusts, which will be sure to tempt us every day. There is something signal in this entering into temptation, that is not the saints' everyday work. It is something that befalls them peculiarly in reference to seduction unto sin, on one account or other, by the way of allurement or fear.

When we permit a temptation to enter into us, then we 'enter into temptation'. Whilst it knocks at the door, we are at liberty; when any temptation comes in and parleys with the heart, reasons with the mind, entices and allures the affections, be it a long or a short time, do it thus insensibly and imperceptibly, or do the soul take notice of it, we 'enter into temptation'.

MAY 23

Sin's Treachery

Peter remembered how Jesus had said to him, 'Before the rooster crows twice, you will deny me three times.' And he broke down and wept.

MARK 14:72

For ourselves, we are weakness itself. We have no strength, no power to withstand. Confidence of any strength in us is one great part of our weakness; it was so in Peter. He that says he can do anything, can do nothing as he should.

A castle or fort may be ever so strong and well fortified, yet if there is a treacherous party within that is ready to betray it on every opportunity, there is no preserving it from the enemy. There are traitors in our hearts, ready to take part, to close and side with every temptation, and to give up all to them; yea, to solicit and bribe temptations to do the work, as traitors incite an enemy.

Do not flatter yourselves that you shall hold out. There are secret lusts that lie lurking in your hearts, which perhaps now stir not, which, as soon as any temptation befalls you, will rise, disturb, cry, disquiet, reduce, and never give up until they are either killed or satisfied. Those who promise themselves that the frame of their heart will be the same under a temptation as it is before, will be woefully mistaken.

Those who now abhor the thoughts of such-and-such a thing, if they once enter into temptation will find their heart inflamed towards it, and all contrary reasonings overborne and silenced. They will deride their former fears and cast out their scruples. Little did Peter think he should deny his Master as soon as he was questioned whether he knew him or not. It was no better when the hour of temptation came; all resolutions were forgotten, all love to Christ buried; the present temptation closing with his carnal fear carried all before it.

MAY

MAY 24

Pride and Ambition

Put on the Lord Jesus Christ, and make no provision for the flesh, to gratify its desires.

ROMANS 13:14

Entering into temptation may be seen in the lesser degrees of it; as, for instance, when the heart begins secretly to like the matter of the temptation, and is content to feed it and increase it by any ways that it may without downright sin.

In particular, a person begins to be in repute for piety, wisdom, learning, or the like—they are spoken of much to that purpose; their heart is tickled to hear of it, and their pride and ambition affected with it. If this person now, with all their strength, pursues the things from which their repute and esteem and glory amongst people spring, with a secret eye to have it increased, they are entering into temptation. If they are not careful, it will quickly render them a slave of lust.

So is it with many scholars. They find themselves esteemed and favoured for their learning. This takes hold of the pride and ambition of their hearts. Hence they set themselves to study with all diligence day and night—a thing good in itself—but they do it that they might satisfy the thoughts and words of others, in which they delight. And so, in all they do, they make provision for the flesh, to gratify its desires.

Some find themselves, perhaps, to be the darlings or glory of their party. If thoughts of this secretly insinuate themselves into their hearts, and influence them into more than ordinary diligence and activity in their way and profession, they are entangled. Instead of aiming at more glory, they need to lie in the dust, in a sense of their own vileness.

MAY 25

Give me neither poverty nor riches… lest I be full and deny you and say, 'Who is the LORD?'

PROVERBS 30:8-9

A season of unusual outward prosperity is usually accompanied with an hour of temptation. Prosperity and temptation go together; yea, prosperity is a temptation, because, without eminent supplies of grace it is apt to cast a soul into a frame and temper exposed to any temptation, and provides it with fuel and food for all. It has provision for lust, and darts for Satan.

The wise man tells us that the 'prosperity of fools destroys them' (Prov. 1:32 KJV). It hardens them in their way, makes them despise instruction, and put the evil day (whose terror should influence them into amendment) far from them. Without a special assistance, it has an inconceivably malignant influence on believers themselves.

We know how David was mistaken in this case: 'I said in my prosperity, "I shall never be moved".' All is well, and will be well. But what was at hand, what lay at the door, that David thought not of? Verse 7, 'you hid your face; I was dismayed' (Ps. 30:6-7). God was ready to hide his face, and David to enter into a temptation of desertion, and he knew it not.

Someone in that state is in the midst of snares. Satan has many advantages against them; he forges darts out of all his enjoyments; and, if they watch not, they will be entangled before they are aware.

You lack that which should poise and ballast your heart. Formality in religion will be apt to creep upon you; and that lays the soul open to all temptations in their full power and strength. Satisfaction and delight in creature-comforts, the poison of the soul, will be apt to grow upon you. In such a time be vigilant, be circumspect, or you will be surprised.

MAY 26

God's Word

The prophets who prophesied about the grace that was to be yours searched and enquired carefully, enquiring what person or time the Spirit of Christ in them was indicating when he predicted the sufferings of Christ and the subsequent glories.

1 PETER 1:10-11

The laws the Old Testament prophets made known, the doctrines they delivered, the instructions they gave, the stories they recorded, the promises of Christ, the prophecies of gospel times they gave out and revealed, were not their own. They were not conceived in their minds, not formed by their reasonings, not retained in their memories from what they heard, not by any means beforehand comprehended by them (1 Pet. 1:10-11). They were all of them immediately from God.

Their tongue in what they said, or their hand in what they wrote, was no more at their own disposal than the pen is in the hand of an expert writer. They were but as an instrument of music, giving a sound according to the hand, intention, and skill of him that strikes it.

Hence, as far as their own personal interests, as saints and believers, did lie in them, they are said 'to make a diligent inquiry into, and investigation' into them. Without this, though their visions were express, so that in them their eyes were said to be open (Num. 24:3-4), yet they understood them not. They studied the writings and prophecies of one another (Dan. 9:2). Thus they attained a saving, useful, habitual knowledge of the truths delivered by themselves and others, by the illumination of the Holy Spirit, through the study of the word, even as we do.

MAY 27

For truly, I say to you, until heaven and earth pass away, not an iota, not a dot, will pass from the Law until all is accomplished.

MATTHEW 5:18

The providence of God has manifested itself no less concerned in the preservation of the sacred writings than of the doctrine contained in them. Hence the malice of Satan has raged no less against the book than against the truth contained in it. The dealings of Antiochus under the Old Testament, and of sundry persecuting emperors under the New, demonstrates no less. And it was no less a crime of old to be one who handed over the books of Scripture to the persecuting authorities than to be one who abandoned the faith.

It is true, we do not have the original signed copies of Moses and the prophets, of the apostles and evangelists, but the copies which we have contain every iota that was in them. There is no doubt that, in the copies we now enjoy of the Old Testament, there are some diverse readings. But yet we affirm, that the whole word of God, in every letter and stroke, as given from him by inspiration, is preserved without corruption. Where there is any variety it is always in things of less importance. God, by his providence preserving the whole entire, suffered this lesser variety to fall out, in or among the copies we have, for the quickening and exercising of our diligence in our search into his word.

MAY 28

God-breathed

Men spoke from God as they were carried along by the Holy Spirit.

2 PETER 1:21

When the word was brought to the prophets, it was not left to their understandings, wisdoms, minds, or memories to order, dispose, and give it out. They were borne, actuated, carried along by the Holy Spirit to speak, deliver, and write all that, and nothing but that which was so brought to them. Their mind and understanding were used in the choice of words (from which arises all the differences in their manner of expression), yet they were so guided, that their words were not their own, but immediately supplied unto them.

And so they gave out the 'words of delight' and 'words of truth' itself. (Eccles. 12:10). Not only the *doctrine* they taught was the word of truth—truth itself (John 17:17)—but the *words* whereby they taught it were words of truth from God himself. What has been thus spoken of the Scripture of the Old Testament, must be also affirmed of the New, with this addition of advantage and pre-eminence: that 'it was declared at first by the Lord' (Heb. 2:3).

Thus God, who himself began the writing of the word with his own finger (Exod. 31:18), lastly commands the close of the immediate revelation of his will to be written in a book (Rev. 1:11). And so he gives out the whole of his mind and counsel to us in writing, as a merciful and steadfast relief against all that confusion, darkness, and uncertainty which the vanity, folly, and looseness of human minds would otherwise have certainly run into.

MAY 29

Redemption!

The redemption that is in Christ Jesus, whom God put forward as a propitiation by his blood.

ROMANS 3:24-25

With what a glorious, soul-appeasing light does the doctrine of satisfaction and atonement by the blood of Christ, the Son of God, come in upon us! This first astonishes, then conquers, then ravishes and satisfies the soul. This is what we looked for. This we were sick for, and knew it not. This is the design of the apostle's discourse in the three first chapters of the Epistle to the Romans. Let anyone read that discourse from Romans 1:18 and onward, and they will see with what glory and beauty, with what full and ample satisfaction, this doctrine breaks out (Rom. 3:21-26).

This meets with people in all their wanderings, stops them in their investigations, convinces them of the darkness, folly, uncertainty, falseness, of all their reasonings about these things—and that with such an evidence and light as at once subdues them, captivates their understanding, and quiets their souls. So was that old Roman world conquered by it; so shall the Islamic world be, in God's good and appointed time.

All mankind, that acknowledge their dependence upon God and relation to him, are naturally (and cannot be otherwise) grievously involved and perplexed in their hearts, thoughts, and reasonings, about the worship of God, acceptance with him (having sinned), and the future enjoyment of him. The doctrine of the Scripture comes in with full, unquestionable satisfaction to all these, suited to the inquirings of every individual soul, with a largeness of wisdom and depth of goodness not to be fathomed. And those who are not persuaded by this, who will not cast anchor in this harbour, let them put to sea once more, if they dare.

MAY 30

Righteous Leaders

I will make your overseers peace and your taskmasters righteousness.

ISAIAH 60:17

If you desire the glory of these nations, labour to promote the interest of Christ in these nations. I am not speaking to you about disputable things, differences among the people of God themselves; nor am I interposing my advice in your civil affairs; but I speak in general about those with whom Christ is present by his Spirit, his chosen ones, against whom there is an old enmity in Satan and the world. The glory of these nations is, that there is a people in them who have Christ in the midst of them; let it be your business to take care for that glory. But how shall we do it?

Labour *personally*, every one of you, to get Christ in your own hearts. I am very far from thinking that a man may not be lawfully called to magistracy, if he be not a believer; or that, being called, he should be impeded in the execution of his trust and place because he is not so. I shall not suspend my obedience whilst I inquire after my lawful governor's conversion. But yet this I say, I confess I can have no great expectation from those whom God loves not and delights not in.

Set yourselves to oppose that *overflowing flood of profaneness*, and opposition to the power of godliness, that is spreading itself over this nation. Know you not that the nation begins to be overwhelmed by the pourings out of a profane, wicked, carnal spirit, full of rage, and contempt of all the work of reformation that has been attempted amongst us? Were our hearts kept up to our good old principles on which we first engaged, it would not be so with us; but innumerable evils have laid hold upon us; and the temptations of these days have made us a woeful prey.

MAY 31

Denominations

Each one of you says, 'I follow Paul' or 'I follow Apollos' or 'I follow Cephas' or 'I follow Christ.' Is Christ divided?

1 CORINTHIANS 1:12-13

What woeful divisions are there amongst this generation of professing Christians! Some are for one way, and some for another; some say one sort are the people of God, some another; some say the Prelatists are so, some the Presbyterians; some the Independents, some the Anabaptists. To this I answer:

1st. It is no party, but the party of Christ in the world, and against the world—the seed of the woman against the seed of the serpent—that I am pleading for (Gen. 3:15). That people, as to their interest in Christ, should be judged from such denominations—which, though they make a great noise in the world, yet, indeed, signify very little things in themselves—is most unrighteous; nor will people find peace in such rash and hasty judgments.

2nd. There may be many divisions amongst the people of God, and yet none of them are divided from Christ, the head. The branches of a tree may be entangled by strong winds, and stricken against one another, and yet none of them be broken off from the tree itself; when the storm is over, every one possesses its own place in quietness, beauty, and fruitfulness. Whilst the strong winds of temptations are upon the followers of Christ, they may be tossed and entangled; but not being broken off from the root, when he shall say to the winds, 'Peace, be still,' they will flourish again in peace and beauty.

We now enter a time when, as Owen put it, 'the former public troubles and disorders in these nations' had been brought to an end, by the restoration of the monarchy under Charles II.

In 1661, Owen published a scholarly and very erudite tome in Latin, with the Greek title Θεολογούμενα παντοδαπὰ, or 'theological affirmations of all kinds', tracing the development of theology in the Bible, from creation to the gospel. That same year, a Franciscan friar called John Vincent Cane wrote a treatise called *Fiat Lux* ('Let there be light!'), on the superiority of Roman Catholicism, which Owen responded to with his own *Animadversions* ('Critical Remarks').

In 1662, Owen was also critical of the idea of compelling ministers to use a set form of words in church services, in his *Discourse concerning Liturgies and their Imposition*. As it turned out, later that year Owen was one of those barred from continuing to work in the academy as a result of the Act of Uniformity and the tragic ejection of many Puritans from the Church of England.

After subsequent years of difficulty, in 1667 he wrote his own plan for how churches ought to function, called *A Brief Instruction in the Worship and Discipline of the Churches of the New Testament*. Alongside this, he also published a shrewd public letter entitled 'Indulgence and Toleration Considered', as well as a tract called *A Peace-Offering in an Apology and Humble Plea for Indulgence and Liberty of Conscience*.

Such pleas fell on deaf ears in the Cavalier Parliament. Foiled in his political hopes, however, Owen continued to work on more scholarly pursuits, publishing in 1668 the first folio volume of his massive commentary on Hebrews.

JUNE 1

True Theology

*My speech and my message were not in plausible words of
wisdom, but in demonstration of the Spirit and of power.*

1 CORINTHIANS 2:4

Everyone agrees we can have no revelation of God, but from God.
So theology rests upon the veracity of him who reveals it. The
object of theology, which in some sense is God himself, differs
infinitely from all objects of all other sciences. So it is impossible
to reduce theology to the rules of other arts and sciences.

The apostle gives an account of Christian theology quite
distant from human wisdom and science. 'My speech,' he says,
'and my preaching (i.e. my science and my doctrine) were not with
enticing words of human wisdom (in which consists all art and
human so-called science), but in demonstration of the Spirit and of
power.' To this, he adds the reason and purpose for this distinction:
'that your faith (or the assent you give to my doctrine) should not
stand in the wisdom of man (as it would do if theology consisted in
the same or like principles, form, and end that the arts and sciences
of philosophers do), but in the power of God' (1 Cor. 2:4-5).

The Lord commanded his apostles that all those great
mysteries which he taught them in private should be publicly
preached to enlighten mankind. The mysteries of the Gentiles'
religion were so called because of their concealment, but the
mysteries of the gospel are so termed from the nature of the
things themselves, which transcend all human capacity, which
is purely natural.

According then to the sense of the apostle, a student of
theology is one who is endued with the Holy Spirit, initiated and
instructed in Christian principles by him who only reveals to us
the mystery of his will by the Spirit of wisdom and revelation
(Eph. 1:17).

JUNE 2

Divine Wisdom

The law of the LORD is perfect, reviving the soul; the testimony of the LORD is sure, making wise the simple.

PSALM 19:7

Theology is a mysterious and divine wisdom which is neither circumscribed by human bounds nor taught by those rudiments that all other arts and sciences use. This sense of it even the heathen themselves have, and perhaps the cause of the various opinions and the wrangling among those who study theology is their endeavour to accommodate it to the rules of other arts and sciences. With these they perplex and darken that doctrine which, in its own nature, is most certain, evident, and clear to the rational understanding, making it ambiguous and uncertain by their attempts to subject the mysteries of divine truth, revealed out of the bosom of God himself, to the arbitrary rules of human sciences.

Learned men have, with much vain labour, framed a structure of learning, comprehended in principles, theorems, and conclusions like other sciences, and this they call theology. But since that doctrine is not self-evident and has no assurance or need of a supernatural faith, and it does not lead to any practical end of theology, it cannot properly be called that. In pursuit of this learning, a certain habit of mind consonant with it is acquired, which the scholastics contend about, affirming that it is neither faith nor natural science.

That knowledge, wisdom, prudence, and learning which God appoints to direct us in the contemplation of himself and his works, to guide us in the obedience we give him and to give us the knowledge of himself which he requires us to have, is called Scripture.

JUNE 3

God's Theology

God, who said, 'Let light shine out of darkness', has shone in our hearts to give the light of the knowledge of the glory of God in the face of Jesus Christ.　2 CORINTHIANS 4:6

God alone knows himself perfectly. This knowledge in God is nothing else but God himself, infinitely wise and understanding. Our knowledge of God is not the same. Our immediate mirror is not God, but his word or gospel, in which with open face, by Christ, we behold the glory of God (2 Cor. 3:18).

God has in his own mind an eternal idea of that truth he would have us know. On this depends all our theology, not directly but on that act of the divine will by which it pleases him to reveal to us this truth. This revelation of the divine mind and will of God is the word of God. To this, all our conceptions of God, his worship, and our obedience ought to be conformable. It is the infallible rule and unchangeable guide of all our science and knowledge.

Theology is divine truth itself, as it is revealed by God. It is his word, doctrine, or light, which is its own credential and evidence. All knowledge of God comes only by his own revelation, and he will have no worship but by his own prescription. For all our obedience depends purely on his will.

Thus, theology is the doctrine of God concerning himself, his works, his will, his worship. Our obedience in everything, our reward, and the punishment of our disobedience is revealed and set forth by him, to the glory of his own name. This scripture is our theology, such that we attribute authority to it as a whole and in every part of it, to everything contained in it.

J U N E   4

Natural Light

God's invisible attributes, namely, his eternal power and divine nature, have been clearly perceived, ever since the creation of the world, in the things that have been made.

ROMANS 1:20

All theology has regard either to the implanted word (and is hence called *natural*) or to the successively revealed word (hence called *supernatural*). In the state of pure nature, theology was implanted and natural in mankind, and is called pure. It was a saving light that consisted in the knowledge of God as our creator, lawgiver, ruler, and rewarder. We call it 'light' because the way scripture uses that word is applicable to all theology.

This light was infused into the soul of mankind in their very creation. It was soon augmented by a revelation of the divine will in the sacramental precept (Gen. 2:16-17). It was to have daily advanced in the contemplation of God's works, and this was sufficient to have rendered them wise in yielding obedience to God according to the covenant of works, accomplishing their own happiness by it, and yielding to God the glory of his divine power, wisdom, grace, and justice.

This light or spiritual wisdom was agreeable to the end for which mankind was made, and necessary for their condition. In itself, it was plainly supernatural (for it was by God's free ordination that mankind should obey him, according to the tenor of a covenant promising eternal reward). Yet, because it was inwardly engrafted and implanted in mankind, in our very creation, we usually say it is natural.

JUNE 5

Creation's Lord

Worthy are you, our Lord and God, to receive glory and honour and power, for you created all things, and by your will they existed and were created.

REVELATION 4:11

It is by all acknowledged that God, by right of creation, is Lord of all the creatures. Hence they all have a necessary dependence on him, and according to their various capacities they celebrate and serve their Creator in fulfilling the law of their creation. Since God made all things for himself, that is, for his own glory, it is just and fitting that the whole creation should give him glory and honour, which the psalmist often calls upon them to do.

People are obliged to render their maker this obedience on account of their being creatures. This the very creation itself sufficiently manifested; and that innate law which was created within mankind was a sufficient guide for them to render such obedience. The sum of the law is that God is to be loved, honoured, and feared as supreme benefactor, sovereign good or happiness, supreme ruler, and rewarder. And because God our creator is most just and holy, therefore we are bound to embrace righteousness and holiness, and persevere in them until they arrive at their ultimate end and perfection.

It is apparent that Adam was endued with the wisdom and moral light that he needed to know God and know the implanted law, and the sacramental legislation (Gen. 2:15-16). Being instructed in this theology, there was certainly nothing else needed to furnish him for the due worship of God, and the holy and happy conduct of his life. This, then, was Adam's theology.

JUNE 6

Reward and Punishment

For this light momentary affliction is preparing for us an eternal weight of glory beyond all comparison.

2 CORINTHIANS 4:17

The covenant, as it was made with Adam, was also known to him. For it is apparent that he knew his duty, and his reward. The sacramental precept that was added did not reveal but seal the covenant. And the reward of it consisted in the everlasting enjoyment of God.

It is a curious, dangerous, and impertinent inquiry to ask how long Adam should have kept going before he enjoyed God as a reward. The time when, and the manner how, neither the nature of the thing itself nor the Scripture acquaints us with.

The first sin manifestly consisted in the total subversion of the moral dependence of the creature upon God. The punishment was separation from God, with that sense of the punishment which retributive justice could not but inflict. After the souls and bodies of sinners were severed in the first death, they were to be again reunited for the suffering of the second death, consisting in eternal separation from God, under grievous tortures, divine power assisting divine justice to uphold them in their misery.

The rewards and punishments under both covenants are for the substance the same. God himself is the reward, and separation from him is the punishment. Under the second covenant, both of them may be said to be increased, as to degrees, for we read of death unto death, and a far more exceeding and eternal weight of glory.

JUNE 7

Broken Covenant

We have put on the new self, which is being renewed in knowledge after the image of its creator.

COLOSSIANS 3:10

We must next consider the vanishing of theology in its first created and native purity, by the entrance of sin, and the consequent abolition of the covenant. The image of God was abolished by the entrance of sin. The implanted law retained no more the nature and use of theology, whose end is the glory of God and the eternal happiness of those who study and practise it. So humanity was, upon the entrance of sin, utterly deprived of all theology. That saving light was extinguished by sin.

No doctrine can properly be called theology which does not rest on some divine covenant, by which those who profess and practice it may please God and, at the last, enjoy him. The covenant which was the foundation of mankind's first theology was abolished, and though God's precepts yet remained pure, no one had the ability to obey them anymore. The doctrine of the covenant was yet most true—'the one who does these things shall live by them'. Yet after the entrance of sin, the covenant itself retained no ability to bring people to God. Neither could mankind be reckoned as in covenant with God, yet they were still in subjection to his commands because of his supreme rule and dominion as their creator and sovereign Lord, which he will always be.

The doctrine propounded in the law, joined with their own innate light, was not sufficient to direct sinners into the way of life, and however earnestly they pursued it, it could not bring them to salvation. For since the entry of sin, to know and obey God as creator, ruler, and rewarder will not bring anyone to salvation, without the knowledge of his grace and mercy in Christ (which it would have done whilst the first covenant was in force).

JUNE 8

Read the Bible!

The unfolding of your words gives light; it imparts understanding to the simple.

PSALM 119:130

Some theological students spend all their time, day and night, poring over theological systems in which the doctrine of the gospel is reduced to various headings, until they surrender to this mould. Yet all true supernatural revelation from God is contained in the holy scriptures. Wisdom consists in true spiritual and saving knowledge of those Scriptures. So, diligent reading and constant meditation on the Scriptures is the absolutely essential thing for aspiring theologians. Everyone knows this, in theory, but very few come at this with the right frame of mind. So many of them neglect this kind of study, to their loss and ruin.

How many spend even a small amount of their time in cursory study of the Scriptures, and even less on meditating on the word, or on listening to the word preached—and yet they still fondly imagine that they will become consummate theologians! They may immerse themselves in ancient and modern theologians. I applaud such diligence. But this is not the same as studying the Scriptures themselves, praying for the illuminating help of the Spirit. Let them hear the Jesuit, Acosta: 'The one who reads the Scriptures with the purity of their soul will have more advantage than the one who attempts to unravel mysteries with many commentaries.'

JUNE 9

Reforming Word

Your word is a lamp to my feet and a light to my path.

PSALM 119:105

It was not Luther nor Calvin, but the word of God, and the practice of the primitive church, that England proposed for her rule and pattern in her reformation; and where any of the reformers forsook them, she counted it her duty, without reflections on them or their ways, to walk in that safe one she had chosen out for herself.

Nor is the preaching of the Protestants, as is pretended, unlike that of the ancients. The best and most famous preacher of the ancient church, whose sermons are preserved, was Chrysostom. We know the way of his proceeding in that work was to open the words and meaning of his text, to declare the truth contained and taught in it, to vindicate it from objections, to confirm it by other testimonies of Scripture, and to apply all unto practice in the close. As far as I can observe, this, in general, is the method used by Protestants, being that indeed which the very nature of the work dictates to them.

JUNE 10

Spiritual Means

Teach me to do your will, for you are my God! Let your good Spirit lead me on level ground!

PSALM 143:10

Protestants conclude that the Scripture, given by God for this purpose, is intelligible to people using the means appointed by God to come to the understanding of his mind and will in it. I know many are pleased grievously to mistake our intention in this inference and conclusion. Sometimes, they claim that we say all places of Scripture, all words and sentences in it, are plain and of an obvious sense, and easy to be understood. And yet this we absolutely deny.

It is one thing to say that *all necessary truth* is plainly and clearly revealed in the Scripture, which we do say; and another, that *every text and passage* in the Scripture is plain and easy to be understood, which we do not say, nor ever thought. To say this would be to contradict our own experience and that of the disciples of Christ in all ages.

Sometimes, people pretend that we believe all the things that are revealed in the Scripture are plain and obvious to everyone's understanding, whereas we acknowledge that the things themselves revealed are many of them mysterious, surpassing the comprehension of anyone in this world. All we maintain is that the propositions in which the revelation of them is made are plain and intelligible to those who use the means appointed by God to come to a right understanding of them.

JUNE 11

Appointed Pastors

Christ gave the apostles, the prophets, the evangelists, the shepherds and teachers, to equip the saints for the work of ministry, for building up the body of Christ.

Ephesians 4:11-12

The chiefest acts and parts of the instituted worship of Christ's public assemblies may be referred to these three heads: *preaching of the word, administration of the sacraments, and the exercise of discipline*. All of these are to be performed with prayer and thanksgiving. The rule for the administration of these things, so far as they are purely of his institution, he gave to his disciples in his appointment of them. Persons, also, he designed to the regular administration of these his holy things in the assemblies of his saints—namely, pastors and teachers—to endure to the end of the world, after those of an extraordinary employment under him were to cease.

The end which Christ aimed at is the edification of his disciples and the glory of God. It is derogatory to the glory, honour, and faithfulness of the Lord Jesus Christ, to affirm that he ceases to bestow gifts for the work of the ministry, whilst he continues and requires the exercise and discharge of that work. What has befallen people, through the wretched sloth, darkness, and unbelief which their wilful neglect of dependence on him, or of stirring up or improving of what they do receive from him, is not to be imputed to any failing on his part, in his promise of dispensing the gifts mentioned to the end of the world. Neither are any of those mischiefs that have accrued to the church by the intrusion of such persons into the place and office of the ministry as were never called nor appointed by him to it.

JUNE 12

Spiritual Profit

As each has received a gift, use it to serve one another, as good
stewards of God's varied grace.

1 PETER 4:10

The edification of the church depends principally on the blessing
of God upon the exercise of those ministerial gifts which are
bestowed on people for that end. The gifts that are bestowed
on ministers are their principal talents, that they ought to trade
with for the profit of their Master (Matt. 25:14-30); that is, the
building up of his house, in which his wealth in this world lies.
Indeed, all the gifts that are bestowed by the Spirit of Christ on
us are given 'for the common good' (1 Cor. 12:7), and they are
required with them to act for God in the edification of the body
of Christ, every one according to their measure (1 Pet. 4:10-11).

The gifts bestowed by Christ on the guides of his church, the
ministers of the gospel, are proportioned and suited to the end
which he aims to accomplish by them. It will undeniably follow
that on the due and regular use and employment of those gifts
which people receive from Christ depends, and that solely, the
edification of his church. Where the gifts bestowed by the Spirit
of Christ on the ministers of his church are used and exercised in
the work of the ministry, according to his mind and will, there,
by his blessing, the edification which he intends will ensue.

Hence, the great direction for the exercise of the work of
the ministry is, to stir up the gift received. Edification, then,
depends on the improvement of gifts, and the improvement of
gifts on their due exercise according to the mind of Christ.

JUNE 13

Bad Shepherds

The weak you have not strengthened, the sick you have not healed, the injured you have not bound up, the strayed you have not brought back, the lost you have not sought, and with force and harshness you have ruled them.

EZEKIEL 34:4

It is the work and duty of the ministers of the gospel to make application of the grace of Christ, of which they are stewards, to the flocks committed to their charge. They are to declare, unfold, tender, and apply the grace of Christ, according to the wants of his disciples, the good of whose souls they watch for in particular.

People who scoff at edification and deride spiritual gifts, who think all religion to consist in the observation of some carnal institution, may think lightly of this. They neither know nor care to come to an acquaintance with the spiritual wants of poor souls, nor do tremble at the threatenings of Christ directed against their negligence and ignorance (Ezek. 34:4). They suppose the whole baptised world is converted to God, and preaching itself is therefore less necessary than it was at the first plantation of the gospel. They esteem the doubts and temptations of believers as needless scruples, and their diligent endeavours to grow in grace and the knowledge of our Lord Jesus Christ, labour lost in hypocrisy. They suppose they can discharge the duty of the ministry by a bare reading of the service-book to their parish, without once inquiring into the spiritual condition of those whose souls they plead to be committed to them.

But those who know the terror of the Lord, and anything of their own duty, will be otherwise minded.

JUNE 14

Acceptable Worship

By faith Abel offered to God a more acceptable sacrifice than Cain, through which he was commended as righteous, God commending him by accepting his gifts.

HEBREWS 11:4

Ever since the entrance of sin into the world, God always had respect to the promise of the Lord Christ and his mediation, in whom alone he will be glorified. It is faith in him which he aimed to begin and increase in all his worship. But he has suited his institutions (which are the means for bringing this about) to that dispensation of light and knowledge of him which he was pleased at any time to grant.

Thus, immediately after the giving of the *promise*, he appointed *sacrifices* as the great means of his worship. This was to glorify himself expressly by people offering to him the principal good things which he had given them. This was to instruct them in the faith and confirm them in the expectation of *the great sacrifice* for sin that was to be offered by the promised seed (Gen. 4:3-4; Heb. 11:4). These were the first instituted worship of God in the world after the entrance of sin. And, to the same general end and purpose, he afterwards added the *Passover*, with its attendant institutions (Exod. 12:3-24). And then, the whole law of institutions contained in ordinances, by the ministry of angels on Mount Sinai (Exod. 20).

So, by sundry degrees, he built up that fabric of his *outward worship*, which was suited, in his infinite wisdom, to his own glory and the edification of his church, until the coming of Christ in the flesh, and the accomplishment of the work of his mediation (Heb. 1:1-2). Then, they were removed by the same authority by which they were instituted and appointed (Col. 2:14, 18-20).

JUNE 15

*I will walk among you and will be your God, and you shall
be my people.*

LEVITICUS 26:12

Question: May not such an estate of faith and perfection in
obedience be attained in this life, that believers may be freed
from all obligation to observe gospel institutions?

Answer: No. For the ordinances and institutions of the
gospel being inseparably joined to the evangelical administration
of the covenant of grace, they may not be left unobserved,
disused, or omitted, whilst we are to walk before God in that
covenant, without contempt of the covenant itself and the
wisdom and authority of Jesus Christ (Heb. 3:3-6; Rom. 6:3-6;
Luke 22:19-20; 1 Cor. 11:23-26; Heb. 10:25; Rev. 2:5, 3:3).

Explanation: All our faith, all our obedience in this life,
whatever may be obtained or attained to in it, it all belongs to
our walking with God in the covenant of grace. In this, God
dwells with people, and they are his people, and God himself is
with them to be their God. Other ways of communion with him,
of obedience to him, of enjoyment of him, on this side of heaven
and glory, he has not appointed nor revealed.

Now, this is the covenant that God has made with his people,
'That he will put his laws into their mind, and write them in
their hearts, and will be to them a God, and they shall be to
him a people; and he will be merciful to their unrighteousness,
and their sins and their iniquities will be remember no more'
(Heb. 8:10-12). There is no grace promised in the covenant to
lead people in this life, or to give them up to a state of perfection,
short of glory. Without a renunciation and relinquishment of
that covenant and the grace of it, these institutions cannot be
omitted or deserted.

JUNE 16

God's Purposes

But you, beloved, building yourselves up in your most holy faith and praying in the Holy Spirit, keep yourselves in the love of God.

JUDE 20-21

Question: What are the chief things that we ought to aim at in our observation of the institutions of Christ in the gospel?

Answer: To sanctify the name of God (Lev. 10:3; Heb. 12:28-29); to own and avow our professed subjection to the Lord Jesus Christ (Deut. 26:17; Josh. 24:22; 2 Cor. 8:5); to build ourselves up in our most holy faith (Eph. 4:11-16; Jude 20); and to testify and confirm our mutual love, as we are believers (1 Cor. 10:16-17).

Explanation: That we may profitably and comfortably, to the glory of God and our own edification, be exercised in the observation of the institutions and worship of God, we are always to consider what are the *ends* for which God has appointed them and commanded our attendance on them. In this way, our observance of them may be the obedience of faith. For, whatever end God has appointed them for, for that end are they useful and effectual, and to no other. If we use them for any other purpose or with any other design, if we look for anything in them or by them except what God has appointed them to communicate to us, we dishonour God and deceive our own souls.

This we ought diligently to inquire into, to know not only *what* God requires of us, but also *why* he requires it, and what he aims at in it. It is well known how horribly many of the institutions of the gospel have been by some abused, by a neglect of the ends of God in them, and imposing new ends of their own upon them, which leads to superstition and idolatry.

JUNE 17

Gospel Glory

If there was glory in the ministry of condemnation, the ministry of righteousness must far exceed it in glory.

2 CORINTHIANS 3:9

The beauty of gospel worship does not in the least depend upon outward ceremonies and their observation. The apostle in sundry places expressly compares the spiritual worship of the gospel with that of the law when the church had a worldly sanctuary and carnal ordinances (Heb. 9:1). It is most evident that the worship of the Old Testament did, for the glory and ornaments of outward ceremonies and the splendour of their observation, far exceed and excel that worship which God commands now. This is suitable to the simplicity of the gospel, which the apostle prefers for glory, comeliness, and beauty, unspeakably above the other. The chief admirers of outward rites and ceremonies can in no way compete for glory with the old worship of the temple. But the apostle compares the law and the gospel, preferring the gospel above the other, which sufficiently proves that the glory of it consists not in any pompous observance of outward ceremonies (2 Cor. 3:7-11).

Through Christ, we have access by one Spirit to the Father (Eph. 2:18). This is the glory of gospel worship and the beauty of it. When people's minds are diverted from this, to look for beauty in the outward preparation of ceremonies, they lose the privilege purchased for believers by the blood of Christ. Instead of furthering the beauty and comeliness of gospel worship, they are apt to lead people into a dangerous error and mistake—namely, that the beauty and excellency of it consists in things far beneath those ceremonies and ordinances of the Old Testament, which yet, in comparison to the worship of the gospel, are called 'worldly, carnal, beggarly', and are said to have 'no glory'.

JUNE 18

God's Presence

Behold, the dwelling place of God is with man. He will dwell with them, and they will be his people, and God himself will be with them as their God.

REVELATION 21:3

To encourage us in our duty, the holy faithful God has given us many *great and precious promises* that he will graciously afford to us: his especial, sanctifying, blessing presence, in our attendance on his worship according to his appointment. He promised of old that he would make glorious 'the place of his feet', or abode amongst his people (Isa. 60:13). He said he would meet them in his sanctuary, the place of his worship, and there dwell amongst them, and bless them, and be their God (Exod. 29:42-45; Deut. 14:23-24). So also the Lord Jesus Christ has promised his presence to the same ends and purposes, to all who assemble together in his name for the observation of the worship which in the gospel he has appointed. 'For where two or three are gathered together in my name, there am I in the midst of them' (Matt. 18:20). And *there* is the tabernacle of God, his gracious dwelling-place with people (Rev. 21:3).

Now, when God offers to us his presence—his gracious, blessing, sanctifying, and saving presence—and that in and by promises which shall never fail, what unspeakable guilt must we needs contract upon our own souls if we neglect or despise the tenders of such grace!

JUNE 19

Dwelling Place

In Christ you also are being built together into a dwelling place for God by the Spirit.

EPHESIANS 2:22

All people are by nature the children of wrath, and belong to the world, which is the kingdom of Satan, and are under the power of darkness (Eph. 2:3). In this state, people are not subjects of the kingdom of Christ, nor suitable to become members of his church. Out of this condition they cannot deliver themselves. They have neither will to do it nor power for it; but they are called out of it. This calling is that which effectually delivers them from the kingdom of Satan, and translates them into the kingdom of Christ.

Sometimes Scripture calls this *regeneration*, or a new birth; sometimes *conversion*, or turning to God; sometimes *vivification*, or quickening from the dead; sometimes *illumination*, or opening of the eyes of the blind. All of these things are carried on by *sanctification* in holiness, and attended with justification and adoption. These are all distinct in themselves, but they all concur to complete that effectual vocation or calling that is required to constitute persons members of the church.

Our Lord Jesus Christ has laid it down as an everlasting rule, that 'unless one is born again, he cannot see the kingdom of God' (John 3:3, 5), requiring regeneration as an indispensable condition in a member of his church, a subject of his kingdom. For his temple is now to be built of living stones (1 Pet. 2:5), people spiritually and savingly quickened from their death in sin. By the Holy Spirit, of which they are partakers, they are made a suitable dwelling place for God (Eph. 2:21-22; 1 Cor. 3:16; 2 Cor. 6:16).

JUNE 20

Church Discipline

I know your works, your toil and your patient endurance,
and how you cannot bear with those who are evil, but have
tested those who call themselves apostles and are not, and
found them to be false.

REVELATION 2:2

The purpose of church discipline is the continuance, increase, and preservation of the church, according to the rule of its first institution (1 Cor. 5:7). This power Christ has given his church for its conservation, without which it must necessarily decay and come to nothing. It is not to be imagined that where any church is called and gathered according to the mind of Christ; he has left it destitute of power and authority to preserve itself in that state and order which he has appointed to it.

One principal cause of the decay of the Asian churches was the neglect of this discipline, the power and privilege of which the Lord had left to them and entrusted them with for their own preservation in order, purity, and holiness. And, therefore, for the neglect of it they were greatly blamed by him (Rev. 2:14-15, 20, 3:1-2); as is also the church of Corinth by the apostle (1 Cor. 5:2); as they are commended who attended to the diligent exercise of it (Rev. 2:2, 3:9). The disuse of discipline has been the occasion of all the defilements, abominations, and confusions that have spread themselves over many churches in the world.

JUNE 21

Tolerating Differences

Behold, how good and pleasant it is when brothers dwell in unity!

PSALM 133:1

It will be utterly superfluous to show how, for three hundred years, there was no one amongst the first Christians who entertained thoughts of outward force against those who differed from the most in the things of Christian religion. And yet, in that space of time, with that principle, the power of religion subdued the world. When the Roman Empire became Christian, the same principle held sway.

So was it all the world over, not to mention the many different observances that were in and amongst the churches themselves, which did not occasion division, much less persecution of one another. And so prevalent is this principle, that despite their design to force people into a uniformity with them, yet it has taken place within the church of Rome itself. There is no nation in which that religion is enthroned, but that there are thousands in it who are allowed their particular ways of worship, and are exempt from the common ordinary jurisdiction of the church.

It seems, therefore, that we are some of the first who ever anywhere in the world, from the foundation of it, thought of ruining and destroying persons of the same religion with ourselves, merely upon the choice of some peculiar ways of worship in that religion. It is reasonable for people to look well to the grounds of what they do, when they act contrary to the principles of the law of nature, expressed in so many instances by the consent of mankind. It is in vain to turn nature out of doors; it will return.

JUNE 22

Endure Suffering

We know that for those who love God all things work together for good, for those who are called according to his purpose.

ROMANS 8:28

The infinitely wise and holy God arranges all things according to the counsel of his own will. He designed our portion in the world so that besides those difficulties which in all ages attend those who are called to profess the truths of the gospel; we are forewarned of sundry evils peculiar to the last days, rendering them 'perilous' (2 Tim. 3:1). It is our duty to apply ourselves to serve his good pleasure in our generation, without being discontent at that station which in his work he has allotted to us. We may be called to suffer according to his will, though nothing will be lost to his holy ends and purposes in the world, but some way or other redound to his glory.

What shall befall us in the course of our pilgrimage, how we shall be treated as to our outward temporary concerns—as it is not in our power to order and determine, so neither ought we to be anxiously concerned about it. All things of that nature belong to his sovereign pleasure, who will make them work together for good for those who love him (Rom. 8:28).

We know that it is only a little while before it will be no grief of heart to us to have done or suffered anything for the name of the Lord Jesus. The old enemy of mankind is never so far asleep whilst any are endeavouring to sow the good seed of the gospel, as not to stir up an opposition to their work, and to labour the ruin of their persons. So we also believe that every sincere endeavour to promote the holy truths and ways of God, according to that measure of light which he is pleased graciously to impart to any of us, is accepted and owned by him who 'rewards those who seek him' (Heb. 11:6).

JUNE 23

The Meekness of Christ

When he was reviled, he did not revile in return; when he suffered, he did not threaten, but continued entrusting himself to him who judges justly.

1 PETER 2:23

Among the many blessed ends of the life of our Lord Jesus Christ in the flesh, he set us a pattern. He gave us an example of that frame of heart and holiness of life by which we may become like our heavenly Father, and be acceptable before him. There was nothing he more emphatically called upon his disciples to endeavour a conformity to him in, than in his meekness, lowliness, gentleness, and tenderness towards all.

These he took all occasions, for our good, to show forth in himself, and to commend unto others. Whatever provocation he met with, whatever injurious opposition he was exposed to, he did not contend, nor cry out, nor cause his voice to be heard with strife or anger. He reproved people's sins with all authority; their groundless traditions in the worship of God he rejected; their errors he refuted by the word: but to their persons he was always meek and tender, as coming to save, and not to destroy— to keep alive, and not to kill.

In the things of man, he referred all to the just authority and righteous laws of men; but in the things of God he never gave the least intimation of severity, but only in his holy threats of future evil in the world to come, upon people's final impenitence and unbelief. 'Coerce, fine, imprison, banish those that apprehend not aright all and everything that I would have them instructed in', are words that never proceeded out of his holy mouth—things that never entered into his gracious heart.

JUNE 24

Progress of Revelation

Long ago, at many times and in many ways, God spoke to our fathers by the prophets.

HEBREWS 1:1

Hebrews 1:1 is about the gradual discovery of the mind and will of God, by the addition of one thing after another at several seasons as the church could bear the light of them, and as it served his main design of reserving all pre-eminence to the Messiah. It denotes the whole progress of divine revelation from the beginning of the world.

The first revelation was made to Adam in the promise of the seed, which was the principle of faith and obedience to the fathers before the flood. The second was to Noah after the flood, in the renewal of the covenant and establishing of the church in his family (Gen. 8:21-22, 9:9-10). The third revelation was to Abraham, in the restriction of the promise to his seed, and fuller illustration of the nature of it (Gen. 12:1-3, 15:11-12, 17:1-2). The fourth was to Moses, in the giving of the law, and the building of the Judaical church in the wilderness. To this, there were three main subservient revelations:

1. To David, which was peculiarly designed to perfect the revelation of the will of God concerning the Old Testament worship (1 Chron. 23:25-32, 28:11-19).

2. To the prophets after the division of the kingdom up to and during the captivity, who pleaded with the people about their defection by sin and false worship.

3. To Ezra, with the prophets that assisted in the reformation of the church after its return from Babylon, who, in an especial manner, incited the people to an expectation of the coming of the Messiah.

These were the principal parts and degrees of the revelation of the will of God, from the foundation of the world until the coming of Christ in his forerunner, John the Baptist.

JUNE 25

God's Final Word

In these last days he has spoken to us by his Son.

HEBREWS 1:2

It is asserted that in the revelation of the gospel, God spoke 'in his Son'. This is the main hinge, on which all the arguments of the apostle in the whole epistle do turn; this bears the stress of all the inferences afterwards by him insisted on.

I take it for granted that the Son of God appeared to the prophets under the Old Testament. Whether he spoke to them immediately, or only by the ministry of angels, is not so certain. It is also granted that there were, in visions, sometimes signs or representations of the person of the Father (e.g. Dan. 7). But that the Son of God did mostly appear to the fathers under the Old Testament is acknowledged by the ancients, and is evident in Scripture.

He it was who is called 'The angel' (Exod. 23:20-21). Both the ancient Jews and Christians generally grant that it is the Messiah that is called 'The angel of the covenant' (Mal. 3:1). The apostle therefore speaks in the rest of Hebrews 1 of those who were angels by nature and no more, and not of him who, being Jehovah the Son, was sent of the Father, and is therefore called his angel or messenger, being so only by office.

There is a difference between the Son of God revealing the will of God in his *divine person* to the prophets, and the Son of God as *incarnate* revealing the will of God immediately to the church. This is the difference here insisted on by the apostle in Hebrews 1:2. Under the Old Testament, the Son of God, in his divine person, instructed the prophets in the will of God; but now, in the revelation of the gospel, taking his own humanity, he taught it immediately himself.

JUNE 26

Pre-eminent Word

For the law was given through Moses; grace and truth came through Jesus Christ.

JOHN 1:17

All the mysteries of the counsel between the Father and the eternal word for the salvation of the elect, with all the way by which it was to be accomplished, through his own blood, were known to Christ. The only reason he did not at once reveal to his disciples the whole counsel of God was because they could not bear anything but that gradual communication of it which he used towards them (John 16:12).

All other prophets, even Moses himself, had no treasure of truth dwelling in them, but apprehended only that particular in which they were enlightened, and that not clearly neither, in its fulness and perfection, but in a measure of light accommodated to the age in which they lived (1 Pet. 1:11-12). The prophets of old saw not to the bottom of the things by themselves revealed; and did therefore both diligently read and study the books of those who wrote before their time, and meditated on the things which the Spirit uttered by themselves, to obtain an understanding in them. But the Lord Jesus had an absolutely perfect comprehension of all the mysteries revealed to him and by him by that divine wisdom which always dwelt in him.

The difference was no less between them in respect of the *revelations themselves*. For although the substance of the will and mind of God concerning salvation by the Messiah was made known to them all, yet it was done so obscurely to Moses and the prophets that ensued, that they all came short in the light of that mystery to John the Baptist, who himself did not rise up, in a clear and distinct apprehension of it, to the least of the true disciples of Christ (Matt. 11:11).

JUNE 27

Gradual Revelation

Behold, these are but the outskirts of his ways, and how small a whisper do we hear of him!

JOB 26:14

God's gradual revelation of himself, his mind and will, to the church, was a fruit of infinite wisdom and care towards his elect. Though all his ways and dispensations are ordered in infinite wisdom, yet we can but stand at the shore of the ocean, and admire its glory and greatness. Little it is that we can comprehend. Yet what may be for our instruction, what may further our faith and obedience, is not hidden from us. These things are evident to us in this gradual discovery of himself and his will:

1. That he overfilled not their vessels. He gave light to them as they were able to bear. Though we know not perfectly what their condition was, yet this we know, that as no generation needed more light than they had for the discharge of the duty that God required of them, so more light would have unfitted them for something or other that was their duty in their respective generations.

2. He kept them in a continual dependence upon himself, and waiting for their rule and direction from him; which, as it tended to his glory, so it was exceedingly suited to their safety, in keeping them in a humble, waiting frame.

3. He so gave out the light and knowledge of himself that the great work which he had to accomplish, that lay in the stores of his infinitely wise will as the end and issue of all revelations—namely, the bringing forth of Christ into the world, in the way in which he was to come, and for the ends which he was to bring about—might not be anticipated. He gave light enough to believers to enable them to receive him, and not so much as to hinder stubborn sinners from crucifying him.

JUNE 28

The Heir of All

In these last days he has spoken to us by his Son, whom he appointed the heir of all things.   HEBREWS 1:2

The mass of Christ's treasure is infinite, the stores of it are inexhaustible; and he is ready, free, gracious, and bountiful in his communications of it to all the subjects of his dominion. This part of his heirship extends to all the grace and mercy that the Father could find in his own gracious heart to bestow, when he was full of counsels of love, and designed to exalt himself by the way of grace. It extends to all the grace and mercy which he himself could purchase by pouring out his blood.

It extends to all that grace which has saved the world of sinners who are already in the enjoyment of God, and which shall effectually save all that come to God by him. And it extends to all that grace which, in the promises of it in the Old Testament, is set out by all that is rich, precious, and glorious; and in the New Testament is called 'treasure', and 'unsearchable riches'. This, being communicated by him to all the subjects of his kingdom, makes every one of them richer than all the potentates of the earth who have no interest in him.

The Father says to him: 'Do you see these poor wretched creatures that lie perishing in their blood and under the curse? Will you undertake to be their saviour and deliverer, to save them from their sins, and the wrath to come?' To which he replies: 'I am content to do your will, and will undertake this work, and that with joy and delight.'

'It shall be,' says the Father, 'as you have spoken, and out of the anguish of your soul you shall be satisfied. Behold, here are unsearchable hidden treasures, not of many generations, but laid up from eternity. Take all these riches into your power, and at your disposal shall they be forever.' This is the noble peculiar foundation of this part of the inheritance of Christ.

JUNE 29

Meditate on the Word

His delight is in the law of the LORD, and on his law he meditates day and night.

PSALM 1:2

God has given Scripture to his servants for their continual exercise day and night in this world. In their inquiry into it, he requires of them their utmost diligence and endeavours. There shall never be any time or strength lost or misspent that is laid out according to the mind of God in and about his word. The matter, the words, the order, the contexture of them, the scope, design, and aim of the Holy Spirit in them, all and every one of them, may well take up the utmost of our diligence—all are divine. Nothing is empty, unfurnished, or unprepared for our spiritual use, advantage, and benefit.

Let us then learn:

1. To admire and, as one said of old, to *adore the fullness of the Scripture*. It is all full of divine wisdom, and calls for our reverence in the consideration of it. And indeed, a constant awe at the majesty, authority, and holiness of God in his word, is the only teachable frame. Proud and careless spirits see nothing of heaven or divinity in the word; but the humble are made wise in it.

2. To stir up and *exercise our faith and diligence* to the utmost in our study and search of the Scripture. It is an endless storehouse, a bottomless treasure of divine truth; gold is in every sand. All the wise people in the world may, everyone for themselves, learn something out of every word of it, and yet leave enough still behind them for the instruction of all those that shall come after them. The fountains and springs of wisdom in it are endless, and will never be dry. We may attain a *true* sense, but we can never attain the *full* sense of any place; we can never exhaust the whole impress of infinite wisdom that is on the word. And how should this stir us up to be meditating in it day and night!

JUNE 30

Preaching the Word

To which of the angels did God ever say, 'You are my Son'?

HEBREWS 1:5

It is lawful to draw consequences from Scripture assertions; and such consequences, rightly deduced, are infallibly true and to be believed. Thus from the name 'Son' given to Christ, the apostle deduces, by just consequence, his exaltation and pre-eminence above angels.

Nothing will rightly follow from truth but what is also truth, and that of the same nature with the truth from which it is derived. So that whatever, by just consequence, is drawn from the word of God, is itself also the word of God, and truth infallible.

To deprive the church of this liberty in the interpretation of the word, is to deprive it of the chiefest benefit intended by it. This is what the whole ordinance of preaching is founded on— that which is derived out of the word has the power, authority, and efficacy of the word accompanying it. Thus, though it is the proper work and effect of the word of God to quicken, regenerate, sanctify and purify the elect—and the word primarily and directly is only that which is written in the Scriptures—yet we find all these effects produced in and by the preaching of the word, when perhaps not one sentence of the Scripture is *verbatim* repeated. And the reason for this is because whatever is directly deduced and delivered according to the mind and appointment of God from the word *is* the word of God, and has the power, authority, and efficacy of the word accompanying it.

JULY

In July, we will be reading from Owen's works published between 1668 and 1671. *The Nature, Power, Deceit, and Prevalency of the Remainders Of Indwelling Sin In Believers* (1668) is a subtle analysis of the moral deceitfulness of the heart, written to guide believers in the exercise of self-examination. The same year, he also published *A Practical Exposition of Psalm 130.* Verse 4, 'with you there is forgiveness, that you may be feared' had been important for his own earlier spiritual life when, as he put it, 'my soul was oppressed with horror and darkness'.

In 1669, he wrote *A Brief Declaration and Vindication of the Doctrine of the Trinity*, which handled the Trinity and the atonement carefully and biblically against those who railed against them. He outlined his views of church and state in *Truth and innocence vindicated in a survey of a discourse concerning ecclesiastical polity, and the authority of the civil magistrate over the consciences of subjects in matters of religion*. He also wrote a preface to an exposition of the Song of Songs by James Durham (1622-1658), a godly minister in Glasgow, who had preached before Cromwell during the civil wars.

In 1670, he continued to defend nonconformity in *Account of the Grounds and Reasons on Which Protestant Dissenters Desire Liberty*, and to defend himself against some unfounded accusations in *Reflections on A Slanderous Libel*. In 1671, he published *Exercitations concerning the name, original, nature, use, and continuance of a day of sacred rest*. This looked at the origins of the Sabbath in creation, the morality of the fourth commandment to keep it holy, and the change of the day to Sunday after the resurrection of Christ.

JULY 1

Indwelling Sin

I find it to be a law that when I want to do right, evil lies close at hand.

ROMANS 7:21

There is an exceeding efficacy and power in the remainders of indwelling sin in believers, with a constant working towards evil. Thus it is in believers; it is a law even *in them*, though not *to them*. Though its rule be broken, its strength weakened and impaired, its root mortified, yet it is a law still of great force and efficacy. Carnal people, in reference to spiritual and moral duties, are nothing but this law. It is in them a ruling and prevailing principle of all moral actions.

The apostle says he found this law. It had been *told* to him there was such a law; it had been *preached* unto him. This convinced him that there was a law of sin. But it is one thing for a person to know in general that there is a law of sin; another thing for them to have an experience of the power of this law of sin in themselves. It is preached to all; all that own the Scripture acknowledge it, as being declared in it. But they are but few who know it in themselves; we should else have more complaints of it than we have, and more contendings against it, and less fruits of it in the world. But this is what the apostle affirms—not that the doctrine of it had been preached to him, but that he found it by experience in himself.

Believers have experience of the power and efficacy of indwelling sin. They find it in themselves; they find it as a law. It has a self-evidencing efficacy to those who are alive to discern it. They that find not its power are under its dominion. Whoever contends against it shall know and find that it is present with them, that it is powerful in them. They shall find the stream to be strong who swim against it, though the one who rolls along with it be insensible of it.

JULY 2

The Law of Sin

*For the law of the Spirit of life has set you free in Christ Jesus
from the law of sin and death.*

ROMANS 8:2

There is—through grace—kept up in believers a constant and
ordinarily prevailing will of doing good, despite the power and
efficacy of indwelling sin to the contrary. This, in their *worst*
condition, distinguishes them from unbelievers in their *best*.

The will in unbelievers is under the power of the law of sin.
The opposition they make to sin, either in the root or branches
of it, is from their light and their consciences; the will of sinning
in them is never taken away. Take away all other considerations
and hinderances and they would sin willingly always.

They will plead, indeed, that they would leave their sins if
they could, and they would gladly do better than they do. But
they do not, they cannot, so choose that which is spiritually
good; only they have some desires to attain that end to which
good leads, and to avoid that evil which the neglect of it tends to.

These also are for the most part so weak and languid that
they make no considerable endeavours against sin. Witness
that luxury, sloth, worldliness, and security, that the generality
of people are even drowned in. But in believers, there is a will
of doing good, a habitual disposition and inclination in their
wills to that which is spiritually good; and where this is, it is
accompanied with answerable effects.

JULY 3

Know Yourself

So then with the mind I myself serve the law of God; but with the flesh the law of sin.

ROMANS 7:25

So we see what wisdom is required in the guiding and management of our hearts and ways before God. Where the subjects of a ruler are in feuds and oppositions one against another, unless great wisdom is used in the government of the whole, all things will quickly be ruinous in that state. There are these contrary principles in the hearts of believers. And if they labour not to be spiritually wise, how shall they be able to steer their course aright?

Many people live in the dark to themselves all their days; whatever else they know, they know not themselves. They know their outward estates, how rich they are, and the condition of their bodies as to health and sickness they are careful to examine; but as to their inward being, and their principles as to God and eternity, they know little or nothing of themselves. Indeed, few labour to grow wise in this matter; few study themselves as they ought, or are acquainted with the evils of their own hearts as they ought. Yet the whole course of their obedience, and consequently of their eternal condition, depends on this. This, therefore, is our wisdom; and it is a needful wisdom if we have any design to please God, or to avoid that which is a provocation to the eyes of his glory.

What diligence and watchfulness is required for a Christian life! There is a constant enemy to it in everyone's own heart. We may well bewail the woeful sloth and negligence that is in most people, even in Christians. They live and walk as though they intended to go to heaven hood-winked and asleep, as though they had no enemy to deal with.

JULY 4

Sin's Home

*Now if I do what I do not want, it is no longer I who do it,
but sin that dwells within me.*

ROMANS 7:20

The flesh, which is the seat and throne of this law, yea, which indeed is this law, is in some sense the man himself, as grace also is the new man. Now, from this consideration of it, that it is an indwelling law inclining and moving to sin as an inward habit or principle, it has sundry advantages increasing its strength and furthering its power.

It always *abides* in the soul—it is never absent. The apostle twice uses that expression, 'It dwells in me' (Rom. 7:17, 20). There is its constant residence and habitation. If it came upon the soul only at certain seasons, much obedience might be perfectly accomplished in its absence; yea, and as they deal with usurping tyrants, whom they intend to thrust out of a city, the gates might be sometimes shut against it, that it might not return. The soul might fortify itself against it. But the soul is its home; there it dwells, and is no wanderer.

Wherever you are, whatever you are about, this law of sin is always in you; in the best that you do, and in the worst. People little consider what a dangerous companion is always at home with them. When they are in company, when alone, by night or by day, all is one, sin is with them. There is a living coal continually in their houses; which, if they are not careful, will set them on fire, and possibly even consume them.

Oh, the woeful security of poor souls! How little do most of them think of this inbred enemy that is never away from home! How little, for the most part, does the watchfulness of any believer answer the danger of their state and condition!

JULY 5

Deceitful Sin

*But exhort one another every day, as long as it is called 'today',
that none of you may be hardened by the deceitfulness of sin.*

HEBREWS 3:13

That sin, indwelling sin, is deceitful, we have the express testimony of the Holy Spirit. Deceitful it is: take heed of it, watch against it, or it will produce its utmost effect in hardening of the heart against God. It is on the account of sin that the heart is said to be 'deceitful above all things' (Jer. 17:9). To the same purpose speaks the apostle: 'The old self is corrupt through deceitful desires' (Eph. 4:22).

Where there is poison in every stream, the fountain must necessarily be corrupt. And thus the account which the apostle gives concerning those who are under the power of sin is, that they are 'led astray' (Titus 3:3). And the life of evil men is nothing but 'deceiving, and being deceived' (2 Tim. 3:13). So our enemy is deceitful. We know he can have no security against one that is deceitful, except in standing upon our guard and defence all our days.

Deceit properly affects the *mind*; it is the mind that is deceived. When sin attempts any other way of entrance into the soul, as by the affections, the mind, retaining its right and sovereignty, is able to give check and control to it. But where the mind is tainted, the dominance must be great; for the mind or understanding is the leading faculty of the soul, and what that fixes on, the will and affections rush after. So it is, that though the entanglement of the affections to sin is often most troublesome, yet the deceit of the mind is always most dangerous, because of the place that it possesses in the soul to guide, direct, choose, and lead.

JULY 6

Love the Cross

But far be it from me to boast except in the cross of our Lord Jesus Christ, by which the world has been crucified to me, and I to the world.

GALATIANS 6:14

As to the object of your affections, in an especial manner, let it be the cross of Christ. The cross of Christ the apostle Paul gloried and rejoiced in; this his heart was set upon. And these were the effects of it: it crucified the world to him, made it a dead and undesirable thing.

If the heart is filled with the cross of Christ, it casts death and undesirableness on 'the lust of the flesh, the lust of the eyes, and the pride of life' (1 John 2:16). It leaves no seeming beauty, no apparent pleasure or comeliness in them. Again, says Paul, 'It crucifies me to the world; makes my heart, my affections, my desires, dead to any of these things.' It roots up corrupt lusts and affections, leaves no principle to go forth and make provision for the flesh, to fulfil the lusts of it.

Labour, therefore, to fill your hearts with the cross of Christ. Consider the sorrows he underwent, the curse he bore, the blood he shed, the cries he put forth, the love that was in all this to your souls, and the mystery of the grace of God in it. Meditate on the vileness and punishment of sin as represented in the cross, the blood, the death of Christ. Shall we give entertainment to that, or hearken to its dalliances, which wounded, which pierced, which slew our dear Lord Jesus? God forbid! Fill your affections with the cross of Christ, that there may be no room for sin. The world once put him out of the house into a stable, when he came to save us; let him now turn the world out of our doors, when he is come to sanctify us.

JULY 7

Dull of Hearing

You have become dull of hearing. For though by this time you ought to be teachers, you need someone to teach you again the basic principles of the oracles of God.

HEBREWS 5:11-12

God does not allow us to be unmindful of the assistance he has afforded us. Commands, exhortations, promises, threatenings, are multiplied to this purpose. He is continually saying to us, 'Why will you wither and decay? Come to the pastures provided for you, and your souls shall live.'

If we see a lamb that has run from the fold into the wilderness, we are not surprised if it is torn apart by wild beasts. If we see a sheep leaving its green pastures to abide in dry barren heaths, we count it no marvel if we see him lean and ready to perish. But if we see sheep pining in full pastures, we judge them to be diseased and unsound. It is indeed no marvel that poor creatures who run away from the pasture of Christ in his ordinances, are torn apart with many lusts, and pine away with hunger and famine. But to see people enjoying all the means of spiritual thriving, yet to decay, not to be fat and flourishing, but rather daily to pine and wither: this suggests some secret powerful disease, whose poisonous and noxious qualities hinder the efficacy of the means they enjoy.

This is indwelling sin. So powerful and poisonous it is, that it can bring leanness on the souls of people in the midst of all precious means of growth and flourishing. It may well make us tremble, to see people living under and using the means of the gospel, preaching, praying, administration of sacraments, and yet grow colder every day, more selfish and worldly.

JULY 8

Listen Up!

Seek the LORD while he may be found; call upon him while he is near.

ISAIAH 55:6

Great opportunities for service neglected and great gifts not improved are often the occasion of plunging the soul into great depths. Gifts are given to trade with for God. Opportunities are the market-days for that trade. To hide away in a handkerchief the one and to let slip the other, will end in trouble and disconsolation (Luke 19:20). Anxieties and perplexities of heart are worms that will certainly breed in the rust of unexercised gifts. God loses a revenue of glory and honour by such slothful souls; and he will make them aware of it. I know some today whom, denied of opportunities for service, are ready to sink into the grave.

When a soul is wrestling with some lust or temptation, God, by his providence, causes some special word, in the preaching of the gospel, or the administration of some ordinance of it, peculiarly suited to the state and condition of the soul, by the ways of rebuke or persuasion, to come near and enter the inmost parts of the heart. The soul cannot but take notice that God is near to it, that he is dealing with it, and calling on it to look to him for assistance. And he seldom gives such warnings to his saints but that he is near them in an eminent manner to give them relief and help. But, if his care and kindness in this is neglected, his following reproofs are usually more severe.

Many believers take little notice of their worldliness, their pride, their passion, their lavish tongues; but the world does, and the gospel is disadvantaged by it. No wonder if they find from the hand of the Lord the bitter fruits of them in the end.

JULY 9

God's Patience

Note then the kindness and the severity of God: severity toward those who have fallen, but God's kindness to you, provided you continue in his kindness.

ROMANS 11:22

Upon the first entrance of sin and the breach of that covenant which God had made with mankind in Adam, he might immediately have executed the threatened curse, and have brought eternal death upon those who sinned. Justice required that it should be so, and there was nothing in the whole creation to interpose so much as for a reprieve or a respite of vengeance. And had God then sent sinning humanity, with the apostate angels who induced them into sin, immediately into eternal destruction, he would have been glorified in his righteousness and severity by and among the angels that sinned not. Or he could have created a new race of innocent creatures to have worshipped him and glorified him for his righteous judgment, even as the elect at the last day shall do for the destruction of ungodly men.

God has not taken this course. He has continued the race of mankind for a long season on the earth. He has watched over them with his providence, and exercised exceeding patience, forbearance, and long-suffering towards them.

The whole world is every day filled with tokens of the power and patience of God; every nation, every city, every family is filled with them. But there is a common abuse of this patience of God visible in the world in all generations.

JULY 10

Forgiveness

Be kind to one another, tenderhearted, forgiving one another, as God in Christ forgave you.

EPHESIANS 4:32

God requires forgiveness in us because of the forgiveness we receive from him. This is to put the greatest obligation on us to forgiveness that we are capable of, and to give the strongest and most powerful motive possible for its performance.

This duty is more directly and expressly required in the New Testament than in the Old. It was required then, but not so openly, so plainly, so expressly as now. So we find a different frame of spirit between those under that dispensation and those under the New Testament. There are found amongst them some such reflections upon their enemies, their oppressors, persecutors, and the like, which were warranted by some actings of the Spirit of God in them, yet, being suited unto the dispensation they were under, do no way become us now, who, by Jesus Christ receive 'grace upon grace' (John 1:16).

So Zechariah, when he died, cried, 'May the LORD see and avenge!' (2 Chron. 24:22); but Stephen, dying in the same cause and manner, said, 'Lord, do not hold this sin against them' (Acts 7:60). Elijah called for fire from heaven (2 Kings 1:10), but our Saviour reproves the least inclination in his disciples to imitate him in this (Luke 9:54-55). And the reason for this difference is because forgiveness in God is, under the New Testament, far more clearly discovered (especially in the nature and cause of it) in the gospel, which has brought life and immortality to light, than it was under the law.

JULY 11

Ponder These Things

Let the word of Christ dwell in you richly.

COLOSSIANS 3:16

Labour to exercise your hearts greatly with thoughts of that abundant grace that is manifested in the way of sinners coming to God, as also of the excellency of the gospel in which it is unfolded. Consider the eternal love of the Father, which is the fountain and spring of this whole dispensation. Consider the inexpressible love of the Son in establishing and confirming it, in removing all hinderances and obstructions by his own blood, bringing forth to beauty and glory this redemption or forgiveness of sin at the price of it. And let the glory of the gospel, which alone makes this discovery of forgiveness in God, dwell in your hearts. Let your minds be exercised about these things. You will find effects from them above all that have, as yet, been brought forth in your souls.

When you have risen above the turmoil of lusts and corruptions in your hearts, the entanglements of your callings, business, and affairs, what have you been able to raise your hearts to? Perplexing fears about your condition, general hopes, without savour or relish, yielding you no refreshment; legal commands, bondage duties, distracted consciences, broken purposes and promises, which you have been tossed up and down with, without any certain rest. And what effects have these thoughts produced? Have they made you more holy and more humble? Have they given you delight in God, and strength for new obedience? Not at all. Where you were, there you still are, without the least progress. But now, bring your souls to these springs, and test the Lord if, from that day, you are not blessed with spiritual stores.

JULY 12

Right Judgment

God has fixed a day on which he will judge the world in righteousness by a man whom he has appointed.

ACTS 17:31

The general who heard one of his soldiers cry out, upon a fresh onset of the enemy, 'Now we are undone, now we are ruined!' called him a traitor, and told him it was not so whilst he could wield his sword. It is not for every private soldier on every danger to make judgment of the battle; that is the work of the general. Jesus Christ is 'the captain of our salvation' (Heb. 2:10); he has undertaken the leading and conduct of our souls through all our difficulties. Our duty is to fight and contend; his work is to take care of the event, and to him it is to be committed.

It is not for you to take the judgment of Christ out of his hand, and to be passing sentence on your own souls. Judgment as to the state and condition of people is committed to Christ, and to him it is to be left. Consider the hard thoughts of what God will do with you, and harsh desponding sentences pronounced against yourselves, will alienate your hearts from God. Such thoughts are very apt to infect the mind with other inclinations, for after a while they will prevail with the soul to look on God as an enemy, as one that has no delight in it; and what will be the consequence of that is easily discernible.

None will continue to love long where they expect no returns. Do not allow your minds to be tainted with such thoughts; and let not God be dishonoured by any such expressions as reflect on that infinite grace and compassion which he is exercising towards you.

JULY 13

Soul Darkness

But I trust in you, O LORD; I say, 'You are my God.' My times are in your hand.

PSALM 31:14-15

David's times of trouble and of peace, of darkness and of light, he acknowledged to be in the hand and at the disposal of God. So it was his duty to wait his time and season for his share and portion in them. During this state, the soul meets with many oppositions, difficulties, and perplexities, especially if its darkness is of long continuance. With some, it abides many years; with some, all the days of their lives. Their hope being deferred, it makes their heart sick (Prov. 13:12), and their spirit oftentimes to faint.

Continuance in waiting is indispensably necessary and assuredly prevails in the end. If upon the eruption of new lusts or corruptions; if upon the return of old temptations, or the assaults of new ones; if upon a revived perplexing sense of guilt, or on the tediousness of working and labouring so much and so long in the dark, the soul begins to say in itself, 'I have looked for light and behold darkness, for peace and yet trouble comes'—it will at length utterly fail, and come short of the grace aimed at.

Do not think to be freed from your entanglements by restless, heartless desiring that it were otherwise with you. Means are to be used that relief may be obtained. Mortification of sin, prayer, meditation, due attendance upon all gospel ordinances; conferring in general about spiritual things, seeking advice about our own state and condition from those who are able to speak a word in season to them that are weary—these are required to this purpose. And in all these are diligence and perseverance to be exercised.

JULY 14

Beautiful Promises

How great is his goodness, and how great his beauty!

ZECHARIAH 9:17

The promises are a declaration of the nature of God, especially of his goodness, grace, and love. God has put an impression of all the glorious excellencies of his nature on his word, especially, as he is in Christ, on the word of the gospel. There, as in a glass, we behold his glory in the face of Jesus Christ. As his commands express to us his holiness, his threatenings, his righteousness, and severity; his promises express his goodness, grace, love, and bounty. And in these things we learn all that we truly and solidly know of God; that is, we know him in and by his word.

The soul that is waiting on or for God, considers the representation which he makes of himself and of his own nature in and by the promises, and receives support and encouragement in its duty. For if God teaches us by the promises what he is, and what he will be to us, we have firm ground to expect from him all fruits of kindness and love. They all express goodness, love, patience, forbearance, long-suffering, pardoning mercy, grace, bounty, with a full satisfactory reward.

Whatever difficulties arise, whatever temptations intervene, or wearisomeness grows upon us, in our troubles, trials, and desertions, let us not entertain such thoughts of God as our own perplexed imaginations may be apt to suggest to us. This would quickly cast us into a thousand impatiences, misgivings, and miscarriages. But the remembrance of and meditation on God in his promises—there appear, yea, gloriously shine forth, that love, that wisdom, that goodness, tenderness, and grace, as cannot but encourage a believing soul to abide in waiting for him.

JULY 15

God the Spirit

Go therefore and make disciples of all nations, baptising them in the name of the Father and of the Son and of the Holy Spirit.

MATTHEW 28:19

The Holy Spirit is a divine, distinct person, and neither merely the power or virtue of God, nor a created spirit. This plainly appears from what is revealed concerning him.

He is placed in the same rank and order, without any note of difference or distinction as to a distinct interest in the divine nature with the other divine persons. He also has the names proper to a divine person only, for he is expressly called 'God' in Acts 5. He who is termed the 'Holy Spirit' (v. 3), and the 'Spirit of the Lord' (v. 9), is called also 'God' (v. 4).

He has personal properties assigned to him: a will (1 Cor. 12:11), and understanding (1 Cor. 2:10). He is the voluntary author of divine operations. He of old cherished the creation (Gen. 1:2). He formed and garnished the heavens. He inspired, acted, and spoke, in and by the prophets (Acts 28:25; 2 Pet. 1:21). He regenerates, enlightens, sanctifies, comforts, instructs, leads, guides, all the disciples of Christ, as the Scriptures everywhere testify.

The same regard is had to him in faith, worship, and obedience, as to the other persons of the Father and Son. For our being baptised into his name, is our solemn engagement to believe in him, to yield obedience to him, and to worship him, as it puts the same obligation upon us to the Father and the Son.

JULY 16

Reason and Revelation

No one knows the Son except the Father, and no one knows the Father except the Son and anyone to whom the Son chooses to reveal him.

MATTHEW 11:27

None can know the Father unless the Son reveals him. Nor will, or does, or can, flesh and blood reveal or understand Jesus Christ to be the Son of the living God, unless the Father reveals him, and instructs us in the truth of it (Matt. 16:17). It is by faith and prayer, and through the revelation of God, that we may come to the acknowledgment of these things, and not by the carnal reasonings of people of corrupt minds.

Reason as it is in this or that person we know to be weak, maimed, and imperfect. So that though we will not admit of anything that is contrary to reason, yet the least intimation of a truth by divine revelation will make me embrace it. Reason, especially in and about things of divine revelation is of very small importance (of none at all) where it rises up against the express testimonies of Scripture.

Many things are *above reason* which are not at all *against it*. It is an easy thing to compel the most curious inquirers of these days to a ready confession of this, by multitudes of instances in things finite and temporary—and shall any dare to deny but it may be so in things heavenly, divine, and spiritual? Nay, there is nothing of the being of God, or his properties, but is absolutely above the comprehension of our reason. We cannot by searching find out God; we cannot find out the Almighty to perfection (Job 11:7).

JULY 17

Christ's Satisfaction

Jesus delivers us from the wrath to come.

1 THESSALONIANS 1:10

The sum of what the Scripture reveals about this great truth, commonly called the 'satisfaction of Christ', may be reduced to these heads:

1. Adam, being made upright, sinned against God; and all mankind, all his posterity, in him: 'By the one man's disobedience the many were made sinners' (Rom. 5:19).

2. By this sin of our first parents, all are brought into an estate of sin and apostasy from God, and of enmity to him. 'For all have sinned and fall short of the glory of God' (Rom. 3:23).

3. In this state all continue in sin against God, nor of themselves can do otherwise: 'None is righteous, no, not one; no one understands; no one seeks for God. All have turned aside; together they have become worthless; no one does good, not even one' (Rom. 3:10-12).

4. The justice and holiness of God, as he is the supreme governor and judge of all the world, require that sin be punished: 'For you are not a God who delights in wickedness; evil may not dwell with you' (Ps. 5:4).

5. God, has also engaged his veracity and faithfulness in the sanction of the law, not to leave sin unpunished. In this state and condition, mankind, had they been left without divine aid and help, must have perished eternally.

6. God, out of his infinite goodness, grace, and love to mankind, sent his only Son to save and deliver them out of this condition.

7. This love was the same in Father and Son.

8. The way, in general, by which the Son of God, being incarnate, was to save lost sinners, was by a substitution of himself, according to the design and appointment of God, in the place of those whom he was to save.

JULY 18

Unchanging Perfection

I the LORD do not change; therefore you, O children of Jacob, are not consumed.

MALACHI 3:6

Some say, 'If God can freely pardon sin, why does he not do it without satisfaction? If he cannot, he is weaker and more imperfect than humans, who can do so.'

Answer: God cannot do many things that we can do; not that he is more imperfect than us, but he cannot do them on the account of his perfection. He cannot lie; he cannot deny himself; he cannot change (Titus 1:2; 2 Tim. 2:13; Mal. 3:6), which people can do, and do every day. To pardon sin without satisfaction, in him who is absolutely holy, righteous, true, and faithful—the absolute, necessary, supreme governor of all sinners—the author of the law and sanction of it (in which punishment is threatened and declared) is to deny himself, and to do what one infinitely perfect cannot do.

'So it follows,' they say, 'that the finite and impotent creature is more capable of extending mercy and forgiveness than the infinite and omnipotent Creator.'

Answer: God, being essentially holy and righteous, having engaged his faithfulness in the sanction of the law, and being naturally and necessarily the governor and ruler of the world—the forgiving of sin without satisfaction would be no perfection in him, but an effect of impotence and imperfection, a thing which God cannot do, as he cannot lie, nor deny himself.

JULY 19

Song of Songs

Let him kiss me with the kisses of his mouth! For your love is better than wine.

SONG OF SOLOMON 1:2

The book of Canticles (Song) is not in any part of it, much less in the whole, a suitable subject for every ordinary person to write about. The matter of it is totally sublime, spiritual, and mystical. The manner of its handling is universally allegorical. So did God think it appropriate in his manifold wisdom to instruct his church of old, whilst it tabernacled under those clouds and shadows whose departure and flying away it so earnestly breathes after in this very book.

God committed to it then in his oracles, the same treasures of wisdom and grace as he does now to us under the gospel, only he so folded them up under types and allegories that they could not clearly and distinctly look into them, he having provided some better things for us, that they without us should not be made perfect (Heb. 11:40).

There was always then a virtual, spiritual light and heat, a mystery of wisdom in this book. But it was so wrapped up, so encircled and enclosed in its manner of expression and universal respect unto Christ, not then actually exhibited, that it shines not forth, it gives not its beauty and glory, until touched and effected by a beam of immediate gospel light, and its covering be taken off by him who removed the veil of Moses and of all the prophets, both from their writings and the minds of those who believe.

JULY 20

Hidden Treasure

The natural person does not accept the things of the Spirit of God, for they are folly to him, and he is not able to understand them because they are spiritually discerned.

1 CORINTHIANS 2:14

I shall not here inquire particularly what express understanding in and of the things divinely revealed in the Song of Songs the church had under the Old Testament, whilst they searched diligently into the grace of Christ here declared, and which his Spirit testified to them in it. Nor shall I stay to manifest how great a weakness as to the true and useful apprehension of the mind of God in this holy allegory, seems to have been upon some whole ages of the Christian church.

This is certain, that ever since this heavenly treasure was committed to the sons of men, such a beauty, glory, and excellency have beamed from the matter contained in it, with the manner of its declaration, and the impress of the wisdom of God in both, that all who have had a due reverence to divine revelation have been filled with a holy admiration of it, and a desire to look into the mystery contained in it. The things contained in it are the deep things of God, which none can search out to perfection but the Spirit of God.

The manner of its delivery is absolutely allegorical, and the proper interpretation of such writing requires great heedfulness, skill, and diligence, both in things spiritual, when their subject is such, and in the nature of those figures of speech. Because of the imperfection and weakness of all, with the curiosities of some who have undertaken this exposition, many mistakes have often ensued.

JULY 21

Jesus' Authority

All authority in heaven and on earth has been given to me.
Go therefore and make disciples of all nations.

MATTHEW 28:18-19

Jesus is the 'Lord of lords, and King of kings'. On this account the gospel, with all the worship instituted in it and required by it, is accompanied with a right to enter into any of the kingdoms of the earth, and spiritually to make the inhabitants of them subject to Jesus Christ, and so to translate them out of the power of darkness into the kingdom of the Son of God. This right is antecedent and paramount to the right of all earthly kings and princes. They have no power or authority to exclude the gospel out of their dominions, and what they exercise of that kind is done at their peril.

Mankind was originally made under a law and constitution of eternal bliss or woe. This state, with regard to his necessary dependence on God and respect to their utmost end, was absolutely unavoidable. All possibility of attaining eternal happiness by themselves, they lost by sin, and became inevitably liable to eternal misery and the wrath to come. Into this condition the Lord Jesus Christ, the supreme Lord of the souls and consciences of men, introduces his law of relief, redemption, and salvation, the great means of mankind's recovery, together with the profession of the way and law of it.

He also lets them know that those by whom it is refused shall perish under that wrath of God which before they were liable to, with a new aggravation of their sin and condemnation, from the contempt of the relief provided for them and tendered to them.

JULY 22

Moral Duties

When Gentiles, who do not have the law, by nature do what the law requires, they are a law to themselves, even though they do not have the law. They show that the work of the law is written on their hearts.

ROMANS 2:14-15

Generally, moral virtues are esteemed to be the duties of the second table of the law (the latter part of the Ten Commandments). For although those who handle these matters more accurately do not so restrict or confine them, yet it is certain that, in vulgar and common acceptation, nothing else is intended by 'moral virtues', or 'duties of morality', but the observation of the precepts of the second table. Nor is anything else meant by those theologians who, in their writings, so frequently declare that it is not morality alone that will render us acceptable to God.

Now, this moral law is nothing but the law of nature, or the law of our creation, which the apostle affirms to be equally obligatory for all, even all the Gentiles themselves (Rom. 2:14-15), and of which the decalogue is summarily expressive. This moral law is, therefore, the law written in the hearts of all people by nature. Let it be, then, that moral virtues consist in the universal observance of the requisites and precepts of the law of our creation, and dependence on God as a result.

J U L Y   2 3

The Lord's Prayer

Pray then like this: 'Our Father in heaven, hallowed be your name.'

MATTHEW 6:9

I am accused of 'blaspheming the Lord's prayer'. This I know, that I do, and ever did, believe that this prayer is part of the canonical Scripture; which I would not willingly blaspheme. I do believe that it was composed by the Lord Jesus Christ himself, and have vindicated it from being thought a collection and composition of such petitions as were then in use among the Jews, as some learned men had, I think unadvisedly, asserted it to be.

I do, and ever did, believe it the most perfect form of prayer that ever was composed, and the words of it so disposed by the divine wisdom of our blessed Saviour that it comprehends the substance of all the matter of prayer to God. I do, and did always, believe that it ought to be continually meditated on, that we may learn from it both what we ought to pray for and in what manner.

However, I do not think that our Lord Jesus Christ, in the giving of this prayer to his disciples, prescribed to them the precise use or repetition of those words, but only taught them what to pray for or how. I have as reverent an esteem for the Lord's prayer as anyone that lives on the earth. It is true, however, that I have said that there were manifold abuses in the rehearsal of it amongst people ignorant and superstitious; and I did deliver my thoughts, it may be, too freely and severely, against some kind of repetition of it.

JULY 24

Deep Things

How great are your works, O LORD! Your thoughts are very deep!

PSALM 92:5

What I have attained to of light and truth is submitted to the judgment of the learned and judicious. The censures of persons heady, ignorant, and proud, who speak evil of those things which they know not, and in what they naturally know corrupt themselves, I neither fear nor value. If any discourses seem somewhat dark or obscure to ordinary readers, I desire they would consider that the foundations of the things discoursed of lie deep, and that no expression will render them more familiar and obvious to all understandings than their nature will allow. Nor must we in any case quit the strengths of truth because the minds of some cannot easily possess themselves of them.

However, I hope nothing will occur but what an attentive reader, though otherwise of an ordinary capacity, may receive and digest. I shall only add, that here is no design of contending with any, of opposing or contradicting any, of censuring or reflecting on those whose thoughts and judgments in these things differ from ours, begun or carried on. Even those by whom a holy day of rest under the gospel and its services are laughed to scorn are by me left to God and themselves. My whole endeavour is to find out what is agreeable to truth about the observance of such a day to the Lord; what is the mind and will of God concerning it; on what foundation we may attend to the services of it, so that God may be glorified in us and by us, and the interest of religion, in purity, holiness, and righteousness, be promoted amongst people.

J U L Y   2 5

Evil Schemes

See, this alone I found, that God made man upright, but they
have sought out many schemes.

ECCLESIASTES 7:29

Solomon tells us that in his investigation of the nature and state
of things in the world, this alone he had found out, that 'God
made man upright, but they have sought out many schemes'
(Eccles. 7:29). And the truth of this we also find by woeful
experience, in all our concerns with respect to God and ourselves.
There is not anything in which people have not found out many
schemes, to the disturbance and perverting of that state of peace
and quietness in which all things were made by God.

Indeed, with the fruits and effects of this perverse apostasy,
and relinquishment of that universally harmonious state of
things in which we were created, the whole world is filled and
overwhelmed with evil. We have the relics of evil to fight with,
even in the repaired condition which in this life, by grace, we are
made partakers of. Some of these evil schemes are ready to mix
themselves into all our ways, actions, and duties—to our own
disturbance, and the perverting of the right ways of God.

An evident instance of this we have in the business of a
day of sacred rest, and the worship of God required on it. God
originally, out of his infinite goodness, gave to mankind a day of
rest, to express to them his own rest and satisfaction in the works
of his hands. It was to be a day of rest for them, and a means
of their entrance into and enjoyment of that rest with himself,
here and forever, which he had ordained for them. But they are
in all things continually finding out new schemes, and various
questions.

JULY 26

Forbearance

Why do you pass judgment on your brother? Or you, why do you despise your brother? For we will all stand before the judgment seat of God.

ROMANS 14:10

God made mankind upright, and gave us the Sabbath, or day of rest, as a token of that condition and pledge of a future eternal rest with himself. Yet, through our many schemes, that very day has become amongst us an occasion and means of much uneasiness and many contentions. This has apparently influenced the minds of all sorts of people to a neglect in the practice of those duties which they acknowledged to be incumbent on them. Some have hotly disputed that there is now no special day of rest to be observed to the Lord, by virtue of any divine precept or institution. Others have granted that if it is to be observed only by virtue of ecclesiastical constitution, people may have various pretences for dispensations from the duties of it. The whole due observance of it is much lost among Christians.

The solemn worship of God is the spring, rule, and measure of all our obedience to him. So it may justly be thought that the neglect of this has been a great, if not a principal occasion of that sad degeneracy from the power, purity, and glory of Christian religion, which all may see and many do complain about at this day in the world. Most people act in themselves and towards others as if they were themselves liable to no mistakes, and that it is an inexpiable crime in others to be in anything mistaken. The consideration of this should affect us with tenderness and forbearance towards those who dissent from us, and whom we therefore judge to err and be mistaken.

JULY 27

Why Weeks?

God blessed the seventh day and made it holy, because on it God rested from all his work that he had done in creation.

GENESIS 2:3

The regular seven-day revolution of time, generally admitted in the world, is a great testimony to the original institution of the Sabbath. Of old it was universal, and is at present received among those nations whose converse was not begun until of late with any of those parts of the world where there is a light gone forth in these things from the Scripture. All nations, I say, in all ages, have from time immemorial made the revolution of seven days to be the second stated period of time. And this observation is still continued throughout the world, unless amongst those who in other things are openly degenerated from the law of nature.

The measure of time by a day and night is directed to sense by the course of the sun: lunar months and solar years are an unavoidable observation to all rational creatures. Therefore, all have reckoned time by days, months, and years, and this is obvious to all. But why the seven-day revolution, or weekly period of time, should make its entrance and obtain universal approval, no one can give an account, but with respect to some impressions on the minds of people from the constitution and law of our nature, with the tradition of a sabbatical rest instituted from the foundation of the world.

JULY 28

Creation Proclaims

God's invisible attributes, namely, his eternal power and divine nature, have been clearly perceived, ever since the creation of the world, in the things that have been made.

ROMANS 1:20

God ordered and designed all his works to be a means of glorifying himself, in and by the obedience of his rational creatures. For God first made all the inanimate things, then animate and sensitive creatures, in their glory, order, and beauty. In and on all these, he implanted a teaching and instructive power, for 'The heavens declare the glory of God, and the sky above proclaims his handiwork' (Ps. 19:1). All creatures are frequently called on to give praise and glory to him. This expresses their nature and order which reveals and manifests him and the glorious excellencies of his nature, which mankind is to contemplate and give glory to him. For after them all was mankind made, to consider and use them all for the end for which they were made, and was a kind of mediator between God and the rest of the creatures, by and through whom he would receive all his glory from them.

This is what our apostle speaks about in Romans 1:19-20. The design of God, as he declares, was to manifest and show himself in his works to mankind. Mankind learning from them 'his invisible attributes' was to 'glorify him as God' as he says.

JULY 29

Covenant Rest

The Lord God commanded the man, saying, 'You may surely eat of every tree of the garden, but of the tree of the knowledge of good and evil you shall not eat, for in the day that you eat of it you shall surely die.'

GENESIS 2:16-17

Mankind in its creation, with respect to the ends of God in it, was constituted under a covenant. That is, the law of his obedience was attended with promises and threatenings, rewards and punishments, suited to the goodness and holiness of God. For every law with rewards and recompenses annexed has the nature of a covenant.

The promise with which mankind was encouraged to obedience, which was that of eternal life with God, did in strict justice exceed the worth of the obedience required. On the other side, the punishment threatened to disobedience, in death and an everlasting separation from God, was such as the righteousness and holiness of God, as our supreme governor and Lord, and the covenant, did require.

Now, this covenant belonged to the law of creation. God might have dealt with mankind by way of absolute sovereignty, requiring obedience of us without a covenant of a reward infinitely exceeding it.

We shall find that so long as God is pleased to establish any covenant with mankind, he has and does invariably require one day in seven to be set apart for praise and glory to himself.

JULY 30

Ancient Hope

I will put enmity between you and the woman, and between your offspring and her offspring; he shall bruise your head, and you shall bruise his heel.

GENESIS 3:15

All acknowledge that a promise of Christ, for the object and guide of the faith of the ancient patriarchs, was given in those words of God immediately spoken to the serpent in Genesis 3:15. The words in themselves seem obscure to any such end or purpose. But there is such light given to them, and the mind of God in them, by the whole ensuing economy, or dealing of God with people, revealed in the Scripture, that no sober person doubts the promissory nature of those words, nor of the intention of them in general, nor of the proper subject of the promise, nor of the grace intended in it.

This promise, therefore, was the immediate object of the faith of the patriarchs of old, the great motive and encouragement to and of their obedience. Yet it will be hard, from the records of Scripture, to prove that any particular patriarch did believe in, trust, or plead that promise, which yet we know that they did all and every one; nor was there any need, for our instruction, that any such practice of theirs should be recorded, seeing it is a general rule that those holy men of God did observe and do whatever he did command them. Wherefore, from the record of a command, we may conclude a suitable practice, though it be not recorded; from a recorded approved practice, on the other side, we may conclude the command or institution of the thing practised, though it be nowhere plainly recorded.

JULY 31

Covenant Republished

If you will indeed obey my voice and keep my covenant, you shall be my treasured possession among all peoples, for all the earth is mine.

EXODUS 19:5

God renewed the knowledge of himself and mankind's duty towards him in the posterity of Abraham. So he gave to them afresh the precepts of the law and covenant of nature, as the guide and rule of their obedience. That this might now be permanent, he reduced the substance of the whole law to 'ten words' or commands, writing them in tablets of stone, which he appointed to be sacredly kept amongst them. The law thus declared and written by him was the same, I say, materially, and for the substance of it, with the law of our creation, or the original rule of our covenant obedience to God.

As to its form or directive power, it was now made external and objective to the mind, which before was principally internal and subjective. It was prefaced with motives peculiar to Israel's state and condition, and its observation continually pressed on them afterwards, with arguments taken from their peculiar relationship to God, with his love and benefits to them. This gave it a new respect, because there was nothing originally in it nor belonging to it but what was equally common to all mankind.

Now, this alteration in the law and covenant of creation, as applied unto the church of the Israelites, did also affect the law of the Sabbath, which was a part of it. It was now no more to them a mere moral command only, equally regarding all mankind, but had a temporary respect given unto it, which was afterwards to be abolished and taken away. So was it with the whole law, and so was it with the Sabbath in particular.

AUGUST

This month, we will be reading Owen's writings from 1672-1674, when he was in his late 50s. In 1672, King Charles II made a Declaration of Indulgence, that he would release nonconformists such as Owen from the strict penal laws that had been enacted against them, and allow them to meet publicly (if they officially registered and were licensed). It was also the year that Owen wrote *A Discourse Concerning Evangelical Love, Church Peace, and Unity; With the Occasions and Reasons of the Present Differences and Divisions about Things Sacred and Religious*.

In 1673, Owen put the finishing touches to the second large folio volume of his huge commentary on Hebrews. The volume covering Hebrews 3-5 was sent to the press in the autumn, and finally published in 1674.

In 1674, Owen kindly wrote a preface to *The Difference Between the Old and New Covenant Stated and Explained* by Samuel Petto from Suffolk, who had been ejected from the Church of England in 1662 but licensed in 1672 as a Congregationalist minister. They shared a deep interest in covenant theology.

That same year, Owen also published his large and comprehensive work on the Holy Spirit, the *Pneumatologia*. Written to counter the rationalism, mysticism, and irreligion of his times, this work was declared the masterpiece of all Owen's writings by the eighteenth-century evangelical, John Newton.

August is a somewhat tragic month for Puritans. August 24th was the infamous day on which the great ejection of the Puritans had taken place in 1662. It was also the date on which Owen was to die, in 1683.

AUGUST 1

Love Enemies

But I say to you, Love your enemies and pray for those who persecute you.

MATTHEW 5:44

We know that God has styled himself the God of love, peace, and order in the church, because they are eminently from him, and highly accepted with him. Love is the new commandment which Jesus Christ has given to his disciples, so he has appointed it to be the bond of perfection to them; which nothing else will ever be, however finely invented for them, or forcibly imposed on them. Without this love, in what relates to church communion, whatever else we are, we are but 'a noisy gong or a clanging cymbal'. And all unity or agreement in outward order not proceeding from and animated by this love, are things in which neither Christ nor the gospel are much concerned.

An endeavour also after one mind and one judgment amongst all believers (Phil. 2:2; 1 Cor. 1:10), to help us keep the 'unity of the Spirit in the bond of peace' (Eph. 4:3) we acknowledge to be indispensably required of us.

All these things—namely, love, peace, and unity—are equally dear to us, yet there are different rules prescribed for the exercise and pursuit of them. Our love is to be catholic, unconfined as the beams of the sun, or as the showers of rain that fall on the whole earth. Nothing of God's rational creation in this world is to be exempted from being the object of our love. And where an exception might seem to be warranted by some people's causeless hatred, with unjust and unreasonable persecution of us, there we are most especially and strictly charged to love, which is one of the noble singularities of Christian religion.

AUGUST 2

Compassion

For the earth shall be full of the knowledge of the LORD as the waters cover the sea.
ISAIAH 11:9

Love toward all mankind in general we acknowledge to be required of us. Even towards the infidel, pagan, and Islamic world, Jews and Gentiles, we owe the duty of love. We desire to be humbled for it as our sin, when we are wanting in the discharge of it. The first natural and genuine effect of love is *compassion*. Compassion for all unbelievers is whatever should deliver them from present or eternal misery—whatever should lead, guide, or bring them to blessedness in the enjoyment of God. The absence of this is accompanied, even in this world, with all that blindness and darkness of mind, all that slavery to sin and the devil, that makes a rational being truly miserable. Unless we have hearts like flint or rock, we cannot but be moved with compassion towards so many perishing souls, originally made like ourselves, in the image of God. If we differ in anything from them it is an effect of mere sovereign grace, and not the fruit of our own contrivance nor the reward of our worth or merit.

Compassion proceeding from love will work by prayer for relief. It is therefore our continual prayer, that God would send out his light and his truth to the utmost parts of the earth, to visit by them those dark places which are yet filled with habitations of cruelty; that he would remove the veil of covering which is yet on the face of many great and populous nations; that 'the whole earth may be filled with the knowledge of the Lord, as the waters cover the sea.'

AUGUST 3

In Christ Alone

There is salvation in no one else, for there is no other name under heaven given among men by which we must be saved.

ACTS 4:12

Some hope to attain salvation or eternal blessedness in the condition that they are in, without the knowledge of Jesus Christ. This we neither believe nor hope concerning them. Nor, to speak plainly, can we desire it should be so. 'For although there may be so-called gods in heaven or on earth—as indeed there are many "gods" and many "lords"—yet for us there is one God, the Father, from whom are all things and for whom we exist, and one Lord, Jesus Christ, through whom are all things and through whom we exist' (1 Cor. 8:5-6).

We know 'there is salvation in no one else' but by Jesus Christ, and that 'there is no other name under heaven given among men by which we must be saved' (Acts 4:12). It is not the giving of the person of Christ absolutely to be a mediator, but the declaration of his name by the gospel, as the means of salvation, that is intended. Hence, our Lord Jesus Christ, giving that commission to his apostles to preach it—'Go into all the world and proclaim the gospel to the whole creation'—adds to it that sentence concerning the everlasting condition of all: 'Whoever believes and is baptised will be saved, but whoever does not believe will be condemned' (Mark 16:15-16). Preaching the gospel and believing in Jesus Christ are the only means of obtaining salvation. So all those who are not made partakers of these must perish eternally. When the apostle affirms that the Jews would have hindered him from preaching to the Gentiles 'that they might be saved' (1 Thess. 2:16), he plainly declares that without it they could not so be.

AUGUST 4

Truly Elect

For with the heart one believes and is justified, and with the mouth one confesses and is saved.

ROMANS 10:10

The real living and spiritual body of Christ is firstly, peculiarly, and properly the *catholic church* militant in this world. These are his elect, redeemed, justified, and sanctified ones, who are savingly united to their head by the same quickening and sanctifying Spirit, dwelling in him in all fulness, and communicated to them by him, according to his promise. This is that catholic church which we profess to believe. It is hidden from the eyes of people, and absolutely invisible in its mystical form, or spiritual saving relation unto the Lord Christ and its unity with him. But it is more or less always visible by that profession of faith in him and obedience to him which it makes in the world, and is always obliged so to do (Rom. 10:10).

This church we believe to be so disposed over the whole world, that wherever there are any societies or numbers of people who ordinarily profess the gospel, and subjection to the kingly rule of Christ by it, with a hope of eternal blessedness by his mediation, we in no way doubt but that there are among them some who really belong to it.

AUGUST 5

Fallen Churches

But I have this against you, that you have abandoned the love you had at first.

REVELATION 2:4

It must be acknowledged that many churches have woefully degenerated, and that any of them may so do. The whole Christian world gives us instances of this today; indeed, we have it confirmed for us in what is recorded concerning various churches in the Scripture itself. They were newly planted by the apostles themselves, and had rules given by them to attend to for their direction. They were obliged in all emergencies to inquire after and receive those commands and directions, which the apostles were enabled infallibly to give to them. And yet, despite these great advantages, we find that sundry of them were suddenly fallen into sinful neglects, disorders, and miscarriages, in doctrine, discipline, and worship. Some of these were reproved and reformed by the great apostle Paul in his epistles; and some of them were rebuked and threatened by the Lord Christ himself immediately from heaven (Rev. 2-3).

Some of them have, by their superstition, false worship, and express idolatry, joined with wickedness of life and persecution of the true worshippers of Christ. So are sundry faithful cities become harlots; and, where righteousness inhabited, there dwell persecuting murderers. Such churches were planted of Christ as wholly noble vines, but are degenerated into those that are bitter and wild (Isa. 5:1-4). Whatever our judgment may be concerning the personal condition of the members of such apostatised churches, it is our indispensable duty to separate from them.

AUGUST 6

I will leave seven thousand in Israel, all the knees that have not bowed to Baal, and every mouth that has not kissed him.

1 Kings 19:18

There may in such apostate churches remain a profession of the fundamental truths of the gospel. And by virtue of this, as they maintain the interest of Christ's visible kingdom in the world, so we no way doubt but that there may be many amongst them who, by a saving faith in the truths they do profess, do really belong to the mystical church of Christ.

An instituted church, therefore, may, by the crimes and wickedness of its rulers and the generality of its members, and their idolatrous administrations in holy things, utterly destroy their instituted estate, and yet not presently all of them cease to belong unto the kingdom of Christ. For we cannot say that those things which will certainly annul church administrations, and render them abominable, will absolutely destroy the salvation of all individual persons who partake in them; and many may secretly preserve themselves from being defiled with such abominations.

So, in the height of the degeneracy and apostasy of the Israelite church, there were seven thousand who kept themselves pure from Baalish idolatry, of whom none were known to Elijah. And therefore did God still continue a respect unto them as his people, because of those secret ones, and because the token of his covenant was yet in their flesh, affording to them an extraordinary ministry by his prophets, when the ordinary ministry by priests and Levites was utterly ceased.

This we are to hope concerning every place where there is any profession made of the name of Christ.

AUGUST 7

Unfruitful Works

Take no part in the unfruitful works of darkness, but instead expose them.

EPHESIANS 5:11

We are neither the authors nor the guides of our own love: he who implants and works it in us has given us rules how it must be exercised. It may work as regularly by sharp cutting rebukes as by the most silken and compliant expressions—by manifesting an aversion to all that is evil, as by embracing and approving of what is good. In all things and cases, it is to be directed by the word. When, under the pretence of love, we leave that rule and go off from any duty which we owe immediately to God, it is will, pride, and self-conceit in us, and not love.

Among all the exhortations that are given us in the Scripture to unity and concord as the fruits of love, there is not one that says we should agree or comply with anyone in their sins or evil practices. But as we are commanded in ourselves to abstain 'from every form of evil' (1 Thess. 5:22), so are we forbidden a participation in the sins of others, and all 'fellowship with the unfruitful works of darkness' (Eph. 5:11). Our love towards such churches is to work by pity, compassion, prayer, instructions; which are due means for their healing and recovery—not by communion with them, by which they may be hardened in the error of their way, and our own souls be subverted.

AUGUST 8

Behold, I establish my covenant with you and your offspring after you.

GENESIS 9:9

The stores of heavenly wisdom, grace, and truth which are treasured up in the divine revelations concerning God's covenants, are far from being fully exhausted, although many have already brought to light excellent and useful instructions in the mind of God and the duty of those who believe. But the thing itself is so excellent, the mystery of it so great, the declaration of it in the Scripture so extensive and diffused throughout the whole body of it from the first to the last, that there is a sufficient ground on which to justify a renewed search into the mind of God in this as revealed in his word.

There is no doubt but the greatest product of divine grace, goodness, and condescension, next to the sending of the only Son of God to take our nature on him, is this of his entering into covenant with us. Nor has anything a greater tendency to the advancement of his own glory. God might have dealt with mankind in a way of sovereignty or mere dominion, as he does with the remainder of the creatures here below. But then it must be acknowledged that, in such a way of rule and procedure, there would not have been that evident demonstration of the divine excellencies, his goodness, righteousness, and faithfulness, as ensues upon the supposition of his condescension to take mankind into covenant with himself. And so it is that he never did nor ever would treat with any of that race any otherwise or on any other terms.

AUGUST 9

Two Covenants

*In speaking of a new covenant, he makes the first one obsolete.
And what is becoming obsolete and growing old is ready to
vanish away.*

HEBREWS 8:13

There are two solemn stated covenants: the one, suited to
the preservation of the state of integrity in which we were
created; and the other to the renovation of the image of God
in us through Jesus Christ, which we had lost by sin. Besides
these, there is mention in the Scripture of various particular
intervening covenants that God made with his church, or with
individual people, at several seasons.

Now, all these did partake of the nature of a divine covenant
in general, and they were also emanations from and particular
expressions or limitations of one or other of the two solemn
covenants mentioned. For a covenant of another kind absolutely,
or more covenants, God never made with mankind.

Yet, under the Old Testament, whilst the wisdom of God
was to be hid in its own mysteries and not clearly brought forth
to light, there was a mixed dispensation. This revealed, for
certain ends, the notion, sense, and power of the first covenant,
and prepared for the introduction of the full revelation and
declaration of the latter by Jesus Christ, who was in all things to
have the preeminence. So it is not easy to discern and distinguish
what belongs to the one in them, and what to the other, or which
covenant they are related to. Here therefore is a blessed field of
sacred truth, in which humble, sober, and judicious people may
exercise themselves, to the great benefit and advantage of the
church of God.

AUGUST 10

Hardening Hearts

Therefore, as the Holy Spirit says, 'Today, if you hear his voice, do not harden your hearts.'

HEBREWS 3:7-8

Many previous sins make way for the great sin of finally rejecting the voice or word of God. The not hearing the voice of God, which is here reproved, is that which is final, which absolutely cuts people off from entering into the rest of God. People do not come to this without having their hearts hardened by depraved lusts and affections.

Hardening of the heart goes before final impenitence and infidelity, as the means and cause of it. Things do not ordinarily come to an immediate issue between God and those to whom the word is preached. I say ordinarily, because God may immediately cut off any person on the first refused tender of the gospel; and it may be he deals so with many. But ordinarily, he exercises much patience towards people in this condition. He finds them in a state of nature; that is, of enmity against him. In this state, he offers them terms of peace, and waits, during the season of his good pleasure, to see what the outcome will be. Many in the meantime attend to their lusts and temptations, and so contract a stubborn senselessness upon their hearts and minds. This, fortifying them against the calls of God, prepares them for final impenitence.

AUGUST 11

Gradual Clarity

In Christ are hidden all the treasures of wisdom and knowledge.

COLOSSIANS 2:3

All things in the Old Testament, both what was spoken and what was done, have a special intention towards the Lord Christ and the gospel. Therefore, in several ways, we may receive instruction from them. As their institutions are our instructions more than theirs, we see more of the mind of God in them than they did; so their mercies are our encouragements, and their punishments our examples.

We know the way by which God was pleased to manifest the counsels of his will in this matter was gradual. The principal degrees and steps of his procedure in this we have already declared (Heb. 1:1). The light of it still increased, from its dawning in the first promise, through all new revelations, prophecies, promises, institutions of worship, until the fullness of time came and all things were completed in Christ.

In him, all the treasures of wisdom and knowledge were to be laid up (Col. 2:3); and all things were to be gathered into a head in him (Eph. 1:10). In him, God designed to give out the express image of his wisdom, love, and grace, yea, of all the glorious properties of his nature. From here, he copied out in various parcels, by prophecies, promises, institutions of worship, actions, miracles, judgments, some partial and obscure representations of what should afterwards be accomplished in the person and kingdom of Christ. These things became types, that is, transcripts from the great idea in the mind of God about Christ and his church, to be at several seasons accomplished among the people of old, to represent what was afterwards to be completed in him.

AUGUST 12

More Light

Whatever was written in former days was written for our instruction, that through endurance and through the encouragement of the Scriptures we might have hope.

ROMANS 15:4

Having reckoned up the faith of the saints under the Old Testament, the apostle adds that 'God had provided something better for us, that apart from us they should not be made perfect' (Heb. 11:40). Neither they nor anything that happened to them was perfect without us. It had not in them its full end nor its full use, being ordained in the counsel of God for our benefit. This privilege God reserved for the church of the New Testament, that it should enjoy that perfect revelation of his will in Christ which the church of the Old Testament did not receive.

See then what use we are to make of the Scriptures of the Old Testament. They are all ours, with all things contained in them. The sins of the people are recorded in them for *our* warning, their obedience for *our* example, and God's dealing with them for *our* direction and encouragement in believing. We are not to look on any parts of them as bare stories of things that are past, but as things directly and peculiarly ordered, in the wise and holy counsel of God, for our use and advantage.

Consider also what is expected from us above those who lived under the Old Testament. Where much is given, much is required. Now we have the additional help of gospel light, with which they were not entrusted. As God in his grace and wisdom has granted to us more light and advantage than to them, so, in his righteousness, he expects from us more fruits of holiness, to his praise and glory.

AUGUST 13

Desert Fathers

Do not harden your hearts as in the rebellion, on the day of testing in the wilderness, where your fathers put me to the test.

HEBREWS 3:8-9

No place, no retirement, no solitary wilderness, will secure people from sin or suffering, provocation or punishment.

The people spoken of in Hebrews 3:7-11 were in a wilderness, where they had many motives and encouragements to obedience, and no means of seduction and outward temptation from others. Yet there they sinned and there they suffered. They sinned in the wilderness, and filled that desert with sins and graves. And the reason for this is because no place as such can of itself exclude the principles and causes either of sin or punishment. People have the principle of their sins in themselves, in their own hearts, which they cannot leave behind them, or get away from by shifting of places, or changing their stations.

The justice of God, which is the principal cause of punishment, is no less in the wilderness than in the most populous cities. The wilderness is no wilderness to him—he can find his paths in all its intricacies. The Israelites came to it by necessity, and so they found it with them; in later times, some have done so by choice—they have retired into wildernesses for the furtherance of their obedience and devotion. In this very wilderness, on the top of Sinai, there is at this day a monastery of people professing themselves to be religious, and they live there to increase religion in them. I once, for some days, conversed with their chief (they call him Archimandrite) here in England. For all I could perceive, he might have learned as much elsewhere.

AUGUST 14

Careful Walking

Blessed is the one who fears the LORD always, but whoever hardens his heart will fall into calamity.

PROVERBS 28:14

Blind confidence in a life of professing Christ, as if the whole of it were a danger-less road, is a ruinous principle (1 Pet. 1:17; Prov. 28:14). 'The prudent sees danger and hides himself, but the simple go on and suffer for it' (Prov. 22:3). It is the highest folly not to look out after dangers, and it usually ends in sorrow, trouble, and punishment.

Fear is necessary in continual exercise; not a fear of distrust or diffidence, of anxious scrupulosity, but of care, duty, and diligence. Continually to fear dangers in all things, brings a useless, perplexing scrupulosity, where people's principle of duty is only a harassed, convinced conscience, and the rule of it is human doctrines and traditions. But where the principle of it is the Spirit of grace, with all this fear there is liberty; where the rule of it is the word, there is safety, peace, and stability.

People at sea that are in the midst of rocks and ridges, and consider it not, will hardly avoid a shipwreck. Livy tells us that Philopoemen, that wary Grecian commander, wherever he went, though he were alone, he was still considering all places that he passed by, how an enemy might possess them and lay ambushes in them to his disadvantage, if he should command an army in those places. By doing this, he became the most wary and expert captain of his age. So should a Christian do: they should always consider how, where, by what means, their spiritual adversaries may ensnare or engage them, and so either avoid them or oppose them.

AUGUST 15

Hold Fast!

For we have come to share in Christ, if indeed we hold our original confidence firm to the end.

HEBREWS 3:14

It is true our persistence in Christ does not depend absolutely on our own diligence. The unalterableness of our union with Christ, on account of the faithfulness of the covenant of grace, is that which does and shall eventually secure it. But yet our own diligent endeavour is such an indispensable means for that end, as that without it, it will not be brought about.

Diligence and endeavours in this matter are like Paul's mariners, when he was shipwrecked at Malta. God had beforehand given him the lives of all that sailed with him in the ship (Acts 27:24); and he believed that it should be even as God had told him (v. 25). So now, the preservation of their lives depended absolutely on the faithfulness and power of God. But yet, when the mariners began to flee out of the ship, Paul told the centurion and the soldiers that unless those men stayed they could not be saved (v. 31). He knew full well that God would preserve them, but also that he would do so in and by the use of means.

If we are in Christ, God has given us the lives of our souls, and has taken upon himself in his covenant the preservation of them; but yet we may say with reference to the means that he has that appointed, when storms and trials arise, unless we use our own diligent endeavours, 'we cannot be saved'. Hence are the many cautions that are given us, not only in Hebrews where they abound, but in other places of Scripture also, that we should take heed of apostasy and falling away.

AUGUST 16

Adoring the Word

You have exalted above all things your name and your word.

PSALM 138:2

God has filled the Scripture with truth. That is why one said well, *Adoro plenitudinem Scripturarum*—'I reverence the fulness of the Scriptures' [Tertullian]. As Psalm 138:2 says, he has exalted his word above all things, and made it more instructive than any other way or means by which he has revealed himself. For not only does the whole Scripture contain the whole counsel of God, concerning his own glory and worship, our faith, obedience, and salvation, but also every parcel of it has in it such a depth of truth as cannot by us be perfectly searched into.

'Open my eyes' says the psalmist, 'that I may behold wondrous things out of your law' (Ps. 119:18). There are wonderful things in the word, if God is pleased to give us light to see it. It is like a cabinet of jewels, that when you pull out one box or drawer and search into it, you find it full; pull out another, it is full; and when you think you have pulled out all, yet still there are some secret recesses in the cabinet, so that if you search further, you will find more. Our apostle seems to have drawn out all the boxes of this cabinet, but making a second search into the words, he finds all these things treasured up, which he had not before intimated nor touched upon. It was said by some of old, that the 'Scripture has fords where a lamb may wade, and depths where an elephant may swim' [Gregory the Great]. And it is true in respect of the perspicuity of some places, and the difficulty of others.

AUGUST 17

Preach the Word

I will meditate on your precepts and fix my eyes on your ways.

PSALM 119:15

I would not speak anything to encourage people in bold adventures, groundless conjectures, and curious pryings into things hidden, secret, and marvellous; but it is humble diligence, joined with prayer, meditation, and waiting on God for the revelation of his will, in the study of the Scripture, upon the account of the fulness of its treasury and the guiding, instructive virtue with which its concerns are accompanied, that I would press after.

I am persuaded that the church of God has, through God's care and faithfulness, had great advantage from those who oppose the truth. To countenance their own errors, they have searched curiously into the words of many testimonies given to the truth. For though they have done this to their own destruction, yet 'out of the eater came something to eat' (Judg. 14:14). For they have imposed a necessity upon us to search with all diligence into every part of some most material passages in the Scripture, and that to the clearing of the truth and the establishing of the minds of many.

It is a defect when people scarce at any time make use of the Scripture in their preaching any further than to make remarks and observations on the obvious sense of any place. They neither enter themselves, nor endeavour to lead their hearers, into the secret and rich recesses of them. Worst of all, some, by their own notions, opinions, curiosities, and allegories, rather draw people away from the Scripture than endeavour to lead them to it.

AUGUST 18

Gospel Rest

While the promise of entering his rest still stands, let us fear lest any of you should seem to have failed to reach it.

HEBREWS 4:1

The true nature of this rest may be discovered from the promise of it; for a promise is said to *remain* of entering into this rest. Now, this promise is none other than the gospel itself as preached to us. This the apostle expressly declares in the next verse. The want of a due consideration of this has led expositors into their mistake in this matter; for they eye only the promise of eternal life given in the gospel, which is but a part of it. That promise concerns only those who do actually believe. Sinners must be interested in the promise of Christ himself, and the benefits of his mediation, before they can lay claim to the promise of eternal life and salvation.

The whole design of the apostle is not to prefer heaven, immortality, and glory, above the law and that rest in God's worship which the people had in the land of Canaan, for none ever doubted this. The rest, therefore, here intended is that rest which believers have an entrance into by Jesus Christ in this world. And this rest in people's consciences from an obligation to an anxious, scrupulous observation of a multitude of carnal ordinances, and that under most severe revenging penalties, is no small part of that rest which our Saviour makes that great encouragement to sinners to come to him (Matt. 11:28-30).

AUGUST 19

Humble Learning

He leads the humble in what is right, and teaches the humble his way.

PSALM 25:9

When people come to the reading and studying of the Scriptures in the confidence of their own skill, wisdom, talent, learning, and understanding, God scorns to teach them. The fruits and effects of this state of things, in people's pride and the severity of God in giving them up to darkness and blindness, we may behold every day. And sometimes, none presume more in this way than those who have as little reason as any to trust to themselves. Many an illiterate person has an arrogance proportionable to their ignorance. And many from whom it was expected, on the account of their condition, that they should be very humble and lowly in mind in their reading of the word, have been revealed in the end, by their being given up to foolish and corrupt errors, to have had their minds filled with pride and self-conceit; without which, they would not have been so.

This is the great preparation for the soul's admittance into the treasury of sacred truths: Go to the reading, hearing, studying of the Scripture, with hearts sensible of your own unworthiness to be taught, of your disability to learn, ready to receive, embrace, and submit to what shall be made known to you. This is the way to be taught by God.

Fleshly and corrupt lusts indulged in people's hearts and minds will make their most industrious search into the Scripture of no advantage to themselves. Love of sin will make all study of the Scripture to be mere lost labour.

AUGUST 20

Days of Flesh

Man is born to trouble as the sparks fly upward.

JOB 5:7

Let us not think it strange, if we have our season of weakness and infirmity in this world, by which we are exposed to temptation and suffering. We are apt, indeed, to complain of such things. The whole nation of professing Christians is full of complaints: one is in want, difficulties, and poverty; another in pain, sickness, and variety of troubles; some are persecuted, some are tempted, some pressed with private, some with public concerns; some are sick, and some are weak, and some are 'fallen asleep'.

These things are apt to make us faint, to despond, and be weary. I know not how others bear up their hearts and spirits. For my part, I have much ado to keep from continual longing after the embraces of the dust and shades of the grave, as a curtain drawn over the rest in another world. In the meantime, every momentary plant that grows up between us and the vehemency of wind and sun, or our frail, fainting natures and spirits, is too much valued by us (Jonah 4:6-7).

These are the days of our flesh, in which these things are due to us, and unavoidable. 'Man is born to trouble as the sparks fly upward' (Job 5:7)—necessarily and abundantly. All complaints, and all contrivances by which we endeavour to extricate ourselves from those innumerable evils which attend our weak, frail, infirm condition, will be altogether vain. And if any, through the flatteries of youth, and health, and strength, and wealth, with other satisfactions of their affections, are not sensible of these things, they are but in a pleasant dream, which will quickly pass away.

AUGUST 21

Soul Food

Like newborn infants, long for the pure spiritual milk, that
by it you may grow up into salvation.

1 PETER 2:2

Before hearing the word, and by way of preparation for it,
there is required in us a desire after the word '*that by it you may*
grow up' (1 Pet. 2:2). The end which we propose to ourselves
in hearing has a great influence on the regulation of the whole
duty. Some hear to satisfy their convictions; some, their curiosity
and inquiry after notions; some, to please themselves; some, out
of custom; some, for company; and many know not why, or for
no end at all. It is no wonder if such persons are slothful in and
unprofitable under hearing the word.

Therefore, in order to rightly discharge this duty, it is
required of us that we consider what is our condition or
stature in Christ; how short we come of that measure in faith,
knowledge, light, and love, which we ought and hope to attain
to. To supply us with this growth and increase, the preaching of
the word is appointed by God as food for our souls, and we shall
never receive it aright unless we desire it and long for it to this
end and purpose.

When we know our weakness, feebleness, and manifold
defects, and come to the word to obtain supplies of strength
suited to our condition, this is the way to thrive under it. And as
for those who have not this desire and appetite, who understand
not a suitableness between the word and their spiritual condition
answerable to that of food to his natural state who is hungry and
desires growth and strength, they will be 'dull in hearing', as to
all the blessed and beneficial ends of it (Heb. 5:11).

AUGUST 22

Son and Spirit

*I tell you the truth: it is to your advantage that I go away, for
if I do not go away, the Helper will not come to you. But if I
go, I will send him to you.*

JOHN 16:7

When God designed the great and glorious work of recovering
fallen mankind and the saving of sinners, to the praise of the
glory of his grace, he appointed, in his infinite wisdom, two great
means for it: the giving of his Son *for* them, and the giving of his
Spirit *to* them. And by this was a way made for the manifestation
of the glory of the whole blessed Trinity, which is the utmost end
of all the works of God.

By this was made gloriously conspicuous: the love, grace,
and wisdom of the Father, in the design and projection of the
whole; the love, grace, and condescension of the Son, in the
execution, purchase, and procurement of grace and salvation for
sinners; and the love, grace, and power of the Holy Spirit, in the
effectual application of all to the souls of people.

From the first entrance of sin, there were two general heads
of the promise of God to mankind, concerning the means of
their recovery and salvation. The one was that concerning the
sending of his Son to be incarnate, to take our nature upon him,
and to suffer for us in it; the other, concerning the giving of his
Spirit, to make the effects and fruits of this effectual in us.

The great promise of the Old Testament, the principal
object of the faith, hope, and expectation of believers, was that
concerning the coming of the Son of God in the flesh, and
the work which he was to perform. The doctrine concerning
the person, the work, and the grace of the Holy Spirit, is the
most peculiar and principal subject of the Scriptures of the New
Testament.

AUGUST 23

Inspiration

*The Preacher sought to find words of delight, and uprightly
he wrote words of truth.*
ECCLESIASTES 12:10

There were three things concurring in the work of writing
Scripture. First, the *inspiration* of the minds of the prophets with
the knowledge and apprehension of the things communicated to
them. Secondly, the *suggestion* of words to them to express what
their minds conceived. Thirdly, the *guidance of their hands* in
setting down the words suggested, or of their tongues in uttering
them to those by whom they were committed to writing. If any
of these were lacking, the Scripture could not be absolutely and
every way divine and infallible.

The Holy Spirit in his work on people's minds does not put a
force upon them, to act any otherwise than they are in their own
natures and with their present endowments and qualifications.
He leads and conducts them in such paths as they are able to
walk in. The words which he suggests to them are such as they
are accustomed to, and he causes them to make use of such
expressions as they were familiar with.

He that uses diverse seals makes different impressions,
though the guidance of them is all equal and the same; and
he that touches skilfully several musical instruments, variously
tuned, makes several notes of music. We may also grant, and do,
that they used their own abilities of mind and understanding
in the choice of words and expressions. But the Holy Spirit,
who is more intimate with people's minds and skills than they
are themselves, did so guide, act, and operate in them, that the
words they fixed upon were as directly and certainly from him as
if they had been spoken to them by an audible voice.

AUGUST 24

New Birth of Old

Truly, truly, I say to you, unless one is born again he cannot see the kingdom of God.

JOHN 3:3

The work of regeneration by the Holy Spirit was wrought under the Old Testament, even from the foundation of the world, and the doctrine of it was recorded in the Scriptures. Yet the revelation of it was obscure in comparison to that light and evidence which it is brought forth into by the gospel.

This is evident from the discourse which our blessed Saviour had with Nicodemus on this subject; for when he acquainted him clearly with the doctrine of it, he was surprised and amazed: 'How can these things be?' (John 3:9). But the reply of our Saviour manifests that he might have attained a better acquaintance with it out of the Scripture: 'Are you the teacher of Israel and yet you do not understand these things?' It would be neither a crime nor negligence in him to be ignorant of this, if God had not revealed it.

This doctrine, therefore—that everyone who will enter into the kingdom of God must be born again of the Holy Spirit—was contained in the writings of the Old Testament (e.g. Deut. 30:6; Ezek. 36:26). But it was so obscurely declared that the principal masters and teachers of the people knew little or nothing of it.

All the elect of God, in their several generations, were regenerate by the Spirit of God. But in that enlargement of truth and grace under the gospel which came by Jesus Christ who brought life and immortality to light, as more persons than of old were to be made partakers of the mercy of it, so the nature of the work itself is far more clearly, evidently, and distinctly revealed and declared.

AUGUST 25

Everlasting Holiness

God is not unjust so as to overlook your work and the love that you have shown for his name in serving the saints, as you still do.

HEBREWS 6:10

Holiness is not confined to this life, but passes over into eternity and glory. Death has no power over it to destroy it or divest us of it. There is not any effect or fruit of holiness, not the least, not the giving of a cup of cold water to a disciple of Christ, but it shall be had in everlasting remembrance, and abide forever in its eternal reward. Nothing shall be lost, but all the fragments of it shall be gathered up and kept safe for ever.

Let no soul fear the loss of any labour, in any of the duties of holiness, in the most secret contest against sin, for inward purity, for outward fruitfulness; in the mortification of sin, resistance of temptations, improvement of grace; in patience, moderation, self-denial, contentment—all that you do know, and what you do not know, shall be revived, called over, and abide eternally in your reward. Our Father, who now 'sees in secret' (Matt. 6:4, 6, 18) will one day reward openly. The more we abound in these things, the more will God be glorified in the recompense of reward.

That love by which we now adhere to God as our chiefest good; that faith by which we are united to Christ, our everlasting head; that delight in any of the ways or ordinances of God in which he is enjoyed, as he has promised his presence in them; that love and good-will which we have for all those in whom is the Spirit, and on whom is the image of Christ—shall be all purified, enhanced, perfected, and pass into glory.

AUGUST 26

Whose Sacrifice?

For you will not delight in sacrifice, or I would give it; you will not be pleased with a burnt offering.

PSALM 51:16

God requires nothing of us to make atonement or satisfaction for our sins, that might compensate for the injuries we have done to him by our apostasy and rebellion. We multiplied sins against him, lived in enmity and opposition to him, and contracted immeasurable debts on our own souls. Terms of peace are now proposed.

'With what shall I come before the LORD, and bow myself before God on high? Shall I come before him with burnt offerings, with calves a year old? Will the LORD be pleased with thousands of rams, with ten thousands of rivers of oil? Shall I give my firstborn for my transgression, the fruit of my body for the sin of my soul?' (Micah 6:6-7). Something of this nature, seems to be a very reasonable inquiry for a guilty self-condemned sinner, when first they entertain thoughts of an agreement with the holy sin-avenging God. This was the foundation of all that cruel and expensive superstition that the world was in bondage to for so many ages. Mankind generally thought that the principal thing which was required of them in religion was to atone and pacify the wrath of the divine Power, and to make a compensation for what had been done against him. And the same principle is still deep-rooted in the minds of convinced sinners: many an abbey, monastery, college, and almshouse has it founded; for in the fruits of this superstition, the priests, which set it to work, always shared deeply.

But it is quite otherwise: in the gospel, there is declared and tendered to sinners an *absolute free pardon* of all their sins, without any satisfaction or compensation made by them.

AUGUST 27

Purifying Spirit

The Spirit will glorify me, for he will take what is mine and declare it to you.

JOHN 16:14

The Holy Spirit proposes, declares, and presents to us the only true remedy, the only means of purification. When people begin to discern their defilements, they are apt to think of many ways for their purging. Though the only fountain for cleansing is near to us, yet we cannot see it until the Holy Spirit opens our eyes. This is an eminent part of his office and work.

The principal purpose of his sending, and consequently of his whole work, was to glorify the Son; as the end and work of the Son was to glorify the Father. The great way by which he glorifies Christ is by showing such things to us (John 16:14). And without his discovery we can know nothing of Christ, nor of the things of Christ; for he is not sent in vain, to show us the things that we can see for ourselves.

To have a true spiritual sense of the defilement of sin, and a gracious view of the cleansing virtue of the blood of Christ, is an eminent effect of the Spirit of grace. Christ is our propitiation through faith in his blood as offered; and he is our sanctification through faith in his blood as sprinkled.

The Holy Spirit actually communicates the cleansing, purifying virtue of the blood of Christ to our souls and consciences, by which we are freed from shame, and have boldness towards God; for the whole work of the application of the benefits of the mediation of Christ to believers is his properly.

AUGUST 28

Being Like God

Beloved, we are God's children now, and what we will be has not yet appeared; but we know that when he appears we shall be like him, because we shall see him as he is.

1 JOHN 3:2

Those who would be like God must be sure to love him, or all other endeavours to that purpose will be in vain. The one who loves God sincerely will be like him.

Under the Old Testament, there was none in his general course so like God as David. He was called, therefore, 'The man after God's own heart' (1 Sam. 13:14), and none ever made greater expressions of love to him, which occur continually in the Psalms. And let people take what pains they can in acts and duties of obedience, if they proceed not from a principle of divine love, their likeness to God will not be increased by them.

All love, in general, casts the mind into the mould of the thing beloved. So love of this world makes people earthly minded; their minds and affections grow earthly, carnal, and sensual. But of all kinds, divine love is most effectual to this purpose, as having the best, the most noble, proper, and attractive object. It is our adherence to God with delight, for what he is in himself, as manifested in Jesus Christ. By it, we cleave to God, and so keep near him, and thereby derive transforming virtue from him. Every approach to God by ardent love and delight is transfiguring.

AUGUST 29

Spiritual Pride

Trust in the LORD with all your heart, and do not lean on your own understanding.

PROVERBS 3:5

Pride, or carnal confidence in our own wisdom and ability of mind for all the ends of our duty towards God, either keeps people's souls under the bondage of darkness and ignorance, or precipitates them into foolish apprehensions or pernicious errors—and this is especially so when it comes to understanding his mind and will. As spiritual pride is the worst sort of pride, so this is the worst degree of spiritual pride, namely, when people do not acknowledge God in these things as they ought to, but lean on their own understandings. This is that which ruined the Pharisees of old, that they could not understand the mind of God in anything unto their advantage.

It is the meek, the humble, the lowly in mind, those that are like little children, that God has promised to teach. This is an eternal and unalterable law of God, that whoever wants to learn his mind and will as revealed in the Scripture must be humble and lowly, renouncing all trust and confidence in themselves.

Whatever people of another frame come to know, they know it not according to the mind of God, nor according to their own duty, nor to their advantage. They know nothing as they ought, nothing to the glory of God, nothing to the spiritual advantage of their own souls. The knowledge of a proud person is the throne of Satan in their mind. To suppose that people full of pride, self-conceit, and self-confidence, can understand the mind of God as revealed in a due manner, is to renounce the Scriptures, or innumerable positive testimonies given in them to the contrary.

AUGUST 30

I will pray with the spirit, and I will pray with the under-standing also.

1 CORINTHIANS 14:15

Praying only by saying or repeating so many words of prayer, whose sense and meaning one perhaps understands not, is unworthy of the disciples of Christ, indeed of rational creatures. 'Present that to your governor; will he accept you or show you favour? says the LORD of hosts' (Mal. 1:8). Neither ruler, nor friend, nor neighbour, would accept it at our hands, if we should constantly make solemn addresses to them without any special design. We must 'pray with our understanding' (1 Cor. 14:15), that is, understand what we pray for.

It is, therefore, indispensably necessary in prayer that we should know what God has promised. God knows our wants, what is good for us, what is useful to us, what is necessary to bring us to the enjoyment of himself, infinitely better than we do ourselves. Indeed, we know nothing of these things but what he is pleased to teach us. These are the things which he has 'prepared' for us, as the apostle speaks (1 Cor. 2:9); and what he has so prepared, he declares in the promises of the covenant, for they are the declaration of the grace and good pleasure which he has purposed in himself.

And so believers may learn what is good for them, and what is lacking in them in the promises, more clearly and certainly than by any other means whatsoever. From them, therefore, do we learn what to pray for as we ought. And this is another reason why people are so barren in their prayers: they know not what to pray for, but are forced into a confused repetition of the same requests by their ignorance of the promises of God.

AUGUST 31

Imitation

Be imitators of me, as I am of Christ.

1 CORINTHIANS 11:1

Due meditation on our great pattern, the Lord Jesus Christ, and the apostles, being followers of them as they were of him, is required of us. The Lord Jesus was the great pattern and example, God in him representing to us that perfection in wisdom which we ought to aim at.

Those who would be really and truly wise in spiritual things, who would either rightly receive or duly improve the gift of the Holy Spirit, ought continually to bear in their heart, their mind, and their affections, this great exemplar and idea of it, even the Lord Jesus Christ in his ministry—namely, what he did, what he said, how on all occasions his condescension, meekness, and authority manifested themselves—until they are changed into the same image and likeness by the Spirit of the Lord.

The same is to be done, in their place and sphere, towards the apostles, as the principal followers of Christ, and who represent his graces and wisdom to us. Their writings, and what is written of them, are to be searched and studied to this very end. Considering how they behaved themselves in all instances, on all occasions, in their testimony, and all administrations of the truth, we may endeavour after a conformity to them, in the participation of the same Spirit with them. It would be no small guidance to us, if on all occasions we would diligently search and consider what the apostles did in such circumstances, or what they would have done.

SEPTEMBER

This month, we will be reading sermons, tracts, books, and prefaces by Owen written in 1674-78. This was a period in which he complained of 'ongoing distressing pains' and was described by one observer as 'often down'. He wrote to a friend that 'I begin to fear that we shall die in the wilderness.' Mary, his wife of thirty-one years, died in 1675.

In this context, Owen delivered two sermons at the so-called Morning Exercises, talks given by Puritan ministers in London: 'How we may Bring our Hearts to Bear Reproof' (on Ps. 141:5) and 'The Testimony of the Church' (on Luke 16:29).

In 1676, he wrote *The Nature of Apostasy from the Profession of the Gospel*, an exposition of Hebrews 6:4-6. He was very concerned 'that among the generality of professed Christians, the glory and power of Christianity are faded and almost utterly lost', and sought to understand how this could happen.

Since justification by faith alone had been declared by Luther to be the article on which a church stands or falls, it is fitting that in 1677 he then published *The Doctrine of Justification by Faith through the Imputation of the Righteousness of Christ, Explained, Confirmed, & Vindicated*.

Owen wrote a preface to his late friend Patrick Gillespie's book *The Ark of the Covenant Opened*, on the covenant between the Father and the Son. Gillespie had worked closely with Cromwell to develop an ecclesiastical settlement for Scotland. Owen also wrote a preface for Elisha Coles's book, *A Practical Discourse of God's Sovereignty*. Coles, a fellow Congregationalist, had been a commissioner for the ejection of scandalous ministers in Oxfordshire during Owen's time as university vice chancellor.

SEPTEMBER 1

Sinful Delicacies

Do not let my heart incline to any evil, to busy myself with wicked deeds in company with men who work iniquity, and let me not eat of their delicacies!

PSALM 141:4

The psalmist requests that, by the power of God's grace influencing his mind and soul, his heart might not be inclined to any communion or society with his wicked adversaries in their wickedness. He also asks that he might be preserved from a liking of, or a longing after, those things which are the baits and allurements whereby people are apt to be drawn into societies and conspiracies with the workers of iniquity. 'And let me not eat of their delicacies' (see also Prov. 1:10-14).

He here describes the condition of people prospering for a season in a course of wickedness. They *first* jointly give themselves up to the practice of iniquity; and *then* together solace themselves in those satisfactions of their lusts which their power and interest in the world furnishes them with. These are 'the delicacies'—an impotent longing and desire for which betrays the minds of unstable persons, into a compliance with ways of sin and folly.

These delicacies are whatever 'the lust of the eyes, the lust of the flesh, or the pride of life' can afford (1 John 2:16). David prays to be delivered from any inclination to all these, especially when they are made the allurements of a course of sin. It is the common practice of wicked people to encourage one another mutually in the enjoyment of these delicacies. The whole of it is but a society in perishing, sensual enjoyments, without control, and with mutual applauses from one another.

SEPTEMBER 2

Righteous Rebukes

Let a righteous man strike me—it is a kindness; let him rebuke me—it is oil for my head.

PSALM 141:5

The psalmist here desires that his reprover may be a righteous person. To give and take reproofs is a dictate of the law of nature, by which everyone is obliged to seek the good of others, *and* to promote it according to their ability and opportunity. The former is directed by that love which is due to others, the latter by that which is due to ourselves.

It does not discharge the one who is reproved from the duty of attending to it, if the one by whom it is managed is not righteous, or is indeed openly wicked. However, it is desirable on many accounts that those who reprove us are themselves righteous, and are esteemed by us so to be. Without the exercise of singular wisdom and humility, all the advantages of a just reproof will be lost, if the allowed practice of greater sins and evils than that reproved is daily chargeable on the reprover.

Hence is that reflection of our Saviour on the useless, hypocritical diligence of people in pulling the speck out of their brother's eyes, whilst they have logs in their own (Matt. 7:3-5). The rule in this case is: if the reprover is a righteous person, consider the reprover first, and then the reproof; if they are otherwise, consider the reproof, but the reprover not at all.

SEPTEMBER 3

Parental Rebukes

The eye that mocks a father and scorns to obey a mother will be picked out by the ravens of the valley and eaten by the vultures.

PROVERBS 30:17

Authoritative reproof is *parental*. Reproof is indeed one of the greatest and most principal duties of parents toward children. Neglect of this has filled us with so many Hophnis, Phineases, and Absaloms (see 1 Sam. 4 and 2 Sam. 13), whose outrageous wickednesses are directly charged on the sinful lenience and neglect in this matter, even of godly parents.

Some parents are openly vicious and debauched even in the sight of their children. In a sensual neglect and contempt of the light of nature they lose all their authority in reproving, as well as all care about it. The most have so little regard to sin as sin, whilst things are tolerably well in outward concerns, that they neglect the reproof of it as such. Many, through a foolish, contemptible dominance of fond affection, will take no notice of the sinful follies, extravagancies, and misbehaviour of their children, until all things grow desperate with them, but soothe and applaud them in such effects of pride, vanity, and wantonness, as ought to be most severely reproved in them. The woeful and dreadful degeneracy of the age in which we live owes much to the horrible neglect of parents in this duty.

There is on many accounts an immediate impress of divine authority on parental reproofs, which children ought to consider. A continuance in the neglect or contempt of them is very often a sign of approaching temporal and eternal destruction.

SEPTEMBER 4

False Accusations

For no transgression or sin of mine, O LORD, for no fault of mine, they run and make ready.

PSALM 59:3-4

If a reproof is false in matter of fact, and we are in no way guilty of it, we must still consider how it may be useful to us.

When someone is fully justified by the testimony of their own conscience, bearing witness to their integrity and innocence, they ought still to attend diligently to their own spirit. We must search our own hearts and ways, whether we have not indeed upon us the guilt of some greater evils than that which is falsely charged on us, or for which we are reproved by mistake.

And if it appears so upon examination, we shall quickly see what little reason we have to rise up with indignation against the charge. And may we not from this see much of the wisdom and goodness of God? He allows us to be exercised with what we can bear, with the impenetrable shield of a good conscience, whilst he graciously hides and covers those greater evils of our hearts, with respect to which we cannot but condemn ourselves.

We must also consider that it is not of ourselves that we are not guilty of the evil suspected and charged against us. No one of sobriety can on any mistake reprove us for anything, be it never so false, but that it is merely of sovereign grace that we have not indeed contracted the guilt of it. Humble thankfulness to God on this occasion for his real preserving grace will abate the edge and take off the fierceness of our indignation against people for their supposed injurious dealings with us.

SEPTEMBER 5

God's Authority

They have Moses and the Prophets; let them hear them.

LUKE 16:29

The holy Scripture of the Old and New Testament is that which we profess to own as the rule of our faith and life, in relation to our future glory. It is then the wisdom of every Christian to inquire why they believe it, and submit to it; whether they are persuaded that it is of God, by God himself, or only by people. For if they can find indeed that they receive it on the authority of God, they may be secure in the truth and sufficiency of it; but if they receive it only on the authority of people, they, being liable to mistakes, may lead us into error, and so we can never be sure that what we own as our rule is indeed the right one, and of God's own prescribing.

If Scripture is not received on right grounds, we will be exposed to innumerable fears and fluctuations, and never walk comfortably nor constantly in our way, when we doubt whether it is the right or a wrong one. The superstructure cannot be better than the foundation; a well-ordered and comfortable life will never be the effect of an ill-grounded belief.

It is good, therefore, in the beginning of our course to be sure of our way, to see both what we believe, and why. Otherwise, we will be either forced to go back, or else swerve from the way, upon as light grounds as we were at first persuaded to engage in it.

SEPTEMBER 6

To the Bible!

They received the word with all eagerness, examining the Scriptures daily to see if these things were so.

ACTS 17:11

The Holy Spirit, in Scripture, calls us to the Scripture itself, and God's authority only in it, and not to the church, for the settling of our belief in its divinity. In the Scripture itself, we have a sufficient argument to move us to believe in its coming from God. In Isaiah 8:20, we are sent 'to the teaching and to the testimony!' The prophets generally propound what they deliver merely in the name and on the authority of God: their usual style is, 'Thus says the Lord' and 'The word of the Lord.' They nowhere send us to the church to know whether it is so or not, but leave it with us, as being of itself (that is, without the testimony of the church) sufficient to convince us. If we will not believe it, at our own peril be it.

In Luke 16:29, Abraham (that is, Christ, whose mind Abraham in this parable is speaking) sends the rich man's brethren to 'Moses and the prophets'. And our Saviour Christ sends the Jews to the Scriptures, bids them 'search' them (John 5:39, and so vv. 46-47). And Luke commends the Bereans, not that they sent up to Jerusalem to the church there, or waited for a general council, to assure them of the divineness of what was preached to them; but that 'they examined the Scriptures daily, to see if those things were so' (Acts 17:11).

All this would be in vain, our labour would be lost in searching the Scriptures and looking into them for confirmation, if there were not something in them sufficient to persuade us of their having God for their author, but at last we must have recourse to the church to assure us of it.

SEPTEMBER 7

Christ's Authority

Not that the testimony that I receive is from man... But the testimony that I have is greater than that of John... And the Father who sent me has himself borne witness about me.

JOHN 5:34-37

On whose authority were the sermons of the prophets received? When they spoke to the people in the name of the Lord, did they ever seek the endorsements of the high priests and governors of the church to establish their doctrine as divine? Their ordinary style is, 'Thus says the Lord' not 'Thus says the church' or 'The church says, that the Lord says thus'.

When our Saviour Christ himself preached, he did not refer himself, as to the divinity of his doctrine, to the authority of the church, nor did any believe it on that account. He did not refer it to the church; for he did not receive testimony from people (John 5:34); no, not from John the Baptist himself, though of no small authority in the Jewish church, and generally taken to be a prophet. He tells the Jews that he had 'greater witness than that of John' (John 5:36): first his works; then his Father himself (v. 37); then the written word (v. 39).

It is clear that those who believed Christ's doctrines did not believe it on the authority of the church. For the church of the Jews was generally corrupt, erred in many things, and therefore was unfit. And it was, especially as to its guides and officers, generally against Christ; and therefore unwilling to give testimony to him. It neither owned him nor his doctrine, so that those who received and believed Christ's preaching, did it on some other account than the testimony of the then present church.

SEPTEMBER 8

Religious Decay

Now the works of the flesh are evident: sexual immorality, impurity, sensuality, idolatry, sorcery, enmity, strife, jealousy, fits of anger, rivalries, dissensions, divisions, envy, drunkenness, orgies, and things like these.

GALATIANS 5:19-21

The state of religion is at this day deplorable in most parts of the Christian world. Among the generality of professed Christians, the glory and power of Christianity are faded and almost utterly lost. The whole world is so evidently filled with the dreadful effects of people's lusts, and sad tokens of divine displeasure, that all things proclaim the degeneracy of our religion, in its profession, from its pristine beauty and glory.

No one can express a greater malice against the gospel, than the one who asserts that the faith, profession, and lives of the generality of Christians are a just representation of its truth and holiness. The 'works of the flesh' have made a broad and open road, that the multitude travel in. It is the way to hell.

There are many who are not given up in the course of their lives to the open practice of such abominations. In that grand defection from the truth and holiness of the gospel which is so prevalent in the world, therefore, the grace of God is greatly to be admired in the small remainders of piety, sobriety, and modesty that are yet left among us. But most are so ignorant of the mysteries of the gospel, so negligent or formal in divine worship, so infected with pride, vanity, and love of the world, so regardless of the glory of Christ and honour of the gospel, that it is no easy thing to find Christian religion in the midst of professed Christians.

SEPTEMBER 9

Gospel Defection

I am afraid I may have laboured over you in vain.

GALATIANS 4:11

Defection from the truth of the gospel has, in some measure and degree, come to pass among Protestants. People grow weary of the truths which have been professed ever since the Reformation. The Reformed religion is by some so unhinged from those pillars of important truths which it depended on, and so sullied by a confused medley of noisome opinions, that its loss in reputation for stability and usefulness seems almost irreparable.

Hence are divisions, debates, and animosities multiplied about the principal articles of our religion. But there is in this matter nothing absolutely new under the sun. No instance can be given of any church or nation in the world, which ever received the profession of the gospel, that did not, sooner or later, either totally or in some considerable degrees, fall away from the doctrine which it reveals and the obedience which it requires.

People deceive themselves if they suppose that the purity of religion will be preserved in confessions and canons, whilst some make it their business to corrupt its truth, and few or none make it their business to preserve its power. It is in vain for any to pretend that the present general visible profession of Christianity reflects the original pattern of it in Scripture, or in the first believers.

The glory of God, the honour of Christ and the gospel, and the eternal welfare of people's souls being eminently concerned, I know not how anyone could have the least satisfaction in the truth and reality of their own Christianity who was not greatly affected with, and did not really mourn for, those suffering in this woeful apostasy.

SEPTEMBER 10

Aggravation

For it is impossible, in the case of those who have once been enlightened, who have tasted the heavenly gift, and have shared in the Holy Spirit, and have tasted the goodness of the word of God and the powers of the age to come, and then have fallen away, to restore them again to repentance.

HEBREWS 6:4-6

It is a great mercy, a great privilege, to be enlightened with the doctrine of the gospel by the effectual working of the Holy Spirit. But, it is such a privilege as may be lost, and end in the aggravation of the sin, and condemnation of those who were made partakers of it. Where there is a total neglect of the due improvement of this privilege and mercy, the condition of such persons is hazardous, as inclining towards apostasy.

There is a knowledge of spiritual things that is purely *natural* and *disciplinary*, attainable and attained without any special aid or assistance of the Holy Spirit. Some, casting themselves on the study of spiritual things, are yet utter strangers to all spiritual gifts. Some knowledge of the Scripture and the things contained in it is attainable at the same rate of pains and study with that of any other art or science.

There is a goodness and excellency in 'the heavenly gift' which may be tasted or experienced in some measure by those who never receive it in its life, power, and efficacy. They may taste: of the word in its truth, not its power; of the worship of the church in its outward order, not in its inward beauty; of the gifts of the church, not its graces. A rejection of the gospel, its truth and worship, after some experience of their worth and excellency, is a high aggravation of sin, and a certain presage of destruction.

SEPTEMBER 11

Excellent Word

They have tasted the goodness of the word of God and the powers of the age to come, and then have fallen away.

HEBREWS 6:5-6

There is a goodness and excellency in the word of God able to attract and affect the minds of people who yet never arrive at sincere obedience to it. There is a special goodness in the word of the promise concerning Jesus Christ and the declaration of its accomplishment.

This goodness and excellency of the word of God consists in its spiritual, heavenly truth. All truth is beautiful and desirable; the perfection of people's minds consists in the reception of it and conformity to it. Whatever is true is also good. So are these things put together by the apostle in Philippians 4:8. And as truth is good in itself, so is it in its effects on people's minds; it gives them peace, satisfaction, and contentment. Darkness, errors, and falsehood, are evils in themselves, and fill people's minds with vanity, uncertainty, superstition, dread, and bondage. It is truth that makes the soul free (John 8:32).

Now, the word of God is the only pure, unmixed, and solid truth: 'Your word is truth' (John 17:17). The truth of the word of God alone is stable, firm, infallible; which gives rest to the soul. How excellent, how desirable, therefore, must it needs be! And what a goodness, to be preferred above all other things, must it be accompanied with! As it is infallible truth, giving light to the eyes and rest to the soul, it is the 'good word of God' (Heb. 6:5).

SEPTEMBER 12

Gospel Threats

For the one who sows to his own flesh will from the flesh reap corruption, but the one who sows to the Spirit will from the Spirit reap eternal life.

GALATIANS 6:8

The severity of God ought to be preached and insisted on in the declaration of the gospel. There is a tendency in corrupted nature to 'presume on the riches of his kindness and forbearance and patience, not knowing that God's kindness is meant to lead you to repentance' and so 'because of your hard and impenitent heart you are storing up wrath for yourself on the day of wrath' as our apostle speaks (Rom. 2:4-5). Considering nothing in God but mercy and long-suffering, and nothing in the gospel but grace and pardon, they are ready to despise them and turn them into lust. By this means, on such mistaken apprehensions, suited to their lusts and corrupt inclinations, heightened by the craft of Satan, do multitudes under the preaching of the gospel harden themselves daily to destruction.

There are others who, although they will not on such wicked pretences give themselves up to their lusts and carnal affections, yet, for want of constant vigilance and watchfulness, are apt to have sloth and negligence, with many ill frames of spirit, increase and grow upon them. Both sorts are to be stirred up by being put in mind of the severity of God. They are to be taught that there are secret powers, accompanying the dispensation of the gospel, continually 'ready to punish every disobedience' (2 Cor. 10:6); and that 'God is not mocked, for whatever one sows, that will he also reap' (Gal. 6:7).

SEPTEMBER 13

Deceptive Rest

For you say, I am rich, I have prospered, and I need nothing, not realising that you are wretched, pitiable, poor, blind, and naked.

REVELATION 3:17

People are apt to please themselves, to approve of their own state and condition, in which they have framed to themselves rest and satisfaction. Churches content themselves with their outward order and administrations, especially when accompanied with secular advantages, and contend fiercely that all is well, and the gospel sufficiently complied with, whilst their outward constitution is preserved and their laws of order kept inviolate. Only a few remain who fruitlessly complain that the glory, power, and purity of Christian religion are lost in the world.

It is known that the judgment of Christ concerning churches, as to their good or bad spiritual estate, is often very distant from their own judgment. It was not only for their sakes, but as a warning to all others in all ages, that it is entered as an everlasting record, that when the church of Laodicea judged and declared without hesitation that she was 'rich and prospered, and had need of nothing', the Lord Christ, 'the Amen, the faithful and true witness' pronounced her 'wretched, pitiable, poor, blind, and naked' (Rev. 3:17). That things at this day are in no better a condition in many, in most churches in the world, is too evident to be denied with any pretence of reverence to the word of God.

SEPTEMBER 14

Be Careful

See to it that no one takes you captive by philosophy and empty deceit, according to human tradition, according to the elemental spirits of the world, and not according to Christ.

COLOSSIANS 2:8

We can never enough admire the profound negligence and security of most churches and professing Christians in the world with respect to a due adherence to the mysteries and truths of the gospel. Some think that they have such a privilege that they can never decline from them or mistake about them, nor have done so in the long tract of sixteen hundred years, although they have been plunged into all manner of wickedness and carnal security.

Others are wanton and careless about their profession, making little difference between truth and error; or suppose that it is no great achievement to abide in the truth in which they have been instructed. And these things have brought most churches and places under the power of apostasy.

The churches planted by the apostles themselves were liable to such defections, and many of them did actually, at least for a season, fall away from very important doctrines of the gospel. It may be they would never have been recovered from this if healing had not been timely applied by apostolical authority and wisdom. So can we, who have not their advantages, nor some of the evidences of the truth which they enjoyed, having all the same causes of apostasy, inward and outward, which they had, expect that we shall be preserved, unless we watchfully and carefully attend to all the ways and means by which we may so be?

SEPTEMBER 15

Preventative Preaching

Preach the word; be ready in season and out of season; reprove, rebuke, and exhort, with complete patience and teaching.

2 TIMOTHY 4:2

The apostle Paul foresaw that a time would come when some would 'not endure sound teaching, but having itching ears they will accumulate for themselves teachers to suit their own passions'. These would 'turn away from listening to the truth and wander off into myths' (2 Tim. 4:3-4). And we may see what course he prescribes for the prevention of this evil, that it might not proceed to a general apostasy. It must also be observed that the advice he gives in this case is a charge for all who are or shall be called to the rule of or ministry in the church.

This course he proposes: 'I charge you in the presence of God and of Christ Jesus, who is to judge the living and the dead, and by his appearing and his kingdom: preach the word; be ready in season and out of season; reprove, rebuke, and exhort, with complete patience and teaching... always be sober-minded, endure suffering, do the work of an evangelist, fulfil your ministry' (2 Tim. 4:1-2, 5).

This is that course and way which he prescribes for the preservation of the truth against the corruptions of people's minds and the craft of seducers. The charge of this duty he gives with so great a solemnity, and urges with so many motives emphatically expressed, that it shows how greatly important he conceived it to be.

SEPTEMBER 16

Gospel Weariness

Having been set free from sin, you have become slaves of righteousness.

ROMANS 6:18

There is no obedience from the heart to the gospel, no possibility of being cast into the mould of the doctrine delivered in it, unless we are made free from the service of sin. We may therefore, without scruple, fix on this as one principal means and cause of that apostasy from the truth of the gospel which has been in the world, and which is yet deplorably progressive. People who love sin and live in sin, whose works are wicked and whose deeds are evil, are all of them in their hearts alienated from the spiritual, holy doctrines of the gospel, and will undoubtedly, on any occasion of temptation or trial, fall away from the profession of them.

This is what has lost the gospel so many princes, nobles, and great men, who for a while made profession of it. All sorts of persons give themselves up to the service of sin. Many are openly shameful, beyond precedent or example among the heathen. Worldliness, pride, ambition, vanity, in all its variety of occasions and objects, with sensuality of life, have even overrun the world. And that which is of the most dreadful consideration is, that the sins of many are accompanied with the highest aggravation of all provocations—namely, that 'they proclaim their sin like Sodom; they do not hide it' (Isa. 3:9), but glory in their shame. In all these things people do really, though not in words, proclaim that they are weary of the gospel, and are ready to leave it; some for any pretence of religion, some for none at all. This was the great cause of that general and almost catholic apostasy that was in the world before the reformation.

SEPTEMBER 17

Truth Transforms

And we all, with unveiled face, beholding the glory of the Lord, are being transformed into the same image from one degree of glory to another.

2 CORINTHIANS 3:18

The philosophers of old contended that there was a beauty in all truth, which would engage the minds and affections of people to it were they able to discern it. If they saw and granted this in things natural and moral, which are earthly and exposed to the common reason of mankind, how much more must it be granted of the truth of things heavenly, spiritual, and divine!

Whatever doctrinal proposition may be made of these things to people's minds, yet the things themselves cannot be comprehended nor spiritually discerned without the illumination of the Holy Spirit. Hence it follows that people may be instructed in the doctrines of truth, yet, continuing under the power of natural darkness, not discern the things themselves in their own spiritual nature and glory, nor have any experience of their power and efficacy.

But we see by open and palpable experience that, despite the knowledge which many have of spiritual things, their minds continue carnal and fleshly, filled with corrupt and depraved affections, and are no way changed into the image or likeness of the things themselves. There needs no farther demonstration that people have never had a spiritual view of or insight into the glory of gospel truths, be their doctrinal knowledge of them what it will, than this: that their minds are not renewed by them, nor transformed into the likeness of them. Where it is thus, they have no stable grounds on which to abide in the profession of the truth against temptation, opposition, or seduction.

SEPTEMBER 18

Enlightenment

Open my eyes, that I may behold wondrous things out of your law.

PSALM 119:18

Pray earnestly for the Spirit of truth to lead us into all truth. For this end is he promised by our Saviour to his disciples (John 16:13). If we learn and receive the truths of the gospel merely in the power and ability of our natural faculties, as we do other things, we shall not constantly abide in them in spiritual trials. What we learn of ourselves in spiritual things, we receive only in the outward form of it; what we are taught by the Spirit of God, we receive in its power. Without his special aid, people may, by their natural sagacity and industry, attain an acquaintance with the doctrines of truth, so as to handle them (like the schoolmen) with incredible subtlety; but they may be far away from establishing knowledge of spiritual things.

That horrible neglect which is among Christians of this one duty of earnest prayer for the teaching of the Spirit of Christ, that scorn which is cast upon it by some, and that self-confidence in opposition to it which prevails in the most, sufficiently manifest of what nature is their knowledge of the truth, and what is likely to become of it when a trial shall befall them. The least spark of saving knowledge inlaid in the minds of the poorest believers by the gracious operation of the Holy Spirit, will be more effectual to their own sanctification, and more powerful against oppositions, than the highest notions or most subtle reasonings that people have attained in leaning on their own understanding.

SEPTEMBER 19

Sufficiency

Not that we are sufficient in ourselves to claim anything as coming from us, but our sufficiency is from God.

2 CORINTHIANS 3:5

The true state of all controversies about the powers of nature and grace is this: that, on the one hand, people's minds and wills are asserted to be self-sufficient as to internal abilities to all duties of obedience necessary to eternal blessedness; on the other, that we have no sufficiency of ourselves, but that all our sufficiency is of God (see 2 Cor. 3:5, 9:8). This principle sprang immediately out of that pride by which we utterly lost what we had (aiming at an enlargement of our self-sufficiency). It was never yet rooted out of the minds of the generality of professed Christians.

In all things, the mind would be its own measure, guide, and rule, continually teeming with these two evils:

1. It exalts *imaginations* of its own, which it loves, applauds, dotes on, and adheres to. This is the origin of heresy, which has given birth, growth, and progress to error; for 'God made man upright, but they have sought out many schemes' (Eccles. 7:29). Seeking out and exalting inventions of our own, in things spiritual and religious, is the principal and most pernicious consequence of our fall from that state of uprightness in which God created us.

2. It makes *itself* the sole and *absolute judge* of what is divinely proposed to it, whether it be true or false, good or evil, to be received or rejected—without desire or expectation of any supernatural guidance or assistance. And whatever is unsuited to its own preconceived imaginations, it is ready to scorn and despise.

SEPTEMBER 20

Infighting

*But if you bite and devour one another, watch out that you
are not consumed by one another.*

GALATIANS 5:15

Apostasy has been very much promoted by persecution. I mean
not that persecution which has befallen the sincere, constant
professors of Christianity from the avowed enemies of it, upon
the account of their profession. This has been the peculiar glory
of our religion, and a notable outward means of the increase of
it. It was the primitive glory of Christian religion that it set out
in the face of a universal opposition from the whole world, and
increased under the fiercest persecutions, until it had finished
that glorious conquest which it was designed for. And not only
did it preserve its being and enlarge its extent under them, but
they were means also to preserve its purity, and to exert its power
in the hearts and lives of its professors. The church never lost
finally either truth or holiness by the violent persecutions of its
avowed enemies.

But I speak not of the outrages committed on the flock of
Christ by wolves in their own skins, but by such as have got
on sheep's clothing. It is professing Christians, persecuting one
another about some differences among themselves concerning
their apprehensions of spiritual things and practice of divine
worship, that I intend. And this has been so great, especially
in the latter ages of the church, that it is questionable whether
there has not greater effusion of the blood of Christians, ruin
of families, and devastation of nations, been made by them
who have professed the same religion in general, than by all the
pagans in the world since the first promulgation of it.

SEPTEMBER 21

National Sins

One of the Cretans, a prophet of their own, said, 'Cretans are always liars, evil beasts, lazy gluttons.' This testimony is true.

TITUS 1:12-13

Want of watchfulness against the insinuation of national vices and the prevailing sins of any present age, has effectually promoted an apostasy from evangelical holiness among the generality of Christians. There are some vices, crimes, or sins that particular nations are peculiarly inclined to, which therefore abound in them. All people are continually encompassed with them, and commonness takes away the sense of their guilt. That which would be looked on in one nation as the greatest debauchery of human nature, is, through custom, in another passed by without any criticism.

The prevalence of the gospel in any nation may be measured by the success it has against known national sins. If these are not in some good measure subdued by it, if people's minds are not alienated from them and made watchful against them, if their guilt appears not naked without the varnish or veil put on it by commonness or custom, whatever profession is made of the gospel, it is vain and useless.

Thus the apostle allows that there were national sins prevalent among the Cretans: 'One of the Cretans, a prophet of their own, said, "Cretans are always liars, evil beasts, lazy gluttons." This testimony is true. Therefore rebuke them sharply, that they may be sound in the faith' (Titus 1:12-13). Whatever their profession was, if they were not delivered by the gospel from the power and practice of these national sins which they were so prone to, they would not long be sound in the faith nor fruitful in obedience.

SEPTEMBER 22

Justified by Faith

Therefore, since we have been justified by faith, we have peace with God through our Lord Jesus Christ.

ROMANS 5:1

It is on all sides agreed that the knowledge of the truth of justification by faith is of the highest importance to people's souls. Anyone who knows themselves to be a sinner, and liable therefore to the judgment of God, must desire to have some knowledge of it, as that alone by which the way of delivery from the evil state and condition they find themselves in is revealed.

Some people, wilfully deluding themselves with vain hopes and imaginations, never once seriously inquire by what way or means they may obtain peace with God and acceptance before him. In comparison with the present enjoyment of the pleasures of sin, they do not value this at all. And it is in vain to recommend the doctrine of justification to those who neither desire nor endeavour to be justified.

But where anyone is really made sensible of their apostasy from God, of the evil of their natures and lives, with the dreadful consequences that follow in the wrath of God and eternal punishment due to sin, they cannot well judge themselves more concerned in anything than in the knowledge of that divine way by which they may be delivered from this condition.

I have had no other design but only to inquire diligently into the divine revelation of that way, and those means, by which the conscience of a distressed sinner may attain assured peace with God through our Lord Jesus Christ. I lay more weight on the steady direction of one soul in this inquiry, than on disappointing the objections of twenty wrangling or fiery disputers.

SEPTEMBER 23

Spiritual Truths

We impart this knowledge in words not taught by human wisdom but taught by the Spirit, interpreting spiritual truths to those who are spiritual.

1 CORINTHIANS 2:13

The Holy Spirit is pleased to make use of many metaphorical expressions, in expressing the most eminent acts in our justification, especially as to our believing, or the acting of that faith whereby we are justified. For any to use them now in the same way, and to the same purpose, is esteemed rude, undisciplined, and even ridiculous; but on what grounds? There is more spiritual sense and experience conveyed by them into the hearts and minds of believers (which is the life and soul of teaching things practical), than in the most accurate philosophical expressions. Those who deny this are themselves really ignorant of the whole truth in this matter.

The propriety of such philosophical expressions belongs and is confined to natural science, but spiritual truths are to be taught, 'in words not taught by human wisdom but taught by the Spirit, interpreting spiritual truths to those who are spiritual' (1 Cor. 2:13). God is wiser than us; the Holy Spirit knows better than the wisest of us all, what are the most expedient ways for the illumination of our minds with that knowledge of evangelical truths which it is our duty to have and attain.

SEPTEMBER 24

Counted Righteous

Abram believed the LORD, and he counted it to him as righteousness.

GENESIS 15:6

The first express record of the justification of any sinner is of Abraham. Others were justified before him from the beginning, but this prerogative was reserved for the father of the faithful, that his justification and the express way and manner of it, should be first entered on the sacred record. So it is: 'He believed the Lord, and it was counted to him as righteousness' (Gen. 15:6). It was 'accounted' to him, or 'imputed' to him, for righteousness. 'But the words "it was counted to him" were not written for his sake alone, but for ours also. It will be counted to us who believe in him' (Rom. 4:23-24). Therefore, the first express declaration of the nature of justification in the Scripture affirms it to be by imputation. As he was justified so are we, and not otherwise.

Under the New Testament, there was a necessity of a more full and clear declaration of the doctrine of it; for it is among the first and most principal parts of that heavenly mystery of truth which was to be brought to light by the gospel (2 Tim. 1:10). The doctrine of justification was fully declared, stated, and vindicated by the apostle Paul. And he does it especially by affirming and proving that we have the righteousness by which we are justified *by imputation;* or, that our justification consists in the *non-imputation* of sin, and the *imputation* of righteousness.

SEPTEMBER 25

Faith and Doctrine

And it shall come to pass that everyone who calls on the name of the LORD shall be saved.

JOEL 2:32

The weight and importance of this doctrine of justification is on all hands acknowledged. It is not a dispute about notions, terms, and speculations, in which Christian practice is little or not at all concerned, but such as has an immediate influence into our whole present duty, with our eternal welfare or ruin.

Those who reject the *imputation of righteousness* do affirm that the faith and doctrine of it overthrows the necessity of gospel obedience, of personal righteousness, and good works, bringing in *antinomianism* and *libertinism* in life. Consequently it must, of necessity, be destructive of salvation in those who believe it, and conform their practice to it. And those, on the other hand, by whom it is believed, seeing they judge it impossible that anyone should be justified before God any other way than by the *imputation of the righteousness of Christ*, do accordingly judge that without it none can be saved.

The latter do not think or judge that all those are excluded from salvation who cannot apprehend, or do deny, the *doctrine* of the imputation of the righteousness of Christ. But they judge that those *to whom righteousness is not really imputed* are so excluded. To believe the *doctrine* of it, or not to believe it, is one *thing*; and to enjoy the *thing*, or not enjoy it, is another. Many people receive more grace from God than they understand or will own. People may be really saved by that grace which doctrinally they do deny; and they may be justified by the *imputation of that righteousness* which, in opinion, they deny to be imputed.

SEPTEMBER 26

Guaranteed

For he has made with me an everlasting covenant, ordered in all things and secure.

2 SAMUEL 23:5

We, on all accounts, stand in need of a surety or guarantor for us, or on our behalf. Without the intervention of such a surety, no covenant between God and us could be firm and stable, or an everlasting covenant, ordered in all things, and sure (2 Sam. 23:5). In the first covenant made with Adam there was no surety, but God and mankind were the immediate covenanters. And although we were then in a state and condition able to perform and answer all the terms of the covenant, yet was it broken and invalidated.

If this came to pass by the failure of the *promise of God*, it was necessary that, on the making of a new covenant, he should have a surety to undertake for him, that the covenant might be stable and everlasting. But this is false and blasphemous to imagine. It was *mankind alone* who failed and broke that covenant: therefore it was necessary, that upon the making of the new covenant (and that with a design and purpose that it should never be annulled, as the former was), we should have a surety and guarantor for us.

For if that first covenant was not firm and stable, because there was no surety to undertake for us, how much less can any other be so, now that our natures have become depraved and sinful! Therefore, we alone stood in need of a surety; and without him the covenant could not be firm and secure on our part. The surety, therefore of this covenant, is a guarantor with God for us.

SEPTEMBER 27

Love and Hate

For this reason the Father loves me, because I lay down my life that I may take it up again.
JOHN 10:17

But it will be said that if our sins, as to the guilt of them, were imputed to Christ, then God must *hate* Christ; for he hates the guilty (Ps. 5). But it is certain that the Lord Christ's taking upon him the guilt of our sins was a high act of obedience unto God (Heb. 10:5-6); and for which the 'Father loved him' (John 10:17-18). There was, therefore, no reason why God should hate Christ for his taking upon him our debt and the payment of it, in an act of the highest obedience to his will.

Secondly, God in this matter is considered as a ruler and judge. Now, it is not required of the severest judge, that, as a judge, he should hate the guilty person. As such, he has no more to do but consider the guilt, and pronounce the sentence of punishment.

But, thirdly, suppose a person, out of a heroic generosity of mind, should become a substitute for another, for his friend, for a good man, so as to answer for him with his life, as Judah undertook to be for Benjamin as to his liberty (Gen. 44:32-34). Would the most cruel tyrant under heaven, that should take away his life, in that case *hate* him? Would he not rather admire his worth and virtue? As such a substitute it was that Christ suffered, and not otherwise.

Fourthly, all the force of this exception depends on the ambiguity of the word *hate*; for it may signify either an aversion or detestation of mind, or only a will of punishing, as in God mostly it does.

SEPTEMBER 28

Bad Medicine

With what shall I come before the LORD, and bow myself before God on high?

MICAH 6:6

Whilst any knowledge of the law or gospel is continued amongst us, people's consciences will at one time or other, living or dying, be really affected with a sense of sin, as to its guilt and danger. Hence that trouble and those disturbances of mind will ensue, as will force people (be they never so unwilling) to seek after some relief and satisfaction. And what will people not attempt who are reduced to the condition expressed in Micah 6:6-7? 'With what shall I come before the LORD, and bow myself before God on high?… Will the LORD be pleased with thousands of rams, with ten thousands of rivers of oil?'

If the true and only relief for the distressed consciences of sinners who are weary and heavy laden is hidden from their eyes—if they have no apprehension of, nor trust in that which alone they may oppose to the sentence of the law, and interpose between God's justice and their souls, in which they may take shelter from the storms of that wrath which abides on those who do not believe (John 3:36)—they will take themselves to anything which confidently tenders them present ease and relief.

Hence many persons, living all their days in an ignorance of the righteousness of God, are often on their sick-beds and in their dying hours, proselyted to a confidence in the ways of rest and peace which others impose upon them. Finding at any time the consciences of people under disturbances, and ignorant of or disbelieving that heavenly relief which is provided in the gospel, they are ready with their applications and medicines.

SEPTEMBER

SEPTEMBER 29

Truth Defamed

The Lord's servant must not be quarrelsome but kind to everyone, able to teach, patiently enduring evil, correcting his opponents with gentleness.

2 TIMOTHY 2:24-25

It is not unworthy of our notice and deepest resentment how zealously affected some people are on behalf of such tenants as stand in direct opposition to the grace of God, and their own eternal happiness. They spare neither arts nor accusations to disgrace the asserters of those very truths that make up the mystery of godliness. Indeed, they scandalise and suppress the truth themselves, as if reason and learning were given to no better ends than to vilify religion. How addicted people are to take in those teachings that are of most fatal consequence. Those principles are far from yielding any effectual influence towards holiness or well-grounded peace, despite their supposed ability to promote them.

But whatever the ends of people are, in defaming the wisdom, sovereignty, and grace of God, the Lord's ends in permitting them are holy and good. We are assured that he would not have suffered those dangerous errors to invade his church, and his glorious truths to be so coarsely and insultingly treated, unless it were to further expose and conquer them.

Therefore, as he has, so he will (of his abundant goodness to the world and faithfulness to his elect) raise up people who with meekness, light, and power shall withstand their furious torrent, and transmit to the following generations those blessed and greatly important truths which the world is so implacably bent against and seeks to eradicate.

SEPTEMBER 30

Covenant Centre

For this is the covenant that I will make with the house of Israel after those days, declares the LORD: I will put my law within them, and I will write it on their hearts.

JEREMIAH 31:33

The doctrine of the covenants is the very centre where all the lines concerning the grace of God and our own duty meet, and in which the whole of religion consists. Hence, people's conceptions of all other sacred truths or doctrines are conformed to the understanding, notions, and conceptions that they have of these covenants of God, and to the doctrine of them as stated in their minds.

Therefore, those who have right apprehensions and a true understanding of these things cannot, in the use of diligence and the means appointed for it, lightly mistake the truth in any other point of weight in the whole compass of religion. In the same way, those who unhappily fall under misapprehensions about them, generally either fluctuate in their own minds about all other evangelical truths, or corrupt and pervert the whole doctrine concerning them. Upon this also depends the regulation of all our entire Christian practice or obedience, as all will acknowledge who have any knowledge of these things.

Very many learned and godly persons have laboured in this subject for the edification of the church. It is not un-useful that the same truth, especially that which is of such great importance as is what concerns the covenant, be variously handled by many, according to the measure of the gift of Christ which they have received. Perfect harmony and universal agreement in all things is the privilege only of the sacred writers who were divinely inspired.

OCTOBER

This month, we will be reading some of Owen's prodigious output during the final years of his life (1678-1683).

Firstly, we will engage with Owen's masterful treatise called *Christologia: Or, a Declaration of the Glorious Mystery of the Person of Christ, God and Man*. This is not so much a defence of Christ's divinity, as an application of that foundational doctrine to the Christian life.

During this period of English history there was a wave of hysteria and conspiracy, mixed with some right concern, about a potential Roman Catholic resurgence. The Roman Catholic Duke of York was heir to the throne, and some tried to have him excluded from the line of succession. Owen's spiritually-minded contributions to these sometimes fierce debates included *The Church of Rome No Safe Guide* (1679), *A Brief and Impartial Account of the Nature of the Protestant Religion* (1682), and *The Chamber of Imagery in the Church of Rome Laid Open* (1683).

In 1680, the third large volume of his Hebrews commentary appeared, on Hebrews 6-10. A year later, he continued to engage in discussions of church polity with *An Enquiry into the Original, Nature, Institution, Power, Order and Communion of Evangelical Churches*. Owen also penned prefaces to works by his friends Stephen Lobb (*The Glory of Free Grace Displayed*), Bartholomew Ashwood (*The Best Treasure*), Samuel Clark (*The New Testament*), and William Benn (*Soul Prosperity*).

His sermon 'An Humble Testimony unto the Goodness and Severity of God in His Dealings with Sinful Churches and Nations' (1681) on Luke 13:1-5 has often been reprinted, as has his book on *The Grace and Duty of Being Spiritually-Minded*. We will read from both of them.

OCTOBER 1

Precious Christ

In the LORD all the offspring of Israel shall be justified and shall glory.

ISAIAH 45:25

To those who believe, Christ is and always has been precious—the sun, the rock, the life, the bread of their souls—everything that is good, useful, amiable, desirable, here or into eternity. In, from, and by him, is all their spiritual and eternal life, light, power, growth, consolation, and joy here—with everlasting salvation hereafter.

By him alone do they desire, expect, and obtain deliverance from that woeful apostasy from God, which is accompanied with whatever is evil, noxious, and destructive to our nature, and which, without relief, will issue in eternal misery. By him are they brought into the nearest alliance and friendship with God, the firmest union to him, and the most holy communion with him that our finite natures are capable of and so lead into the eternal enjoyment of him.

For in him 'shall all the offspring of Israel be justified, and shall glory' (Isa. 45:25). For Israel shall be this impregnable rock, this precious foundation. In the defence of these truths they contended in prayers, studies, travels, and writings, against the swarms of seducers by whom they were opposed.

OCTOBER 2

Image of God

He is the image of the invisible God, the firstborn of all creation.

COLOSSIANS 1:15

A mere external doctrinal revelation of the divine nature and properties, without any exemplification or real representation of them, was not sufficient to the end of God in the manifestation of himself. This is done in the Scripture. But the whole Scripture is built on this foundation, or proceeds on this supposition—that there is a real representation of the divine nature to us, which it declares and describes.

There was such a notion in the minds of all, that some representation of God, in which he might be near to them, was necessary. This arose from the consideration of the infinite distance between the divine nature and their own, which allowed of no measures between them. So, God himself has declared that, in his own way, such a representation was needful.

All this is done in the person of Christ. He is the complete image and perfect representation of the Divine Being and excellencies. I do not speak of it absolutely, but as God proposes himself as the object of our faith, trust, and obedience. Hence, it is God, as the Father, who is so peculiarly represented in him and by him; as he says: 'Whoever has seen me has seen the Father' (John 14:9).

OCTOBER 3

Prophetic Christ

The prophets who prophesied about the grace that was to be yours searched and enquired carefully, enquiring what person or time the Spirit of Christ in them was indicating when he predicted the sufferings of Christ and the subsequent glories.

1 PETER 1:10-11

It is true, we have under the gospel many unspeakable advantages from the prophetic office of Christ, above what they enjoyed under the Old Testament. But he was the prophet of the church equally in all ages. Only he has given out the knowledge of the mind of God in different degrees and measures; that which was most perfect being for many reasons reserved to the times of the gospel. The sum of which is, that God designed him for a pre-eminence above all in his own personal ministry.

Some may inquire how the Lord Christ could be the prophet of the church before he took our nature on him and dwelt among us. Shall they also ask how he is the prophet of the church now he has left the world and is gone to heaven, so that we neither see him nor hear him anymore? If they shall say that he is so by his Spirit, his word, and the ministry which he has ordained—I say, so was he the prophet of the church before his incarnation also.

To confine the offices of Christ, as to their virtue, power, and efficacy, to the times of the gospel only, is utterly to evacuate the first promise, with the covenant of grace founded on it. Those who suppose that the respect of the church to Christ, in faith, love, trust, and instruction, commences from the date of his incarnation have their minds secretly influenced by a disbelief of his divine person.

OCTOBER 4

Veil Removed

> *The law has but a shadow of the good things to come instead of the true form of these realities.*
>
> HEBREWS 10:1

God gave them representations and prefigurations of his office and work. He did so by the high priest of the law and the tabernacle, with all the sacrifices and services belonging to it. All that Moses did, as a faithful servant in the house of God, was but a 'testimony of those things which were to be spoken after' (Heb. 3:5). But the apostle tells us that all those things had but a 'shadow of good things to come, and not the very image of the things themselves' (Heb. 10:1). And although they are now to us full of light and instruction, evidently expressing the principal works of Christ's mediation, yet were they not so to them.

For the veil is now taken off from them in their accomplishment, and a declaration is made of the counsels of God in them by the gospel. The meanest believer may now find out more of the work of Christ in the types of the Old Testament, than any prophets or wise men could have done of old.

Therefore they always earnestly longed for their accomplishment—that the day might break, and the shadows fly away by the rising of the Sun of Righteousness with healing in his wings (Mal. 4:2). But as to his person, they had glorious revelations concerning it; and their faith in him was the life of all their obedience. Of the same nature were all his personal appearances under the Old Testament, especially that most illustrious representation made of him to the prophet Isaiah (Isa. 6, 9:6). Nevertheless, their conceptions concerning them were dark and obscure.

OCTOBER 5

Christ's Love

Behold, I stand at the door and knock. If anyone hears my voice and opens the door, I will come in to him and eat with him, and he with me.

REVELATION 3:20

The love of Christ is always the same and equal to the church. But there are peculiar seasons of the manifestation and application of a sense of it to the souls of believers. So it is when it is witnessed to them, or shed abroad in their hearts by the Holy Spirit. Then is it accompanied with a constraining power, to oblige us to live for him who died for us, and rose again (2 Cor. 5:14-15). And this sense of his love we might enjoy more frequently than for the most part we do, were we not so much wanting unto ourselves and our own concerns. For although it is an act of sovereign grace in God to grant it to us, and affect us with it (as it seems good to him), yet is our duty required to dispose our hearts to its reception.

Were we diligent in casting out all that 'filthiness and rampant wickedness' (James 1:21) which corrupts our affections, and disposes the mind to abound in vain imaginations; were our hearts more taken away from the love of the world, which excludes a sense of divine love; if we meditated more on Christ and his glory—we should more frequently enjoy these constraining visits of his love than now we do.

He makes intimation of his love and kindness to us. But often we neither hear his voice when he speaks, nor open our hearts to him. So we lose that gracious, refreshing sense of his love which he expresses in that promise, 'I will come in to him and eat with him'. The expression is metaphorical, but the grace expressed is real, and more valued than the whole world by all who have experience of it.

OCTOBER 6

Sincere Love

If you love me, you will keep my commandments.

JOHN 14:15

Some may think that they love Christ, but indeed do not so. That love is not sincere and uncorrupted which proceeds not from faith, and is not a fruit of it. Those who do not first really believe on Christ, can never sincerely love him. It is faith alone that works by love towards Christ and all his saints. If, therefore, any do not believe with that faith which unites them to Christ—which purifies the heart within and is outwardly effectual in duties of obedience—whatever they may persuade themselves concerning love to Christ, it is but a vain delusion. Where their faith is dead, their love will not be living and sincere.

Love, which arises from false ideas and representations that people make of Christ, or have made of him in their minds, is also not sincere. People may draw images in their minds of what they most fancy, and then dote upon them. So some think of Christ only as a glorious person exalted in heaven at the right hand of God, without farther apprehensions of his natures and offices. So the Roman missionaries represented him to some of the Indians—concealing from them his cross and sufferings. But every false notion concerning his person or his grace—what he is, has done, or does—corrupts the love that is pretended to him.

Shall we think that they love Christ by whom his divine nature is denied? Or that those who disbelieve the reality of his human nature do so? Or those by whom the union of both in the same person is rejected? There cannot be true evangelical love to a false Christ, such as these imaginations do fancy.

OCTOBER 7

Perfume of Death

Your anointing oils are fragrant; your name is oil poured out;
therefore virgins love you.

SONG OF SONGS 1:3

If our minds are not filled with these things—if Christ does not dwell plentifully in our hearts by faith (Eph. 3:17)—we are strangers to the life of faith. Take one instance from among the rest—namely, his death. Have they the heart of a Christian, who do not often meditate on the death of their Saviour, who do not derive their life from it? Who can look into the gospel and not fix on those lines which either immediately and directly, or through some other paths of divine grace and wisdom, lead them to this?

And can any have believing thoughts concerning the death of Christ, and not have their heart affected with ardent love for his person? Christ in the gospel is 'publicly portrayed as crucified' before us (Gal. 3:1). Can any by the eye of faith look on this bleeding, dying Redeemer, and suppose love for his person to be nothing but the work of fancy or imagination?

They know the contrary, who are 'always carrying in the body the death of Jesus' as the apostle speaks (2 Cor. 4:10). As his whole 'name' in all that he did, is 'as ointment poured forth,' for which 'the virgins love him' (Song 1:3)—so this precious perfume of his death is that with which their hearts are ravished in a peculiar manner.

OCTOBER 8

Christ's Example

Walk in love, as Christ loved us and gave himself up for us, a fragrant offering and sacrifice to God.

EPHESIANS 5:2

Christ's meekness, lowliness of mind, condescension to all sorts of persons—his love and kindness to mankind—his readiness to do good to all, with patience and forbearance—are continually set before us in his example. It is required that 'the same mind be in us that was in Christ Jesus' (Phil. 2:5), and that we 'walk in love, as he also loved us' (Eph. 5:2).

One Christian who is meek, humble, kind, patient, and useful to all; that condescends to the ignorance, weaknesses, and infirmities of others; that passes by provocations, injuries, contempt, with patience and with silence, unless where the glory and truth of God call for a just vindication; that pities all sorts of people in their failings and miscarriages, who is free from jealousies and evil theories; that loves what is good in all people, and all people even when they are not good, nor do good—such a Christian more expresses the virtues and excellencies of Christ than thousands can do with the most magnificent works of piety or charity, where this frame is lacking in them.

For people to pretend to follow the example of Christ, and in the meantime to be proud, wrathful, envious, bitterly zealous, calling for fire from heaven to destroy others, or fetching it themselves from hell, is to cry, 'Hail to him!' and to crucify him afresh.

OCTOBER 9

Leading Losers

I think that God has exhibited us apostles as last of all, like men sentenced to death, because we have become a spectacle to the world, to angels, and to men.

1 CORINTHIANS 4:9

The Bible is a divine revelation of the whole will and mind of God in all things that are necessary to his glory and our salvation. This it frequently testifies of itself; and, since it is such a divine revelation, its testimony must be granted to be infallibly true. Both these assertions the apostle expressly joins together (2 Tim. 3:15-17).

The holy apostles succeeded to the personal ministry of our Lord Jesus Christ, as to this conduct of people's souls. Such power was committed to them by him who sent them, 'even as the Father sent me' (John 20:21). Such assurance was there in their conduct, through infallible inspiration, and the presence of the Holy Spirit with them in an extraordinary manner, that all people were bound to give themselves up to their guidance.

However, they judged that there was no duty more incumbent on them than to make it evident to all the world that they neither sought nor would accept of any temporal advantages for themselves by the trust reposed in them. They were content that their portion in this world should lie in all the extremities and calamities of it. And this they willingly submitted to, that all might be encouraged to trust them in their everlasting affairs, when they saw what losers they were by it in this world, without desire, hope, or expectation of any better condition.

OCTOBER 10

Hidden Revelation

*Our Saviour Christ Jesus abolished death and brought life
and immortality to light through the gospel.*

2 TIMOTHY 1:10

Truth was stored up in the prophecies, promises, and institutions of the Old Testament, but so stored up that it was in a great measure hidden also. It was brought forth to light, and made manifest in the gospel.

For whereas it is said that the great mystery of the manifold wisdom of God was hidden in him from the beginning of the world (Eph. 3:9-10), the meaning is not that it was so hidden in the will and purpose of God that he had made no intimation of it; for he had done so variously from the foundation of the world, or the giving of the first promise. But he had so laid it up and stored it in his sacred revelation that it was much hidden from the understanding of the best of people in all ages, until it was displayed and brought forth to light by the gospel.

All that glorious evidence of the grace of God which now appears to us in the writings of the Old Testament, is from a reflection of light on them from the New Testament, or the revelation of God by Jesus Christ. And therefore the whole church of the Jews, although they were in the entire possession of those writings of the Old Testament for so many ages, never understood so much of the mystery of the will and grace of God declared in them as every ordinary believer under the gospel is enabled to do.

If we have the privilege and advantage of those oracles of God which were committed to them, incomparably above what they attained to, certainly greater measures of holiness, and greater fruitfulness in obedience, are expected from us than from them.

OCTOBER 11

Gifts and Grace

But by the grace of God I am what I am, and his grace toward me was not in vain.

1 CORINTHIANS 15:10

The sovereign will, pleasure, and grace of God is that alone which puts a difference among people, especially in the church. He makes people great or small, high or low, eminent or obscure, as it seems good to him. 'He raises up the poor from the dust; he lifts the needy from the ash heap to make them sit with princes and inherit a seat of honour. For the pillars of the earth are the LORD's, and on them he has set the world' (1 Sam. 2:8); which is plentifully testified to elsewhere.

Why was it that the twelve poor fishermen were made apostles, to 'sit on twelve thrones, judging the twelve tribes of Israel' (Matt. 19:28) and becoming princes in all nations? Who made the most glorious apostle of the first and fiercest persecutor? (Gal. 1:13) Was it not he who 'has mercy on whom he will have mercy' and is 'gracious to whom he will be gracious?' (Exod. 33:19; Rom. 9:15). It is laid down as a universal rule, that no one has anything in this kind but what they have freely received; nor does anyone make themselves to differ from others (1 Cor. 4:7).

God lays the foundation of all spiritual differences among people in his sovereign decree of eternal election (Rom. 9:11-16; Eph. 1:4). Amongst those who are chosen, he calls them when and how he pleases, both to grace and employment or work. As to grace, gifts, and spiritual endowments, the Holy Spirit 'apportions to each one individually as he wills' (1 Cor. 12:11). Let everyone, then, be content with their lot and condition. Let God be owned in all his gifts and grace.

OCTOBER 12

Spiritual Worship

Take my yoke upon you, and learn from me, for I am gentle and lowly in heart, and you will find rest for your souls. For my yoke is easy, and my burden is light.

MATTHEW 11:29-30

The gospel is easy and gentle, in opposition to the burden and insupportable yoke of the old institutions and ordinances. So are all the commands of Christ to believers, as the whole system of his precepts, whether for moral obedience or worship, declares: 'Take my yoke upon you, and learn from me, for I am gentle and lowly in heart, and you will find rest for your souls. For my yoke is easy, and my burden is light' (Matt. 11:29-30). So the apostle tells us that 'his commandments are not burdensome' (1 John 5:3).

But concerning this ease of gospel-worship some things must be observed, as to the persons to whom it is so easy and pleasant. It is so only to those who, being 'weary and heavy laden' come to Christ that they may have rest, and learn of him. That is, to convinced, humbled, converted sinners, who believe in him.

To all others, it proves an insupportable burden, and that which they cannot endure to be obliged to. Hence the generality of people who, although professing the Christian religion, are quickly weary of evangelical worship, and find out endless inventions of their own, by which they are better satisfied in their divine services. Therefore they have multiplied ceremonies, fond superstitions, and downright idolatries, which they prefer before the purity and simplicity of the worship of the gospel. People of unspiritual minds cannot delight in spiritual worship.

OCTOBER 13

The Present Truth

I found it necessary to write appealing to you to contend for the faith that was once for all delivered to the saints.

JUDE 3

God is pleased to exercise and try the faith of the church by heresies, which are fierce, persistent, and subtle oppositions made to the truth. Now none of them, which aim at any consistency in and with themselves, or are of any real danger unto the church, did ever reject *all* gospel truths. Some general principles they will allow, or they would leave themselves no foundation to stand on in their opposition to others. Those, therefore, singly opposed by them at any time—such as the deity or satisfaction of Christ, justification by faith, and the like—being so opposed, become 'the present truth' of the age (2 Pet. 1:12).

A truth may come under this qualification by persecution as well as by heretical opposition. Satan is always awake and attentive to his advantages: and therefore though he hates all truth, yet he does not at all times equally attempt upon everything that is so. He waits to see an inclination in people, from their lusts, or prejudices, or interests in this world, against any special truth or way of divine worship which God has appointed. When he finds things so ready prepared, he falls to his work, and stirs up persecution against it. This makes that truth to be 'the present truth' to be contended for, as that in which God will try the faith and obedience and patience of the church.

OCTOBER 14

Interceding

He is able to save to the uttermost those who draw near to God through him, since he always lives to make intercession for them.

HEBREWS 7:25

So great and glorious is the work of saving believers to the utmost, that it is necessary that the Lord Christ should lead a mediatory life in heaven, for the perfecting and accomplishment of it. 'He always lives to make intercession for us.' It is generally acknowledged that sinners could not be saved without the death of Christ; but that believers could not be saved without the life of Christ following it, is not so much considered (see Rom. 5:10, 8:34-35, etc).

Perhaps some think that when he had declared the name of God, and revealed the whole counsel of his will; when he had given us the great example of love and holiness in his life; when he had fulfilled all righteousness, redeemed us by his blood, and made atonement for our sins by the offering of himself; confirming his truth and acceptance with God in all these things by his resurrection from the dead, in which he was 'declared to be the Son of God with power' (Rom. 1:4)—that he might have now left us to deal for ourselves, and to build our eternal safety on the foundation that he had laid.

But, alas! When all this was done, if he had only ascended into his own glory, to enjoy his majesty, honour, and dominion, without continuing his life and office in our behalf, we would have been left poor and helpless. Both we and all our right to a heavenly inheritance would have been made a prey to every subtle and powerful adversary.

OCTOBER 15

Tender Priest

We do not have a high priest who is unable to sympathise with our weaknesses, but one who in every respect has been tempted as we are, yet without sin.

HEBREWS 4:15

The intercession of Christ is the great evidence of the continuance of his love and care, his pity and compassion towards his church. Had he only continued to rule the church as its king and lord, he would have manifested his glorious power, his righteousness, and faithfulness. 'The sceptre of his kingdom is a sceptre of righteousness' (Ps. 45:6). But mercy and compassion, love and tenderness, are constantly ascribed to him as our high priest (see Heb. 4:15, 5:1-2). So the great exercise of his sacerdotal office, in laying down his life for us and expiating our sins by his blood, is still peculiarly ascribed to his love (Gal. 2:20; Eph. 5:2; Rev. 1:5).

Therefore these properties of love and compassion belong peculiarly to the Lord Christ as our high priest. All people, who have any spiritual experience and understanding, will acknowledge how great the interest of believers is in these things, and how all their consolation in this world depends on them. The one whose soul has not been refreshed with a due apprehension of the unspeakable love, tenderness, and compassion of Jesus Christ, is a stranger to the life of faith, and to all true spiritual consolation.

OCTOBER 16

Perfect Sacrifice

Behold, the Lamb of God, who takes away the sin of the world!

JOHN 1:29

No sacrifice could bring us to God, and save the church to the utmost, but that in which the Son of God himself was both priest and offering. We needed such a high priest, who offered himself once for all. This was one of the greatest effects of infinite divine wisdom and grace. His incarnation, in which he had a body prepared for him for this purpose, his call to his office by the oath of the Father and anointing of the Spirit, his sanctifying himself to be a sacrifice, and his offering up himself through the eternal Spirit to God, are all full of mysterious wisdom and grace. All these wonders of wisdom and love were necessary to this great end of bringing us to God.

Every part of this transaction, all that belongs to this sacrifice, is so filled up with perfection, that no more could be required on the part of God. Nor is anything lacking, to give countenance to our unbelief. The person of the priest, and the offering itself, are both the same: the Son of God. One view of the glory of this mystery, how satisfactory is it to the souls of believers!

A distinct consideration of the person of the priest and of his sacrifice will evidence this truth to the faith of believers. What could not this priest prevail for, in his intervention on our behalf? Must he not needs be absolutely successful in all he aims at? Were our cause entrusted to any other hand, what security could we have that it should not miscarry? And what could not this offering make atonement for? What sin, or whose sins could it not expiate? 'Behold the Lamb of God, which taketh away the sin of the world.'

OCTOBER 17

True Worship

We have such a high priest, one who is seated at the right hand of the throne of the Majesty in heaven, a minister in the holy places, in the true tent that the Lord set up, not man.

HEBREWS 8:1-2

The church has lost nothing by the removal of the old tabernacle and temple, all being supplied by this sanctuary, true tabernacle, and minister. The Jews would by no means part with the glory and worship of the temple. They chose rather to reject Christ and the gospel than to part with the temple and its outward, pompous worship. And it is almost incredible how the vain mind of mankind is addicted to an outward beauty and splendour in religious worship. Take it away, and for most you destroy all religion itself—as if there were no beauty but in painting; no evidence of health or vigour of body, but in warts and tumours.

The Christians of old suffered in nothing more from the prejudice of the whole world, Jews and Gentiles, than in this: that they had a religion without temples, altars, images, or any solemnity of worship. And in later ages, people did not cease until they had brought into Christianity itself a worship vying for external order, ceremony, pomp, and painting, with whatever was in the tabernacle or temple of old; coming short of it principally in this, that *that* was of God's institution for a time, but *this* was the invention of weak, superstitious, and foolish people.

Hence is there at this day so great a contest in the world about tabernacles and temples, modes of worship and ceremonies. For they judge that God will be satisfied with their carnal ordinances in the church. But to those who believe, Christ is precious (1 Pet. 2:7).

OCTOBER 18

Admire Christ

Christ has obtained a ministry that is as much more excellent than the old as the covenant he mediates is better.

HEBREWS 8:6

We can never sufficiently admire the love and grace of our Lord Jesus Christ, in undertaking this office for us. The greatness and glory of the duties which he performed in the discharge of it, with the benefits we receive thereby, are unspeakable. They are the immediate cause of all grace and glory. Yet we are not absolutely to rest in them, but to ascend by faith to the eternal spring of them. This is the grace, the love, the mercy of God, all acted in a way of sovereign power. These are everywhere in the Scripture represented as the original spring of all grace, and the ultimate object of our faith, with respect to the benefits which we receive by the mediation of Christ.

The condescension of the Son of God to undertake the office of the ministry on our behalf is unspeakable, and for ever to be admired. Especially will it appear so to be when we consider who it was that undertook it, what it cost him, what he did and underwent in the pursuance and discharge of it, as it is all expressed in Philippians 2:6-8. Not only what he continues to do in heaven at the right hand of God belongs to this ministry, but all that he suffered also upon the earth. His ministry, in the undertaking of it, was not a dignity, a promotion, a revenue (Matt. 20:28). He came not to be served but to serve. It is true, his ministry issued in glory, but not until he had undergone all the evils that human nature is capable of undergoing. And we ought to undergo anything cheerfully for him who underwent this ministry for us.

OCTOBER 19

Stable Covenant

In Christ all things hold together.

COLOSSIANS 1:17

No covenant between God and mankind ever was, or ever could be stable and effectual, as to the ends of it, that was not made and confirmed in Christ. God first made a covenant with us in Adam. In him we all sinned, by breach of covenant. The Son of God had not then interposed himself, nor undertaken on our behalf. The apostle tells us that 'in him all things hold together' (Col. 1:17)—without him, they have no consistency, no stability, no duration. So was this first covenant immediately broken. It was not confirmed by the blood of Christ.

Those who suppose that the efficacy and stability of the present covenant depend solely on our own will and diligence, surely know little of themselves, and less of God. No external administration of a covenant of God's own making, no obligation of mercy on the minds of people, can enable them to be steadfast in covenant obedience, without an effectual influence of grace from and by Jesus Christ.

If God casts people out of his special care, upon the breach of his covenant, this is the highest judgment that in this world can fall on any persons. And we are concerned in all these things. For although the covenant of grace is stable and effectual for all who are really partakers of it, yet as to its external administration, and our entering into it by a visible profession, it may be broken, to the temporal and eternal ruin of persons and whole churches. Take heed of the golden calf.

OCTOBER 20

Gospel Priests

To him who loves us and has freed us from our sins by his blood and made us a kingdom, priests to his God and Father, to him be glory and dominion forever and ever. Amen.

REVELATION 1:5-6

This was the great privilege of the priests under the Old Testament, that they alone might and did enter into the sanctuary, and make an approach to God. And this privilege they had as they were types of Christ, and not otherwise. It was a great part and a great means of that state of servitude and fear in which the people or the body of the church was kept. They might not so much as come near the pledges of God's presence. It was forbidden them under the penalty of death and being cut off; of which they sadly complained (Num. 17:12-13).

This state of things is now changed under the gospel. It is one of the principal privileges of believers, that, being made kings and priests to God by Jesus Christ, this distinction as to special gracious access to God is taken away (Rev. 1:5-6; Ephesians 2:18; Romans 5:2).

Yet there are and ought to be officers and ministers in the house of God, to dispense the holy things of it, and to minister in the name of Christ. For in their so doing they do not hinder, but promote, the approach of the church into the presence of God; which is the principal end of their office. And as this is their peculiar honour, for which they must be accountable (Heb. 13:17), so the church of believers itself ought always to consider how they may duly improve and walk worthy of this privilege, purchased for them by the blood of Christ.

OCTOBER 21

Church Meetings

Let us consider how to stir up one another to love and good works, not neglecting to meet together, as is the habit of some, but encouraging one another, and all the more as you see the Day drawing near.

HEBREWS 10:24-25

These assemblies were of two sorts: 1. Stated, on the Lord's Day, or first day of the week (1 Cor. 16:2; Acts 20:7); 2. Occasional, as the duties or occasions of the church required (1 Cor. 5:4). The end of these assemblies was twofold: 1. The due performance of all solemn stated, orderly, evangelical worship, in prayer, preaching of the word, singing of psalms, and the administration of the sacraments. 2. The exercise of discipline, or the watch of the church over its members, with respect to their walking and lifestyle, that in all things it should be such as becomes the gospel, and gives no offence: so to admonish, exhort, and 'provoke one another to love and good works' to comfort, establish, and encourage those who were afflicted or persecuted, to relieve the poor, etc. Such assemblies were constantly observed in the first churches.

These assemblies were the life, the food, the nourishment of their souls. These assemblies were those which exposed them to sufferings, as those whereby they made their profession visible, and evidenced their subjection to the authority of Christ, by which the unbelieving world is enraged. This in all ages has prevailed on many, in times of trial and persecution, to withdraw themselves from these assemblies; and those who have done so are those 'fearful and unbelieving' ones who in the first place are excluded from the new Jerusalem (Rev. 21:8).

OCTOBER 22

Riches and Treasures

God chose to make known how great among the Gentiles are the riches of the glory of this mystery, which is Christ in you, the hope of glory. Him we proclaim, warning everyone and teaching everyone with all wisdom, that we may present everyone mature in Christ.

COLOSSIANS 1:27-28

The wisdom and grace of God in Christ Jesus are frequently in the Scripture expressed by the name of riches and treasures (e.g. Col. 2:3). These it is the duty of believers in all ages diligently to search after, to inquire into, and possess for themselves.

It may be that more diligence has not been used in this inquiry into the doctrinal revelation of them, or with more success, in any age than in this age in which we live. But they continue to be 'unsearchable' (Eph. 3:8) as to their immeasurable dimensions, their breadth and length and depth and height in degrees of fulness (Eph. 3:18-19).

Therefore, after the most diligent search made into these things by the best and wisest of people, there is still and ever will be, new work for the church whilst it is in this world, to inquire further into these treasures. Nothing but the sight of Christ himself in glory can give us a full comprehension of them. Whilst we are here below, no one can exercise their spiritual wisdom and faith about a more noble, useful, and beneficial object. Those who are not only wise for themselves in this but communicate to others the knowledge that they have obtained of these unsearchable treasures, and their insight into them (that they also may be made partakers of them) deserve well in an eminent manner of all that do believe.

OCTOBER 23

Joining Church

Go therefore and make disciples of all nations... teaching them to observe all that I have commanded you.

MATTHEW 28:19-20

It is the duty of everyone who professes faith in Christ Jesus, and takes due care of their own eternal salvation, voluntarily and by their own choice to join themselves to some particular congregation of Christ's institution, for their own spiritual edification, and the right discharge of his commands.

This duty is prescribed to those only who profess faith in Christ Jesus, who own themselves to be his disciples, that call Jesus Lord. For this is the method of the gospel: that first, people by the preaching of it are made disciples, or brought to faith in Christ Jesus, and then are taught to do and observe whatever he commands (Matt. 28:18-20)—first to 'believe' and then to be 'added to the church' (Acts 2:41-47). People must first join themselves to the Lord, or give themselves up to him, before they can give themselves up to the church, according to the mind of Christ (2 Cor. 8:5).

We are not, therefore, concerned at present about those who either do not at all profess faith in Christ Jesus, or else, through ignorance of the fundamental principles of religion and wickedness of life, destroy or utterly render useless that profession. We do not say it is the duty of such persons—that is, their immediate duty—in the state they are in, to join themselves to any church. Indeed, it is the duty of every church to refuse them their communion whilst they abide in that state. There are other duties to be in the first place pressed on them, by which they may be qualified for this.

OCTOBER 24

Gospel Discipline

Am I my brother's keeper?

GENESIS 4:9

Without gospel discipline the duties of church-societies cannot be observed nor the ends of them attained. The neglect, the loss, the abuse of this, is what has ruined the glory of Christian religion in the world, and brought the whole profession of it into confusion. Because of this, the fervency and sincerity of true, evangelical, mutual love have been abated, yea, utterly lost. The continuation of it amongst the generality of Christians is but vainly pretended; little or nothing of the reality of it in its due exercise is found. And this has happened because of the neglect of evangelical discipline in churches, or the turning of it into a worldly domination.

That mutual watch over one another that ought to be in all the members of the church, the principal evidence and fruit of love without pretence, is also lost by this. Most people are rather ready to say, in the spirit and words of Cain, 'Am I my brother's keeper?' (Gen. 4:9) than to attend to the command of the apostle, 'exhort one another every day, as long as it is called "today", that none of you may be hardened by the deceitfulness of sin' (Heb. 3:13), or comply with the command of our Saviour, 'If your brother sins against you, go and tell him his fault, between you and him alone' (Matt. 18:15).

By this means likewise is the purity of communion lost, and those received as principal members of churches who, by all the rules of primitive discipline, ought to be cast out of them. This is to be considered in the choice we are to make of what churches we will join ourselves to.

OCTOBER 25

Justice Demanded

And will not God give justice to his elect, who cry to him day and night? Will he delay long over them? I tell you, he will give justice to them speedily.

LUKE 18:7-8

God manifests himself to be a God who hears prayers, regarding the cries of his poor and distressed witnesses in the world. When the world abounds in provoking sins, especially in blood and persecution, there is a cry to God from those who have suffered, and those who do suffer, in heaven and earth, for vengeance on obstinate, impenitent sinners (see Luke 18:7-8; Rev. 6:10).

The voices of all those who have suffered to death in foregoing ages, for the testimony of Jesus, and are now in heaven in a state of expectancy of complete glory, with all those of them whose sighs and groans under their oppressors do at present ascend to the throne of God, have the sense in them by divine interpretation that punishment should be inflicted on impenitent sinners. This is plainly expressed by our Saviour in that place of the gospel affirming that he will avenge his elect speedily, who cry to him day and night. In this, God will vindicate his glory, as the God who hears prayers.

A sense of this divine truth is a great and effectual means of God's rule in the hearts of people in the world, setting bounds to their lusts, and restraining that abundance of wickedness and villainy which would otherwise take away the distinction, as to sin, between the earth and hell.

OCTOBER 26

Two Sins

My people have committed two evils: they have forsaken me, the fountain of living waters, and hewed out cisterns for themselves, broken cisterns that can hold no water.

JEREMIAH 2:13

Two sins will be the ruin of this nation:

1. The first is *atheism*—an abomination that these parts of the world were unacquainted with until these latter ages. I speak of that which is called practical atheism—when people live and act as if they were influenced by dominant thoughts that there is no God. This exerts itself especially two ways: in cursed oaths and blasphemous swearing by which the highest contempt is cast on the divine name and being; and boldness, confidence, and security in sinning.

2. *The loss of the power of that religion* whose outward form we do retain. We are all Protestants, and will abide to be of the Protestant religion. But are people changed, renewed, converted to God, by the doctrine of this religion? Are they made humble, holy, zealous, fruitful in good works by it? Have they experience of the power of it in their own souls? The glory, the power, the efficacy of it are, if not lost and dead, yet greatly decayed; and an outward carcass of it only abides, in articles of faith and forms of worship. Unless God is pleased by some renewed outpouring of his blessed Spirit from above to revive and reintroduce a spirit of life, holiness, zeal, readiness for the cross, conformity to Christ, and contempt of the world in and among the churches which profess the Protestant religion, he will take away the hedge of his protecting providence, which now for some ages he has kept about them, and leave them for a spoil to their enemies.

OCTOBER 27

Earthly-Minded

To set the mind on the flesh is death, but to set the mind on the Spirit is life and peace.

ROMANS 8:6

There is a way of being earthly minded which consists in an inordinate affection for the things of this world. It is that which is sinful, which ought to be mortified. Yet some who are really and truly spiritually-minded may, for a time at least, be under such an inordinate affection for and care about earthly things that they may be justly said to be earthly-minded. And where it is thus, this grace can never thrive or flourish, it can never advance to any eminent degree.

There are more ways of spiritual and eternal death than one, as well as of natural death. All that die have not the plague, and all that perish eternally are not guilty of the same profligate sins. The covetous are excluded from the kingdom of God no less severely than fornicators, idolaters, adulterers, and thieves (1 Cor. 6:9-10). But there is a degree of being earthly-minded which they suppose their interest, advantages, relations, and occasions of life calls for, which they want to be a little indulged in.

They think well of others who are spiritually-minded in an eminent degree, at least they do so as to the thing itself in general; for when they come to particular instances of this or that person, for the most part they esteem what is beyond their own measure to be little better than pretence. But, in general, to be spiritually minded in an eminent degree, they cannot but esteem it a thing excellent and desirable—but it is for those who are more at leisure than they are; their circumstances and occasions require them to satisfy themselves with an inferior measure.

OCTOBER 28

Spiritually-Minded

For from within, out of the heart of man, come evil thoughts, sexual immorality, theft, murder, adultery, coveting, wickedness, deceit, sensuality, envy, slander, pride, foolishness.

MARK 7:21-22

Our thoughts are like the blossoms on a tree in the spring. You may see a tree in the spring all covered with blossoms, so that nothing else of it appears. Multitudes of them fall off and come to nothing. Often, where there are most blossoms there is least fruit. But yet there is no fruit, be it of what sort it will, good or bad, but it comes in and from some of those blossoms. People's minds are covered with thoughts, as a tree with blossoms. Most of them fall off, vanish, and come to nothing, end in vanity; and sometimes, where the mind most abounds with them, there is the least fruit; the sap of the mind is wasted and consumed in them. But there is no fruit which actually we bring forth, be it good or bad, but it proceeds from some of these thoughts.

'As a man thinks in his heart, so is he' (Prov. 23:7 KJV). Ordinarily, voluntary thoughts are the best measure and indication of the frame of our minds. As the nature of the soil is judged by the grass which it brings forth, so may the disposition of the heart by the predominance of voluntary thoughts; they are the original actings of the soul, the way by which the heart puts forth and empties the treasure that is in it, the waters that first rise and flow from that fountain.

Every man's heart is his treasury, and the treasure that is in it is either good or evil, as our Saviour tells us. The more you spend of the treasure of your heart in any kind, the more will you abound in treasure of the same kind.

OCTOBER 29

Mind Delight

Set your minds on things that are above, not on things that are on earth.

COLOSSIANS 3:2

The objects of our daily thoughts and meditations are to be: the glory of his presence, as God and man eternally united; the discharge of his mediatory office, as he is at the right hand of God; the glory of his present acting for the church, as he is the minister of the sanctuary and the true tabernacle which God has fixed and not people; the love, power, and efficacy of his intercession, by which he takes care for the accomplishment of the salvation of the church; and the approach of his glorious coming for judgment.

Let us not mistake ourselves. To be spiritually-minded is not to have the notion and knowledge of spiritual things in our minds; it is not to be constant, no, nor to abound, in the performance of duties: both of which may be where there is no grace in the heart at all. It is to have our minds really exercised with delight about heavenly things, the things that are above, especially Christ himself as at the right hand of God.

So think of eternal things as continually to lay them in the balance against all the sufferings of this life. It is very probable that we shall yet suffer more than we have done. Those who have gone before us have done so; it is foretold in the Scripture that if we want to live a godly life in Christ Jesus we must do so (2 Tim. 3:12).

OCTOBER 30

Glorious Worship

Since we have confidence to enter the holy places by the blood of Jesus, by the new and living way that he opened for us through the curtain, that is, through his flesh, and since we have a great priest over the house of God, let us draw near with a true heart in full assurance of faith.

HEBREWS 10:19-22

All light into the true glory of evangelical worship, all perceptions of it, all experience of its power, was, amongst the most, lost in the world. Those who had the conduct of religion could discern no glory in these things, nor obtain any experience of their power. What, then, shall they do? They set their inventions to work to find out ceremonies, vestments, gestures, ornaments, music, altars, images, paintings, with prescriptions of great bodily veneration. This pageantry they call the beauty, the order, the glory, of divine worship.

The beauty and glory which carving, and painting, and embroidered vestures, and musical incantations, and postures of veneration give to divine service, they can see and feel, and, in their own imagination, are sensibly excited to devotion by them.

But instead of representing the true glory of the worship of the gospel, in which it excels that under the Old Testament, they have rendered it altogether inglorious in comparison to it; for all the ceremonies and ornaments which they have invented for that end come unspeakably short, for beauty, order, and glory, of what was appointed by God himself in the temple—scarce equalling what was among the pagans.

OCTOBER 31

Protestant Religion

I have applied all these things to myself and Apollos for your benefit, brothers, that you may learn by us not to go beyond what is written.

1 CORINTHIANS 4:6

The Protestant religion may be considered either as it is religion in general—that is, Christian religion—or as it is distinct from and opposite to another pretended profession of the same religion, because of which it is called Protestant.

In the first sense of it, it derives its original from Christ and his apostles. What they taught to be believed, what they commanded to be observed in the worship of God—all of it, and nothing but that—is the Protestant religion. Nothing else belongs to it; in nothing else is it concerned. These, therefore, are the principles of the religion of Protestants, into which their faith and obedience are resolved:

1. What was revealed to the church by the Lord Christ and his apostles is the whole of that religion which God will and does accept.

2. So far as is needful to the faith, obedience, and eternal salvation of the church, what they taught, revealed, and commanded is contained in the Scriptures of the New Testament, witnessed to and confirmed by those of the Old.

3. All that is required of us that we may please God, be accepted with him, and come to the eternal enjoyment of him, is, that we truly believe what is so revealed and taught, yielding sincere obedience to what is commanded in the Scriptures.

If in anything it is found to deviate from this—they are ready to renounce it. Here they live and die; from this foundation they will not depart: this is their religion.

NOVEMBER

This month, we will be listening in to sermons and talks which Owen gave throughout the reign of Charles II. During this period, Owen was excluded from ministry in the national church, but he was able still (despite official opposition) to pastor a small Congregational gathering in London. To them he preached on a variety of biblical texts, and many of these sermons were recorded for posterity by Sir John Hartopp MP, a member of the congregation skilled in shorthand.

When Sir John's daughter died in infancy, Owen wrote to his wife, Elizabeth. The letter may reveal a little of how Owen himself dealt with the death of ten of his own children in infancy. He wrote: 'Every work of God is good; the Holy One in the midst of us will do no iniquity; and all things shall work together for good to those who love him, even those things which at present are not joyous, but grievous… Your dear infant is in the eternal enjoyment of the fruits of all our prayers; for the covenant of God is ordered in all things, and sure. We shall go to her; she shall not return to us… But this I will beg of God for you both that you may not faint in this day of trial—that you may have a clear view of those spiritual and temporal mercies with which you are yet entrusted (all undeserved)—that sorrow of the world may not so overtake your hearts as to prevent you carrying out any duties, to grieve the Spirit, to prejudice your lives… God in Christ will be better to you than ten children, and will so preserve your remnant, and to add to them, as shall be for his glory and your comfort.'

Owen also delivered talks to church meetings on various practical cases of conscience, which we will also read from in the following extracts.

NOVEMBER 1

Not Forsaken

For Israel and Judah have not been forsaken by their God, the LORD of hosts, but the land of the Chaldeans is full of guilt against the Holy One of Israel.

JEREMIAH 51:5

From the height of profaneness and atheism, through the filthiness of sensuality and uncleanness, down to the lowest oppression and cheating, the land is filled with all sorts of sin.

But England is not yet utterly forsaken by the Lord its God, the Lord of hosts, though the land be filled with sin.

God has reserved a remnant among us who make use of this space and season to apply themselves to the throne of grace, and to cry mightily for mercy. God has not taken his Holy Spirit from us. God has not said, by any open work or secret intimation of providence, 'Pray no more for this people; my heart shall not be toward them.' He has not said so, and, therefore, there are yet among us precious souls who do lift up prayers to God night and day, not only for themselves and families, not only for the church of God, but for this poor land of our birth.

We pray that, if it is the will of God, we may not see it soaked in blood—that God would not come forth to destroy it with a curse—that God would pity, and spare, and have mercy upon it—that he would not make it an 'Akeldama'—a field of blood (Acts 1:19). There are many cries to God to this purpose. So there are some who make use of this space and season God has given us.

NOVEMBER 2

The Devil's Misery

You believe that God is one; you do well. Even the demons believe—and shudder!

JAMES 2:19

Faith does not consist solely in the assent of the mind to the truth of the promises, or of any promise. When one affirms anything to us, and we say we believe them—that is, that the thing they speak is true—then there is this assent of the mind. Without this, there is no faith. But this alone is not the faith we speak of. This alone and solitary the devils have, and cannot choose but have it, James 2:19. They believe that which makes them tremble, on the authority of God who reveals it.

But you will say, 'The devil believes only the threats of God—that which makes him tremble; and so his belief is not a general assent, but partial—and is thereby distinguished from our assent; which is to all that God has revealed, and especially the promises.'

I answer: The devil believes the promises no less than he does the threats of God; that is, that they are true, and shall be accomplished. It is part of his misery, that he cannot but believe them. And the promises of God are as much suited to make him tremble as his threatenings. The first promise to us was couched in a threatening to him (Gen. 3:15). And there is no promise in which a threatening to him is not couched. Every word concerning Christ, or grace by him, speaks his downfall and ruin. Indeed, his destruction lies more in promises than threats. Promises are what weaken him daily, and give him a continual foretaste of his approaching destruction.

NOVEMBER 3

Loving Father

The LORD, the LORD, a God merciful and gracious, slow to anger, and abounding in steadfast love and faithfulness, keeping steadfast love for thousands, forgiving iniquity and transgression and sin.

EXODUS 34:6-7

Let us consider God himself, even the Father; and that declaration of his love, kindness, tenderness, readiness, and willingness to receive poor believers, which he has made of himself in Christ Jesus. According as our apprehensions are of him, and his heart towards us, so will the settlement of our souls in cleaving to him by believing be.

We are, amongst people, free and easy with those whom we know to be of a kind, loving, compassionate disposition; but full of doubts, fears, and jealousies when we have to deal with those who are morose, peevish, and difficult. Entertaining hard thoughts of God, ends perpetually in contrivances to fly and keep at a distance from him, and to employ ourselves about anything in the world rather than to be treating and conversing with him. What delight can anyone take in him whom they conceive to be always furious, wrathful, ready to destroy? Or, what comfortable expectation can anyone have from such a one?

Consider, then, in some particulars, what God declares of himself, and see, in the exercising of your thoughts on this, whether it is not effectual to engage your hearts to steadfastness in believing the promises, and closing with the Son of his love tendered in them.

NOVEMBER 4

Greater Glory

We are God's house, if indeed we hold fast our confidence and our boasting in our hope.

HEBREWS 3:6

Whilst the first tabernacle was standing, before Christ by his death had removed it and the worship that accompanied it, there was no immediate admission unto God. The way into the holy of holies not made with hands, which we now make use of in gospel worship, was not yet laid open, but the worshippers were kept at a great distance, making their application to God by outward, carnal ordinances. The tabernacle being removed, now a way is made, and an entrance is given to the worshippers, into the holy of holies, in their worship. How is that obtained? By what means? It is 'by the blood of Jesus Christ'—by the rending of his flesh (Heb. 10:19-20).

That fear and bondage in which people were kept under the law is now removed, and in its place a spirit of children going to their father with reverent boldness, is given to us. This, I say, adds to the glory, beauty, and excellency of gospel worship. There is not the meanest believer but, with their most broken prayers and supplications, has an immediate access to God, and that as a Father; nor the most despised church of saints on the earth but it comes with its worship into the glorious presence of God himself.

In the worship of the gospel, the saints have an access through Christ unto God himself in their own persons, and that continually. The Lord Jesus sees more beauty and glory in the weakest assemblies of his saints, coming together in his name, and acted and guided in his worship and ways by his Spirit, than ever was in all the worship of Solomon's temple when it was in its glory.

NOVEMBER 5

Spiritual Power

'And as for me, this is my covenant with them,' says the LORD: 'My Spirit that is upon you, and my words that I have put in your mouth, shall not depart out of your mouth, or out of the mouth of your offspring, or out of the mouth of your children's offspring,' says the LORD, 'from this time forth and forevermore.'

ISAIAH 59:21

The Lord Jesus Christ has promised to send his Spirit to believers, to enable them, both for matter and manner, in the performance of every duty required in the word (Isa. 59:21). He will give his word and Spirit. The promise of the one and the other is of equal extent and latitude. Whatever God proposes in his word to be believed, or requires to be done—*that* he gives his Spirit to us for, to enable us to believe and do accordingly.

There is neither promise nor precept, but the Spirit is given to enable believers to answer the mind of God in them; nor is the Spirit given to enable us for any duty, but what is in the word required. Those who require duties which the word enjoins not, have need of other assistances than what the Spirit of grace will afford them; and those who pretend to be led by the Spirit beyond the bounds of the word, need to provide themselves with another gospel.

It is the Holy Spirit who works in believers faith, love, delight, fervency, watchfulness, perseverance—all those graces that give the soul communion with God in his worship—and in Christ renders their prayers effectual.

NOVEMBER 6

Pressing On

Do you not know that in a race all the runners run, but only one receives the prize? So run that you may obtain it.

1 CORINTHIANS 9:24

If our obedience is to be 'walking with God', it is required that it be a constant, progressive motion towards a mark before us. Walking is a constant progress. The one who is walking towards a place that they have in their eye may stumble sometimes and, perhaps, also fall. But yet, whilst their design and endeavour lies towards the place aimed at—whilst they lie not still when they fall, but get up again and press forward—they are still, from the chief aim of their acting, said to walk that way.

But now, let this person sit down, or lie down in the way, and you cannot say they are walking; much less can you say that they are walking that way, if they walk quite contrary. So is it in that obedience which is walking with God. 'I press on,' says the apostle, 'toward the goal' (Phil. 3:14); 'I follow after it' (3:12). And he bids us 'so run that you may obtain the prize' (1 Cor. 9:24).

There is a constant pressing forwards required in our obedience. David says, 'I follow hard after God' (Ps. 63:8 KJV). The enjoyment of God in Christ is the mark before us; our walking is a constant pressing towards it. To fall into or perhaps fall under a temptation, hinders not but that a person may still be said to be walking, though they make no great speed, and though they defile themselves by their fall. But to sit down and give up—to engage in a way, a course of sin—this is that which is called walking contrary to God, not with him (Lev. 26:40).

NOVEMBER 7

True Sight

For the LORD sees not as man sees: man looks on the outward appearance, but the LORD looks on the heart.

1 SAMUEL 16:7

God does not judge as people judge. People judge according to the seeing of the eye, and the hearing of the ear; but God searches the heart. Little do we know what is in the heart of people—what transactions there are or have been between God and them, which, if they were drawn forth, as they shall be one day, the righteousness of God in his procedure would shine as the sun. Rest on this: we know much less of the matter on the account of which God judges, than we do of the rule by which he judges. Most things are to him otherwise than to us.

God is the great Judge of all the world—not of this or that particular place; and so he disposes of all as may tend to the good of the whole and his glory in the universality of things. Our thoughts are bounded—much more our observation and knowledge—within a very narrow compass. That may seem deformed to us which, when it lies under an eye that at once has a view of the whole, is full of beauty and order.

If someone was able to see at once only one small part of a goodly statue, they might think it a deformed piece; whilst the one who sees it as a whole is assured of its due proportion and comeliness. All things in all places, of the ages past and to come, lie at once naked before God. He disposes of them so that, in their intertwining and answer one to another, they shall be full of order—which is properly righteousness.

NOVEMBER 8

Walk Humbly

He has told you, O man, what is good; and what does the LORD require of you but to do justice, and to love kindness, and to walk humbly with your God?

MICAH 6:8

This is the import of the expression at the beginning of the verse, 'What does the Lord your God require of you?' You may cast about in your thoughts to other things, in which you may be more delighted, or, as you suppose, may be more acceptable to God. Be not mistaken; this is the great thing that he requires of you: to walk humbly with him.

Everyone is most concerned in that which is their great purpose; the bringing about of that is of most importance to them; the great exercise of their thoughts is whether they shall succeed in this or not. The chief end of believers is the glory of God. This, I say, is so, or ought to be so. For this purpose they were made, redeemed to this purpose, and purchased to be his own people. Now, the Scripture everywhere teaches, that the great means of our glorifying God, is by our humble walking with him.

You may have many thoughts that God is glorified by works of miracles, and the like, amazing and dazzling the eyes of the world. Be it so; but in the most eminent manner, it is by your bearing fruit (John 15:8). You know the general rule that our Saviour gives his followers: it is from our good works that people give glory to God (Matt. 5:16). Walking according to this rule, we adorn the doctrine of the gospel in all things.

Christ Pleading

And they shall know that I am the LORD. I have not said in vain that I would do this evil to them.

EZEKIEL 6:10

It may be observed, that in such seasons when Christ has any great and notable work to bring forth in the world, he does by his Spirit deal with the hearts and consciences of the most wicked and vile; which, when the secrets of all hearts shall be discovered at the last day, will exceedingly exalt the glory of his wisdom, patience, goodness, holiness, and righteousness. So did he with those before the flood, as is evident from Genesis 6:3. When an utter destruction was to come, he says, his Spirit shall strive with them no more—that is, about their sin and rebellion.

That this Spirit was the Spirit of Christ, and that the work of dealing with these ungodly men was the work of Christ, and that it was a fruit of long-suffering, Peter declares in 1 Peter 3:18-20. And if he deals thus with a perishing world, by a work that perishes also—how much more does he do an effectual work upon the hearts of his own! It is the Spirit that speaks to the churches in all their trials (Rev. 2:7).

By this means, Christ pleads with his saints; secretly and powerfully judging their lusts, corruptions, failings—consuming and burning them up. He first, by frequent motions and instructions, gives them no rest in any unequal path; then reveals to them the beauty of holiness, the excellence of the love of Christ, the vanity and folly of everything that has interrupted their communion with him. Thus, he fills them with godly sorrow, renunciation of sin, and cleaving to God—which is the very promise that we have (Ezek. 6:10).

NOVEMBER 10

Heresies

I hear that there are divisions among you. And I believe it in part, for there must be factions among you in order that those who are genuine among you may be recognised.

1 Corinthians 11:18-19

Satan pours out a flood of abominations on purpose to bring an ill report upon the truth and light that is sent out by Christ. The great prejudice against truth in the world is that it is new. 'He seems to be a preacher of foreign divinities' they say of Paul, because he preached Jesus and the resurrection (Acts 17:18). To increase this prejudice, the devil sends forth his darkness. This enables the world to load the truth itself with reproaches.

God permits this to be so to test those who are careless in their profession of faith. There must be heresies, that the approved may be recognised (1 Cor. 11:19). Most people are apt to content themselves with a lazy profession. They will hold to the truth whilst nothing appears but truth. Let error come with the same pretences and advantage—they are for that also. Now, God delights to judge such persons even in this world, to manifest that they are not of the truth—that they never received it or loved it. And he sifts and tries the elect by it.

God also permits it, to set a greater lustre and esteem upon truth. Truth, when it is sought after, when it is contended for, when it is experienced in its power and efficacy, is rendered glorious and beautiful; and all these, with innumerable other advantages, it has by the competition that is set up against it by error.

NOVEMBER 11

Self-righteousness

When you have done all that you were commanded, say, 'We are unworthy servants; we have only done what was our duty.'

LUKE 17:10

Take heed of a degeneration into self-righteousness. Intentions to holiness have more than once been ruined by Satan through this deceit; they have set out upon conviction, and ended in Pharisaism.

Some, really convinced of the vanity of an empty profession and of boasting of saintship upon the account of faith and light without holiness and godliness, fall to disputing and contending for the absolute necessity of holiness and strict obedience, of fruitfulness and good works. But Satan here gets an advantage from people's natural spirits, their heats and contentions, and insinuates an inherent righteousness, on account of which we should expect to be accepted by God for the justification of our persons. So he prevailed upon the Galatians.

Self-righteousness prevails from a secret self-pleasing, that is apt to grow on people's minds from a dedication in the performance of duties. This is what the Heart-searcher aims to prevent in his command, that 'when you have done all that you were commanded, say, "We are unworthy servants; we have only done what was our duty"' (Luke 17:10). That is, in the secrets of our hearts to sit down in a sense of our own worthlessness.

'God, I thank you I am not like other people' (Luke 18:11) is apt to creep into the heart in a strict course of duties. This quickly produces the deadly, poisonous effect of spiritual pride; which is the greatest assimilation to the nature of the devil that the nature of mankind is capable of.

NOVEMBER 12

Reformation

Since all these things are thus to be dissolved, what sort of people ought you to be in lives of holiness and godliness, waiting for and hastening the coming of the day of God.

2 PETER 3:11-12

Reformation is the great thing that we have been talking of for many years. The more that light for it has broken forth amongst us, the more unreformed has the body of the people been. The light of truth has been accompanied with so many scandals in some, and with so little power and evidence in the most, that prejudices have been strengthened in the minds of people against all that has been pretended or professed.

We are contemptible to the nation, in our pressing after reformation whilst we are divided amongst ourselves. We are conformable to the world, whilst we proclaim our un-mortified lusts, pride, covetousness, ambition, revenge, self-seeking. Would all the people of God stir up themselves to show forth the power of that faith and life they have received, and so take away advantage from stubborn opposers of the gospel, and give an eminent example to others, who now abhor them on the account of many prejudices that they have taken, the nations would be more awakened to their duty than now they are.

Were we agreed and united on this principle, that we would jointly and severally make this our design, what work might be wrought in families, councils, counties, cities! Now, reformation is acknowledged to be the means, the only means, of the preservation of a nation, and this the only means of that.

NOVEMBER 13

Unashamed

For whoever is ashamed of me and of my words, of him will the Son of Man be ashamed when he comes in his glory and the glory of the Father and of the holy angels.

LUKE 9:26

Not to be ashamed of the gospel of Christ, but to own it, avow it, and profess it as a thing holy and honourable in all the duties it requires, against all reproaches and persecutions that are in the world, is the indispensable duty of every one who desires to be saved by the gospel.

Jesus said, 'For whoever is ashamed of me and of my words, of him will the Son of Man be ashamed when he comes in his glory and the glory of the Father and of the holy angels' (Luke 9:26). The whole sum of the gospel is comprised in this—the person of Christ and the words of Christ. The person of Christ takes up the whole work of the promise; the words take up all the commands and institutions of Christ. We have heard before what it is to be ashamed of them. And what shall be the end of such? The Son of man shall be ashamed of them, when he shall come in his own glory, and his Father's glory.

There can be no greater weight put upon words, to strike awe and dread into people's minds. The Son of Man, who loved us, redeemed us, gave his life for us, shall come again, though now he be absent and we think things are put off for a season. And then he will inquire into our posture towards the gospel. At which time he will appear in all his own glory, the glory given him on the account of his doing his Father's will, and the glory of his Father and the holy angels. Certainly, we should be extremely troubled then to hear Christ say, 'I am ashamed of you.'

NOVEMBER 14

Power of God

I am not ashamed of the gospel, for it is the power of God for salvation to everyone who believes.

ROMANS 1:16

The gospel is the instrument God puts forth to effect his great and mighty works in the world. Preaching is looked upon as a very foolish thing in the world. 'We preach Christ crucified... folly to the Gentiles' (1 Cor. 1:23). But God has chosen this foolish thing to confound the wise. And though the preachers of it are very weak, mere earthen vessels, God has chosen this weak thing to bring to nought things that are strong and mighty—the things of this world.

Therefore it is called 'The word of God's grace, which is able to build us up, and to give us an inheritance among all those who are sanctified' (Acts 20:32). The plain preaching of it has this power upon people's souls, to convince them, convert them, draw them home to God; to expose them to all troubles in this world; to make them let go their reputation and livelihood, and expose themselves even to death itself. It is the power of God to these ends and purposes; God has made it his instrument for that end.

If it were the power of God to give peace and prosperity to a nation, or to heal the sick, no one need or ought to be ashamed of it. But to be the power of God for so excellent an end as the eternal salvation of people's souls, makes it much more glorious.

It would be sad for people to keep corn from the poor, or medicine from the sick who lie dying; but to keep the word of God from people's souls that they might be saved—Lord, lay it not to the charge of any!

NOVEMBER 15

Amazing Love

And above all these put on love, which binds everything together in perfect harmony.

COLOSSIANS 3:14

Love, and its exercise, is the principal grace and duty that is required among, and expected from, the saints of God, especially as they are engaged in church-fellowship.

The world neither has nor knows what this love is. Variance, strife, and wrath entered by sin; for when we fell away from the love of God, and from his love to us, it is no wonder if we fell into a hatred and variance among ourselves. The love of God was originally, in the state of innocency, the bond of perfection: when that was broken, all the creation fell into disorder—all mankind, in particular, into that state described by the apostle: 'passing our days in malice and envy, hated by others and hating one another' (Titus 3:3).

There is carnal and natural love still in the world, that follows necessarily upon natural relations; the same is in some degree in brutes themselves. There is also a love that arises from a society in sin, in pleasure—from a similar sense of humour in conversation, or of political goals—to which heads you may reduce all the love in the world. But all these are utter strangers to this evangelical love. And therefore, when it was brought to light by the gospel, there was nothing that amazed the heathen world so much as to see this new love among Christians. It was even a proverb among them: 'See how they love one another!' To see persons of different sorts, different nations, tempers, degrees, high and low, rich and poor, all knit together in love, was the great thing that amazed the heathen world.

NOVEMBER 16

New Love

A new commandment I give to you, that you love one another:
just as I have loved you, you also are to love one another.

JOHN 13:34

The reason why this was a new commandment was because there was no quickening, enlivening example of it to express the power of love, under the Old Testament. This was reserved for Christ. He comes and gives that glorious instance of love, in his condescension in all that he did, and in all that he suffered. He shows that there was something in love that they never before had an instance of in the world. Consequently, the command for love is this: 'Have this mind among yourselves, which is yours in Christ Jesus' (Phil. 2:5)—'just as I have loved you, you also are to love one another' (John 13:34). And then it is a new commandment indeed, which it was not before.

'By this,' says he, 'all people shall know that you are my disciples: if the great example I have set you, the great command I have given you, and the great work I came into the world about, was to renew love; by love people will know that you are my disciples, and not else.' We have no other way to evidence ourselves to be disciples of Christ. People's gifts and wisdom will not do it; if there is no love, the world has no reason to conclude that we are the disciples of Jesus Christ.

It is love in which the communion of saints principally consists. There is great talk about communion of saints and certainly, it is a great thing. We may observe it had a place in all the ancient creeds of the church: where they profess to believe in God, in Christ, and in the Holy Spirit, they profess also to believe the communion of saints, which shows it to be a thing of great importance.

NOVEMBER 17

National Salvation

Save, O LORD, for the godly one is gone; for the faithful have vanished from among the children of man.

PSALM 12:1

When the good are very few, and the bad are very bad, inevitable destruction lies at the door of that place or nation. If either of these are otherwise, there is yet hope. If there had been but ten good men in Sodom, it would have been spared (Gen. 18:32). If the sin of the Amorites had not been come to the full, they would not have been ruined (Gen. 15:16). If the good, therefore, are not very few, or the bad very bad, there is yet hope; but where both concur in a professing nation, as in this, which was the visible church of God, unavoidable destruction is at the door; there is neither hope nor recovery, and therefore, they that endeavour to make people good, to increase the number of the good, they not only endeavour to save their own souls, but they endeavour to save the nation from ruin.

And we will place our plea and our cause there—in which we are engaged in this world against the world and those that do reproach us—that our design is to save the nation as far as we are able. For it is to increase the number of the good, to convert people to God, the consequence of which is to preserve the nation. And it will at last be found, that those who are useful in this, do more for the preservation of the nation than armies or navies can do. But when the prophet says, 'The godly has perished from the earth, and there is no one upright among mankind' (Micah 7:2), it is hyperbole, intimating that there are but few that are either good or upright.

NOVEMBER 18

Given Up

God gave them up in the lusts of their hearts to impurity.

ROMANS 1:24

The first thing God does when he hardens people's hearts in punishment is to give them up to their own lusts. It is directly expressed, 'Therefore God gave them up in the lusts of their hearts' (Rom. 1:24). When God leaves people and gives them up to pursue their own lusts with delight and greediness, then he is hardening them. And this is a visible judgment of God at this day: he takes away shame, fear, all restraint and disadvantages, and gives people up to their hearts' lusts.

The second thing is, that God gives people up to Satan, to blind them, darken them, harden them; for he is 'the god of this world, who blinds the eyes of people' (2 Cor. 4:4). The principal way by which he works at this day is by being a lying spirit in the mouth of the false prophets as it was in the business of Ahab. When Satan went to seduce Ahab to go up to Ramoth-gilead, he did it by being a lying spirit in the mouths of the false prophets (1 Kings 22). God is visibly at work in the world with this judgment, giving people up to Satan, acting in the mouths of the false prophets, who cry, 'Peace, peace!' to all sorts of sinners, when God speaks not one word of peace.

The third way by which God judicially gives people up to hardness of heart is by supplying them in his providence with opportunities to draw out their lusts. They shall have opportunity for them. It is commonly given for one of the darkest dispensations of divine providence towards people, when it orders things so that they shall have opportunities to accomplish their lusts and go on in their ways, administered to them.

NOVEMBER 19

Ancient Battle

I will put enmity between you and the woman, and between your offspring and her offspring; he shall bruise your head, and you shall bruise his heel.

GENESIS 3:15

There are these four things in this promise:

1. That there shall always be a two-fold seed in the world: the seed of the serpent, and the seed of the woman.

2. That these two seeds shall always be at enmity. There shall be an everlasting conflict, from the entrance of sin to the end of it—and such an enmity as shall be carried on by the highest and most severe warfare. The enmity is spiritual, but the warfare is often outward. The first manifestation of this enmity was in blood. Cain killed Abel. Why? Because he was of the evil one. And so it has been carried on by blood from that day to this.

3. That either seed has a leader: there is 'he and you', that is, Christ and Satan. Christ is the leader of the seed of the woman, the captain and head of it in this great conflict; Satan, as he was the head of the apostasy from God, continues the head of his seed, the generation of vipers, to try out the contest with Christ unto the end.

4. The victory shall always be to the seed of the woman. It is said, indeed, 'you shall bruise his heel'—Christ's heel, in his sufferings, both in his own person and those of the church. But on the other hand, it is said likewise, 'He shall bruise your head'—break your power and strength—conquer you.

This was the foundation of the Old Testament. And though things were often brought to great distress—sometimes by apostasy and sometimes by persecution—yet this promise carried it, and delivered over the church safe into the hand of Christ.

NOVEMBER 20

Mourning

Pass through the city, through Jerusalem, and put a mark on the foreheads of the men who sigh and groan over all the abominations that are committed in it.

EZEKIEL 9:4

We ought greatly to mourn for the public abominations of the world and of the land in which we live. In Ezekiel 9, God sends out his judgments and destroys the city; but before, he sets a mark upon the foreheads of the men who sigh for all the abominations that are done in the midst of it. I would only observe this, that such only are the servants of God, let people profess what they will, 'who mourn for the abominations that are done in the land'. The mourners in the one place are the servants of God in the other.

And truly, brethren, we are certainly to blame in this matter. We have been almost well-contented that people should be as wicked as they want, and we sit still and see what will come of it. Christ has been dishonoured, the Spirit of God blasphemed, and God provoked against the land of our birth, and yet we have not been affected with these things. I can truly say in sincerity, I bless God, I have sometimes laboured with my own heart about it. But I am afraid we all of us come exceedingly short of our duty in this matter.

'My eyes shed streams of tears,' says the psalmist, 'because people do not keep your law' (Ps. 119:136). Horrible profanation of the name of God, horrible abominations which our eyes have seen and our ears heard, and yet our hearts have been unaffected with them! According to the Scripture rule, there is no one of us who can have any evidence that we shall escape outward judgments that God will bring for these abominations, if we have not been mourners for them.

NOVEMBER 21

Preparing for Death

So teach us to number our days that we may get a heart of wisdom.

PSALM 90:12

Let us take heed of being surprised with death. We know not how soon we may be called on by death. It may not come in an ordinary course, by long sickness, and give us warning; nor when we have lived all the years of our life which are 'threescore years and ten' as the psalmist speaks (Ps. 90:10); we may be surprised with it when we look not for it. Let this, then, be fixed upon our minds, that whatever our state and condition is—some are strong, young, and healthy, and some of us are old and feeble, going out of the world—there are none of us but may be surprised with it.

There is no maintaining of a quick, holy, lively frame of mind but by a diligent contemplation of things that are above. Our wisdom in this case is to labour to keep up this spiritual view of eternal things, in a holy contemplation of and cleaving to them in our affections, or death will be surprising.

Death is a messenger sent of God; he knocks at the door, and what comes he for? To perfect the frame you are in, that you may see heavenly things more clearly. He is come to free you from that deadness you are burdened with, that darkness you are entangled with, and to set you at perfect liberty in the enjoyment of those things your souls cleave to. How, then, can your souls but bid this messenger welcome? Pray, then, that God would keep up your souls, by fresh supplies of his Spirit, to a constant view of heavenly things.

NOVEMBER 22

Offended!

Woe to the world for temptations to sin! For it is necessary that temptations come, but woe to the one by whom the temptation comes!

MATTHEW 18:7

Be not afraid of the great multiplication of scandalous temptations at this day in the world. The truths of the gospel and holiness have broken through a thousand times more offences. They have broken through heresies and blasphemies, and poverty and persecution. God has still preserved his people, who have broken through and got the conquest over the greatest temptations.

People are offended by the cross of Christ, by the poverty of Christ, by people that have preached the gospel, and by those who have professed it. They are offended by innumerable swarms of blasphemous heretics who have professed the name of Christ from the beginning, and by false reports that have been cast on Christians (who are reported generally throughout the world to be a vile generation of wicked people). The truth and grace of God have conquered all these offences, and prevailed over them all, and will do so again if we keep close to truth and the power of religion.

NOVEMBER 23

Stormy Seas

But we are not of those who shrink back and are destroyed,
but of those who have faith and preserve their souls.

HEBREWS 10:39

There will, even after sincere believing and closing with Christ, be many a heavy charge brought against a soul from the law, and the guilt of sin in the conscience. Now, in such a case, the inquiry is, what does the soul abide by when it is shaken?

If someone goes only on mere convictions, on such shaking impressions of the guilt of sin, they will be very ready and inclined in their own mind to tack about to some other relief. They put out fair for their voyage—the storm arises—the ship will not carry them—they must tack about for another harbour. I have known it so with some, and experienced, when the wind has set very strong that way with myself—when the guilt of sin has been charged with all its circumstances—the soul has been hardly able to keep its hold, but resolved all the same that 'I will trust to Christ'.

But sometimes the soul comes about to self again—'I must remedy this, and bring relief for this myself; I cannot abide by it, and live wholly upon Christ; but when the storm is over, then I will set out to sea again.' I say, this is no good sign to me when things are so; but when a soul in all those charges that sometimes come upon it abides the issue and says, 'Here I will trust on Christ, let the worst come upon me!'—this I call a permanence in our choice against opposition. I hope you have experience of it.

NOVEMBER 24

Church Society

*Let us then with confidence draw near to the throne of grace,
that we may receive mercy and find grace to help in time of need.*

HEBREWS 4:16

How cold we are grown in valuing the ordinances of Christ, and the society of his people for edification! How little is the church society upon our hearts, which some of us remember when it was the very joy of our souls! Truly, we have reason to lift up our cry to God, that he would return and visit the churches, and pour out a new, fresh, reviving spirit upon them, that we fall not under the power of these decays till we come to formality, and God withdraws himself from us, and leaves us; which he seems to be at the very point of doing.

So, brethren, let us remember our own church, that God would in a special manner revive the spirit of life, power, and holiness among us; that he would be pleased to help the officers of the church to discharge their duty, and not suffer them to fall under any decay of grace or gifts, unfitting of them to the discharge of their office to the edification of the church. Let us pray that he would help them also to beware and take heed of formality in the exercise of gifts in their administration; and that he would take care of us, since we are apt to fall under these things. Let us pray that we may be moved by the Spirit of God, and enlivened by the grace of God, in all things we do.

Have any of us any particular occasions in reference to temptations, trials, and troubles? We may bear it upon our hearts to the Lord this day. The Lord help us to know the plague of our own hearts, and to be enabled to plead with the Lord for grace and mercy to help us in every time of need!

NOVEMBER 25

Don't Drift

Therefore we must pay much closer attention to what we have heard, lest we drift away from it.

HEBREWS 2:1

Have a care that your head in notion and your tongue in talk do not too quickly empty your hearts of truth. We are apt to lay it up in our heads by notions, and bring it forth in talk, and not let it be in our hearts; this weakens spiritual life greatly. You hear the word preached; and it is of great importance what account we shall give of the word that has been preached to you. For we who preach must give an account of our preaching, and so must you of what you hear; many a good word is spoken, truly, and yet we see but little fruit of it. And the reason of this is that some, when they hear it, take no farther regard of it, but 'let it slip' as the apostle says and drift away.

It is not the treachery of our memories, but of our hearts and affections, that makes the heart like a broken vessel. The word slips away when your affections are only exercised in a carnal way; it quickly finds its way to depart from the heart that gives it no better hospitality. We talk away a sermon and the sense of it, which robs us both of the sermon and the fruit of it. A person hears a good word of truth, and, instead of taking the power of it into their heart, they take the notion of it into their mind, and are satisfied with that. But this is not the way to thrive.

God grant that we may never preach to you anything but what we may labour to have an experience of the power of in our own hearts. May we profit ourselves by the word with which we design to profit others! And I pray God grant that you also may have some profit by the word dispensed to you.

NOVEMBER 26

Contemplation

We all, with unveiled face, beholding the glory of the Lord, are being transformed into the same image from one degree of glory to another.

2 CORINTHIANS 3:18

There is an abiding with Christ in our minds. Now this, to me, is in contemplation and thoughts of him night and day. 'On my bed by night I sought him whom my soul loves' says the spouse (Song 3:1). It is to consider very much the person of Christ, to contemplate him as vested with his glorious office, and as entrusted and designed by the Father to this work. 'We all,' says the apostle, 'with unveiled face, beholding the glory of the Lord, are being transformed into the same image from one degree of glory to another' (2 Cor. 3:18). My brethren, that which you and I are aiming at is to be 'transformed into the same image', that is, into the image and likeness of the glory of God in Christ.

I dare boldly say, for those of us who have reason to have daily apprehensions of our going out of the world, and leaving this state of things, that we have no greater desire nor is there anything more frequent in our minds than this, that we may be more and more changed into that image before we go out of this world. We are looking for perfection in likeness to Christ. Aged Christians especially will bear witness, that there is nothing now we long for more than to be more and more changed into the image and likeness of Christ.

This is the advice I would give you who are aged Christians and not likely to continue long in this world: exercise yourselves in immediate contemplations on Christ. All the teachings you have had from ministers, the principal end of them has been to enable you to this.

NOVEMBER 27

Inclinations

But each person is tempted when he is lured and enticed by his own desire.

JAMES 1:14

The inclination of constitution gives particular advantages to particular sins. Some may be very much inclined to envy; some to wrath and passion, and others to sensual sins—gluttony, drunkenness, uncleanness. It has been much from the fallacy of the devil that people have been apt to plead constitution and the inclination of their constitution as excuses for their sin. 'I am apt to be passionate in my nature,' says one; 'I am cheerful,' says another, 'and love company.' They make their natural inclinations to be a cover and excuse for their sin.

If grace does not cure constitution-sins, it has cured none; and that we can have no trial of the efficacy of grace, if we have it not in curing constitution-sins. The great promise is that grace shall change the nature of the wolf and the lion, of the bear, the asp, and the adder, and that they shall become as lambs (Isa. 11)—which it can never do, if it does not change it by a habitual counter-working of inclinations arising from constitution. If grace, being habitual, does not change the very inclination of constitution, I know not what it does.

Brethren, I take it for granted the vilest of those lusts which our Saviour and his apostles warn us against, to mortify and crucify, may be working in the hearts and minds of the best of us. Therefore, look to yourselves. But when the mind and soul is frequently and greatly urged upon and pressed with a particular lust and corruption, this does not prove that particular lust and corruption to be habitually prevalent, for it may be a temptation.

NOVEMBER 28

Condescension

For thus says the One who is high and lifted up, who inhabits eternity, whose name is Holy: 'I dwell in the high and holy place, and also with him who is of a contrite and lowly spirit.'

ISAIAH 57:15

If a great, a mighty king or prince of the earth had made a covenant with us, and confirmed it solemnly by his oath, to take care of all our concerns—so carnal and so fleshy are we, that it would give us great relief against imminent danger and hazards. But who has made this covenant with us? God has made it.

Consider the condescension of God on account of his greatness. You may observe in sundry places, that where God mentions his covenant, or the fruits of his covenant, he often mentions his greatness with it. 'For thus says the One who is high and lifted up, who inhabits eternity; I dwell with him also' (which is God's covenant) 'who is of a contrite and humble spirit' (Isa. 57:15). That the high and the lofty One, the great and the glorious God, should enter into this covenant with poor dust and ashes, worms of the earth as we are!—the Lord help us to understand it.

Condescension is endearing and satisfying. If a person who is great in the world condescends to respect and be familiar towards those who are poor, who are beggars, it is looked on as a very great matter. But there is an infinite distance between God and us, between the high and the lofty One, the glorious God, the possessor of heaven and earth, and poor dust and ashes. That he should take us into covenant, and engage himself by oath for the accomplishment of it; that he should be ours, and that we should be his—no heart can fully conceive this condescension.

NOVEMBER 29

Sufficiency

God is able to make all grace abound to you, so that having all sufficiency in all things at all times, you may abound in every good work.

2 CORINTHIANS 9:8

It will be a relief, if we consider God's all-sufficiency to satisfy our souls in every state and condition. This he made the ground of his covenant with Abraham: 'I am God Almighty.' And if there is any lack in God, we are freed from the terms of the covenant. This aggravates the sin of our instability, and our not taking up full satisfaction in him. 'Have I been a wilderness to you, or a barren heath?' says God, 'Have I been as waters that fail?' Have we, at any time in our own experience, lacked anything? Our want arises because we will not admit, we will not receive; or we long after other things, which God is not pleased we should have.

There is in God an all-sufficiency of grace and mercy to pardon us. There is an all-sufficiency of spiritual strength to support us and carry us through all our difficulties. There is an all-sufficiency of goodness and beauty to satisfy us. And there is an all-sufficiency of power and glory to reward us.

There is also an all-sufficiency in God to reward us when we shall be here no more. The lion lies at the door—death is ready to seize upon us—let our condition be what it will, we are entering into eternity. But God has engaged himself by covenant to be our God. He has promised to carry us through the dark shade, and to crown our souls with glory: 'Be faithful unto death, and I will give you the crown of life' (Rev. 2:10).

NOVEMBER 30

Heartfelt Joy

I tell you, there is joy before the angels of God over one sinner who repents.

LUKE 15:10

Let us inquire whether we have found, or do find, this joy in our own hearts. Is the remembrance of the closing of our hearts with Christ a song of love to us (Ps. 45)? Truly, if our loves are earnest and intent upon *other* things, we find joy and refreshment in *them*; but are we not dead and cold to the thoughts of this great and excellent advantage, of being betrothed to Christ, as all believers are? If so, it is but a sad evidence we are truly so betrothed.

Alas! If a poor beggar, a deformed creature, should be married to a great prince, would she not be joyfully aware of it? We are poor, deformed, woeful, sinful, polluted creatures, and for us to be taken into this relationship with Jesus Christ!—where are our hearts? Why do we not rejoice in the Lord with joy that is inexpressible and filled with glory (1 Pet. 1:8)? Is it not because Christ has not our whole hearts? Because we are not so entirely with him and for him in our affections as is fitting for this relationship? Because the world has too much hold upon us?

Shall God rejoice, and Christ rejoice—shall it be a song of love to God and Christ that we are brought into this relationship, and these dull hearts of ours are no farther affected with it? We ought to be ashamed to think how little we are concerned about such a great a privilege—how little lifted up above the world, and alienated from the world it makes us—if, indeed, we are partakers of this mercy.

DECEMBER

This month, we will read from some of those works which did not see the light until after Owen's death. The final volume of his almost two-million-word-long commentary on Hebrews was published in 1684. The nineteenth-century Scottish minister, Thomas Chalmers, pronounced that this commentary was 'the greatest work of John Owen... a work of gigantic strength as well as gigantic size; and he who has mastered it is very little short, both in respect to the doctrinal and practical of Christianity, of being an erudite and accomplished theologian.'

1684 also saw the publication of *Meditations and Discourses on the Glory of Christ*. This may be seen as a series of reflections on John 17:24, a very suitable text for a Christian approaching their death: 'Father, I desire that they also, whom you have given me, may be with me where I am, to see my glory that you have given me because you loved me before the foundation of the world.' Indeed, two days before he died, Owen wrote to a friend that 'I am going to him whom my soul has loved, or rather who has loved me with an everlasting love—which is the whole ground of my consolation.'

A Treatise of the Dominion of Sin and Grace (based on Romans 6:14) was published by his second wife and widow, Dorothy, in 1688. Twenty-five short talks which Owen had given before the administration of the Lord's Supper between 1669 and 1682 were recorded in shorthand by Sir John Hartopp at the time, and published by his granddaughter in 1760.

John Owen died on 24th August 1683, aged sixty-seven. He is buried in Bunhill Fields in London, near Isaac Watts (chaplain to the Hartopp family who later succeeded Owen as pastor of his London church) and John Bunyan.

DECEMBER 1

Admiring Love

Though he was in the form of God, he did not count equality with God a thing to be grasped, but emptied himself, by taking the form of a servant, being born in the likeness of men. And being found in human form, he humbled himself by becoming obedient to the point of death, even death on a cross.

PHILIPPIANS 2:6-8

There is no love like the love between Christ and the souls of believers. The love of Christ is an ocean—we cannot fathom it. The best act of our souls towards Christ's love is admiration, astonishing admiration, till the heart is quite overwhelmed with it, till our thoughts and understandings are, as it were, lost. The soul is taken out of itself, and laid in the dust as nothing, to be swallowed up in a holy contemplation of the unspeakable, inconceivable love of Jesus Christ.

This love is inimitable because nothing but infinite, divine power and wisdom could work such an effect as was the condescension of the Son of God—out of his love to take our nature upon him, to become flesh as we are. Therefore, this love has the preeminence above all other loves. He stoops so low, that he says 'I am a worm, and not a man' (Ps. 22:6). He comes to the lowest condition mankind can be reduced to in this condescension, and surely this has a pre-eminence above all other loves.

The love of Christ was manifested in his suffering in that condition. He suffered to bear the guilt of our sins, so to take away the wrath of God; he suffered to wash away the filth of our sins, so to take away shame and confusion from our souls; he suffered to redeem us from the world, poor captive creatures as we were, that we might be his own.

DECEMBER 2

Justice and Grace

For our sake he made him to be sin who knew no sin, so that in him we might become the righteousness of God.

2 CORINTHIANS 5:21

I would remember, if the Lord help me, the *sovereignty* of God the Father, his *justice*, and his *grace*: His sovereignty, 'He made him'—God the Father made him; his justice, 'He made him to be sin'—a sacrifice and an offering for sin; and his grace, 'That we might be made the righteousness of God in Christ.'

1. The *sovereignty* of God. This sovereignty of God extends itself to all persons chosen, and shows for whom Christ should be made sin; for he was not made sin for all, but for those who became 'the righteousness of God in him'. The whole foundation of this great transaction lies in the sovereignty of God over persons and things, in reference to Christ. Let us, then, remember to bow down to the sovereignty of God in this ordinance of the Lord's supper.

2. There is the *justice* of God. 'He made him to be sin'—imputed sin to him, reckoned to him all the sins of the elect, caused all our sins to meet upon him, made him a sin-offering, a sacrifice for sin, laid all the punishment of our sins upon him. To this end, he sent him forth to be a propitiation for sin, to declare his righteousness. The Lord help us to remember that his righteousness is in a special manner exalted by the death of Christ. He would not save us any other way but by making him sin.

3. There is *the grace* of God, which manifests itself in the aim and design of God in all this. What did God aim at? It was 'that we might become the righteousness of God in him'—that we might be made righteous, and freed from sin.

DECEMBER 3

Proclaiming

For as often as you eat this bread and drink the cup, you proclaim the Lord's death until he comes.

1 CORINTHIANS 11:26

The ordinance is firstly *commemorative:* 'Do this in remembrance of me.' There is no greater joy to the heart of sinners, and a person knows not how to give greater glory to God, than to call the atonement of sin to remembrance. How sweet is that offering that brings to our remembrance the atonement made for all our sins! That is pleasing and acceptable to God, and sweet to the souls of sinners.

Secondly, it has a peculiar *profession* attending it. The apostle says, 'you proclaim the Lord's death until he comes'; you make a profession and manifestation of it. Those who look towards Christ, and do not put themselves in a way of partaking of this ordinance, they refuse the principal part of that profession which God calls them to in this world. The truth is, we have been apt to content ourselves with a profession of moral obedience, but it is a profession of Christ's institution by which alone we glorify him in this world. 'I will have my death shown forth,' says Christ, 'and not only remembered.' The use of this ordinance is to show forth the death of Christ.

Thirdly, it is a *federal* ordinance, in which God confirms the covenant to us, and calls us to make a recognition of the covenant to God. The covenant is once made; but we know that we stand in need that it should be often transacted in our souls—that God should often testify his covenant to us, and that we should often actually renew our covenant engagements to him. God never fails nor breaks his promises, so that he has no need to renew them, but testify them anew: we break and fail in ours, so that we have need actually to renew them.

DECEMBER 4

Christ's Faith

I will put my trust in him.

Christ had a double faith in reference to his death: one with respect to himself, and his own interest in God; and the other with respect to the cause whose management he had undertaken, and the success of it.

The Lord Christ had faith in reference to *his own person* and to his own interest in God. The apostle declares that because 'the children were partakers of flesh and blood, Christ also did partake of the same' (Heb. 2:14) that he might die to deliver us from death. He brings a text of Scripture in confirmation of this, which is taken out of Psalm 18:2, 'I will put my trust in him.' In that great and difficult work that Christ did undertake, to deliver and redeem the children, he was all along carried through it by faith and trust in God.

He gives a great instance of his faith when he was departing out of the world. He looked through all the clouds of darkness round about him towards the rising sun—through all storms, to the harbour—when he cried those words 'Father, into your hands I commend my spirit' with a loud voice, and gave up the ghost. It is the highest act of faith upon a stable foundation, such as will not fail, to give up a departing soul into the hands of God; which Jesus Christ here did for our example. Some die with presumption; some in the dark, but faith can go no higher than to give up a departing soul into the hands of God, upon a sure and stable ground.

DECEMBER 5

Examination

*Let a person examine himself, then, and so eat of the bread
and drink of the cup.*

1 CORINTHIANS 11:28

There were many disorders in this church at Corinth, in various
ways—in schisms and divisions, in neglect of discipline, in false
opinions, and particularly in a great abuse of the administration
of this great ordinance of the supper of the Lord. And though I
do not, I dare not, I ought not, to bless God for their sin, yet I
bless God for his providence. Had it not been for their disorders,
we would all have been much in darkness on this subject. The
correction of their disorders contains the principal rule for
church communion and the administration of this sacrament
that we have in the whole Scripture. This might have been
hidden from us, but God suffered them to fall into disorder on
purpose that, through their fall, in them and by them he might
instruct his church in all ages to the end of the world.

The apostle is here rectifying abuses about the administration
of the Lord's supper, which were many. He gathers up all
directions into this one general rule of self-examination. This
extends itself to the whole due preparation of our souls for the
actual participation of this ordinance. There is a preparation
necessary for the celebration or observance of all solemn
ordinances.

DECEMBER 6

Pliable Spirit

Be not like a horse or a mule, without understanding, which must be curbed with bit and bridle, or it will not stay near you.

PSALM 32:9

There is no particular, set time, neither as to the day or season of the day, as to the beginning or ending of it, that is determined for this duty of partaking of the supper in the Scripture. But the duty itself being commanded, the time is left to our own prudence, to be regulated according to what duty requires.

There are two things that will greatly guide us:

1. The time ought to be so fixed, that the duty may leave a savour upon the soul unto the time of the celebration of the ordinance itself.

2. Providential occurrences and intimations are great rules for the choosing of time and season for duties. God loves a pliable spirit, that upon every look of his eye will be guided to a duty. But those who are like horses and mules, that must be held with a strong rein, that will not be turned until God puts great strength to it, are possessed with such a frame of spirit as God approves not. You are left at liberty to choose a time—but observe any intimation of providence that may direct to that time.

DECEMBER 7

Look on Him

When they look on me, on him whom they have pierced, they shall mourn for him, as one mourns for an only child.

ZECHARIAH 12:10

I shall now speak a little to the duty itself of preparation for that ordinance. The duty may be reduced to these four heads: meditation, examination, supplication, expectation. They are all given us in one verse (Zech. 12:10), though not directly applied to this ordinance.

1. Meditation: 'They shall look upon him.' This is not to be performed in any way but by the meditation of faith. Our looking upon Christ is by believing meditation. Looking is a fixing of the eye; faith is the eye of the soul: to look, is to fix faith in meditation.

2. Examination: this produces the mourning here mentioned. For though it is said, 'They shall mourn for him', it was not to mourn for his sufferings, for so he said, 'Weep not for me' (Luke 23:28)—but to mourn because of those things in which they were concerned in his sufferings. It brings us to repentance, which is the principal design of this examination.

3. There is supplication: for there shall be poured out a spirit of grace and supplication (Zech. 12:10a).

4. There is expectation: this is included also in looking to Christ. He has placed his name upon his ordinances, and there he is. Go to them with expectation, and rise from the rest of the duties with this expectation.

DECEMBER 8

Horrible Guilt

For the death he died he died to sin, once for all, but the life he lives he lives to God.

ROMANS 6:10

The first part of this duty of preparation consists in *meditation*, and meditation is a duty that, by reason of the vanity of our own minds, and the variety of objects which they are apt to fix upon, even believers themselves find as great a difficulty as any.

The principal object of meditation, in our preparation for this ordinance, is *the horrible guilt and provocation that is in sin.* There is a representation of the guilt of sin made in the cross of Christ. There was a great representation of it in the punishment of angels; a great representation of it is made in the destruction of Sodom and Gomorrah; both these are proposed to us in a special manner in 2 Peter 2:4-6, to set forth the heinous nature of the guilt of sin. But they come very short; indeed, give me leave to say that hell itself comes short of representing the guilt of sin, in comparison to the cross of Christ.

And the Holy Spirit would have us mind it, where he says, 'He made him sin for us' (2 Cor. 5:21). 'See what comes of sin,' says he, 'what demerit, what provocation there is in it.' To see the Son of God praying, crying, trembling, bleeding, dying; God hiding his face from him; the earth trembling under him; darkness round about him—how can the soul but cry out, 'O Lord, is this the effect of sin? Is all this in sin?' Here, then, take a view of sin. Others look on it in its pleasures and the advantages of it, and cry, 'Is it not a little one?' as Lot said of Zoar (Gen. 19:20), but look on it in the cross of Christ, and there it appears in another hue. 'All this is because of my sin', says the contrite soul.

DECEMBER 9

Christ's Sufferings

It was before your eyes that Jesus Christ was publicly portrayed as crucified.

GALATIANS 3:1

You know I usually speak a few words to prepare us for this ordinance. You know it is an ordinance of calling to remembrance: 'Do this in remembrance of me.' This great ordinance of the Lord's supper is not to call iniquity to remembrance, but it is to call to remembrance the putting an end to iniquity: God will make an end of sin, and this ordinance is our solemn remembrance of it.

Now, there are sundry things that we are to call to remembrance. I have endeavoured to help you to call the *love* of Christ to remembrance. The Lord, I trust, has guided my thoughts now to direct you to call the *sufferings* of Christ to remembrance. It is our duty, in this holy ordinance, solemnly to call to remembrance the sufferings of Christ.

It is said of the preaching of the gospel, that Jesus Christ is 'publicly portrayed as crucified before our eyes' in it (Gal. 3:1). And, if Christ is evidently crucified before our eyes in the preaching of the gospel, Christ is much more evidently crucified before our eyes in the administration of this ordinance, which is instituted for that very end.

And certainly, when Christ is crucified before our eyes, we ought deeply to consider his sufferings. It would be a great sign of a hard and senseless heart in us, if we were not willing, in some measure, to consider his sufferings upon such an occasion. We are, therefore, solemnly to remember them.

DECEMBER 10

Imputation

With his wounds we are healed.

ISAIAH 53:5

In Deuteronomy 21, a sacrifice is appointed for expiation of an uncertain murder; that is, when a man was killed, and no one knew who killed him, so no one was liable to punishment but there was guilt upon the land. The elders of the nearest city, to take away the guilt, were to cut off the neck of a heifer, by God's appointment; and that took away the guilt. Thus did God instruct the church under the Old Testament in this great, sovereign act of his wisdom and righteousness, in transferring the guilt of sin from the church to Christ.

Therefore the prophet says, 'The LORD has laid on him the iniquity of us all' (Isa. 53:6). What then? 'With his wounds we are healed' (Isa. 53:5). The wounds were all due to us, but they were due to us for our iniquities, and for no other cause. Now, our iniquities being transferred to Christ, all the wounds came to be his, and the healing came to be ours.

To the same purpose the apostle says, 'For our sake he made him to be sin who knew no sin, so that in him we might become the righteousness of God' (2 Cor. 5:21). As we are made the righteousness of God in him, so he is made sin for us. We are made the righteousness of God in him by the imputation of his righteousness to us; for our apostle is to be believed, that righteousness is by imputation: 'God imputes righteousness' says he (Rom. 4:6 KJV). We have no righteousness before God but by imputation; and the righteousness of God, which God ordains, approves, and accepts, is the righteousness of Christ imputed to us.

DECEMBER 11

Faith Alone

By faith the people of old received their commendation.

This only we may observe in general, that it is faith alone which, from the beginning of the world, in all ages, under all dispensations of divine grace and all alterations in the church-state and worship, has been the only principle in the church of living to God, of obtaining the promises, of inheriting life eternal. And it continues so to be, to the consummation of all things. Faith can do all things that belong to the life of God; and without it nothing can be done. Spiritual life is by faith (Gal. 2:20); and victory (1 John 5:4); and perseverance (1 Pet. 1:5); and salvation (Eph. 2:8; 1 Pet. 1:9): and so they were from the beginning.

It is faith alone which, from the beginning of the world (or from the giving of the first promise), was the means and way of obtaining acceptance with God. There has been great variety in the revelations of the object of this faith. The faith of some, as of Noah and some others, was principally and signally exercised on special objects, but it is faith of the same nature and kind in all from first to last that gives acceptance with God. And all the promises of God, as branches of the first promise, are in general the formal object of it; that is, Christ in them, without faith in whom none was ever accepted with God.

The faith of true believers from the beginning of the world was fixed on things future, hoped for, and invisible; that is, eternal life and glory in a special manner. So vain is the imagination of those who affirm that all the promises under the Old Testament respected only things temporal.

DECEMBER 12

Faith in God

By faith Sarah herself received power to conceive, even when she was past the age, since she considered him faithful who had promised.

HEBREWS 11:11

The formal object of faith in the divine promises is not the things promised in the first place, but God himself—in his essential excellencies of truth or faithfulness, and power. To fix our minds on the things promised themselves, to have an expectation of the enjoyment of them (mercy, grace, pardon, glory) without a previous acquiescence of mind in the truth and faithfulness of God, or faith in God himself as faithful and able to accomplish them, is but a deceiving imagination.

Every promise of God has this consideration tacitly annexed to it: 'Is anything too hard for the Lord?' There is no divine promise, no promise of the new covenant, but when it comes to the trial, as to our closing with it, we apprehend as great a difficulty and improbability of its accomplishment to us as Sarah did of conceiving. All things seem easy to those who know not what it is to believe, nor the necessity of believing; they do so to those also who have learned to abuse the grace of God expressed in the promises, and to turn it into wantonness. But poor, humble, broken souls, burdened with sin, and entangled in their own darkness, find insuperable difficulties, as they apprehend, in the way of the accomplishment of the promises. This is their principal retreat in their distress, 'Is anything too hard for the Lord?' This God himself proposes as the foundation of our faith in our entering into covenant with him.

DECEMBER 13

Self-denial

By faith Moses, when he was grown up, refused to be called the son of Pharaoh's daughter, choosing rather to be mistreated with the people of God than to enjoy the fleeting pleasures of sin.

HEBREWS 11:24-25

The work of faith in all ages of the church, as to its nature, efficacy, and method of its actings, is uniform and the same. They had not of old a faith of one kind, and we of another. This in general is the design of the apostle to prove in Hebrews 11. It has been varied in its degrees of light by outward revelations, but in itself from first to last it is still the same.

The first act of purely evangelical faith is *self-denial* (Matt. 16:24; Luke 9:23). And what greater instance of it, unless it were in Jesus Christ himself, can be given since the foundation of the world, than in what is here recorded of Moses? He was in the quiet possession of all the secular advantages which a man not born of the royal family could enjoy, and perhaps in a just expectation of them also. His personal eminency above others, joined with his high place and dignity, procured him all the popular veneration which he could desire. For him now, voluntarily and of his own accord, to relinquish them all, and to commit himself to dangers, poverty, banishment, without any prospect of relief—and that merely on the account of the promise of Christ—must be acknowledged to be comprehensive of all the acts, parts, and duties of evangelical self-denial.

Moses left not his outward enjoyments until he had crucified his heart to them, esteeming them but loss and dung in comparison of Christ (Phil. 3:8), and what was in him to be enjoyed.

DECEMBER 14

Disgrace

Moses considered the reproach of Christ greater wealth than the treasures of Egypt, for he was looking to the reward.

Hebrews 11:26

Christ and the church were considered from the beginning as one mystical body. What the one underwent, the other is esteemed to undergo the same. Hence it is said that 'in all their affliction he was afflicted' (Isa. 63:9). And the apostle Paul calls his own sufferings, 'what is lacking in Christ's afflictions' (Col. 1:24)—namely, what belonged to the full allotment of sufferings for that mystical body of which Christ is the head. And in this sense also, the afflictions of the church are the afflictions of Christ.

Somewhat of that which is here called 'the reproach of Christ' is called by the same apostle 'the marks of Jesus in his body' (Gal. 6:17), or the stripes which he endured, with the marks of them that remained, for the sake of Jesus Christ.

All sorts of afflictions, persecutions, and oppressions on the account of the profession of the truth, are intended. The world can neither justify nor countenance itself in its persecutions of the church, unless they first cover it all over with reproaches. So dealt they with our Lord Jesus Christ himself. They attempted not to take away his life, before the rage of the people was by all manner of reproaches stirred up against him. So it is in all the persecutions and sufferings of the church. They are always represented as heretics, schismatics, or seditious persons, opposite to all good order in church and state, before they are exposed to violence. And this also is usually accompanied with contempt, scorn, mocking, and false accusations.

DECEMBER 15

Peace with All

Strive for peace with everyone, and for the holiness without which no one will see the Lord.

HEBREWS 12:14

We must 'strive for peace with everyone'. We are not to do it by a compliance with them in any evil, nor by a neglect of any duty, nor by anything that impinges on holiness towards God. We must eternally bid defiance to that peace with people which is inconsistent with peace with God.

The worst of people are not excepted out of this rule—not our enemies, not our persecutors. We are still to follow peace with them all. Let this alone be fixed, that we are not obliged to anything that is inconsistent with holiness, that is contrary to the word of God, that is adverse to the principles and light of our own minds and consciences, for the obtaining of peace with any or all the people in the world, and this rule is absolute and universal.

A spirit which is apt and ready for strife and contention, to give and receive provocations, to retain a sense of injuries, is quite contrary to what the gospel requires of us. The glory of the kingdom of Christ is frequently promised under the name of peace, with a cessation of wars and contentions among people. It is evidence of how little of the power of the gospel remains at present in the minds of people in the world, when all things amongst those who are called Christians are filled with hatred, strife, persecutions, and savage wars.

DECEMBER 16

Immoral and Unholy

*See to it that no one is sexually immoral or unholy like Esau,
who sold his birthright for a single meal.*

HEBREWS 12:16

Hebrews puts together 'sexual immorality' and 'unholiness', and
that probably for these three reasons:

1. Because they are, as it were, the heads of the two sorts of
sins that people may be guilty of, namely, sins of the flesh, and
sins of the mind (Eph. 2:3).

2. Because they usually go together. Those who are sexually
immoral habitually always grow profane and unholy. And
profane persons, of all other sins, are apt to think lightly of
sexual immorality. These things are written with the beams of
the sun in the days in which we live.

3. They are the especial sins whose relinquishment by
sincere repentance is most rare. Few sexually immoral or profane
persons ever come to repentance.

The apostle places these evils at the door of final apostasy, and
more than intimates the difficulty, if not the moral impossibility,
of the recovery of those who are guilty of them. Those who are
forsaking the profession of holiness usually fall into immorality,
as experience testifies. Yet in this place the apostle does not intend
every such person as may, through temptation, be surprised into
that sin; but those who live in this sin, who are sexually immoral
habitually—such as are placed at the head of those who shall
never inherit the kingdom of God (1 Cor. 6:9). Such are to be
excluded out of the church, as a certain pledge and token of their
exclusion out of heaven.

DECEMBER 17

Let brotherly love continue.

The power and glory of Christian religion are exceedingly decayed and debased in the world. Next to faith in Christ Jesus, and the profession of this, the life and beauty of Christian religion consists in the mutual love of those who are partakers of the same heavenly calling, which all pretend to. And this is that upon which the Lord Christ has laid the weight of the manifestation of his glory in the world, namely, the love that is among his disciples. It was foretold as the peculiar glory of his rule and kingdom. But there are only a few footsteps now left of it in the visible church. There are only some marks that it has been there, and dwelt there of old.

Brotherly love, as to its lustre and splendour, is retired to heaven, abiding in its power and efficacious exercise only in some corners of the earth, and secret retirements. Envy, wrath, selfishness, love of the world, with coldness in all the concerns of religion, have possessed the place of it. And in vain shall people wrangle and contend about their differences in opinions, faith, and worship, pretending to design the advancement of religion by an imposition of their persuasions on others. Unless this holy love is again introduced among all those who profess the name of Christ, all the concerns of religion will more and more run into ruin.

DECEMBER 18

Dominant Sins

Keep back your servant also from presumptuous sins; let them not have dominion over me! Then I shall be blameless, and innocent of great transgression.

PSALM 19:13

The psalmist, treating with God in prayer about sin, acknowledges that there are in all people unsearchable errors of life, beyond all human understanding or comprehension, with such daily sins of infirmity as stand in need of continual cleansing and pardon. He says, 'Who can discern his errors? Declare me innocent from hidden faults' (Ps. 19:12). But yet he supposes that these things are consistent with a state of grace and acceptation with God. He had no thought of any absolute perfection in this life, of any such condition as should not stand in need of continual cleansing and pardon.

But he speaks immediately of another sort of sin, which will certainly prove destructive to people's souls wherever they are (v. 13). This is the hinge upon which the whole cause and state of my soul turns: Although I am subject to many sins of various sorts, yet under them all, I can and do maintain my integrity, and covenant uprightness in walking with God; where I fail, I am kept within the reach of cleansing and pardoning mercy, continually administered to my soul by Jesus Christ. But there is a state of life in this world in which sin has dominion over the soul acting itself presumptuously, with which integrity and freedom from condemning guilt are inconsistent. This state, therefore, which alone is eternally ruinous to people's souls, he deprecates with all earnestness, praying to be kept and preserved from it.

DECEMBER 19

Inner War

Beloved, I urge you as sojourners and exiles to abstain from the passions of the flesh, which wage war against your soul.

1 PETER 2:11

Sin still abides in and dwells with believers. Those who think otherwise know neither themselves, nor what sin is, nor what the grace of the gospel consists in. There is the 'flesh' remaining in everyone, which 'lusts against the Spirit' (Gal. 5:17); it adheres to all the faculties of our souls, which is why it is called the 'old self' (Rom. 6:6), in opposition to the renovation of our minds and all the faculties of them, called the 'new self' (Eph. 4:24), or 'new creation' in us (2 Cor. 5:17).

But the old self continually works to provide for and fulfil its own lusts (Rom. 13:14). It so abides in believers in various degrees that it may put forth its power in them to obtain victory and dominion over them. It rules over all unbelievers, all that are under the law; it will strive to do the same in those who believe and are under grace. Hence it is said to fight and war in us (Rom. 7:23) and to war against our souls (1 Pet. 2:11). Now, it thus fights, and wars, and contends in us for dominion, for that is the end of all war; whatever fights, it does it for power and rule. The design of sin lies not in the particular temptation, but to make it a means to obtain dominion over the soul.

This should keep believers always on their guard against all the motions of sin, though the matter of them seem but small; for the aim and tendency of every one of them is dominion and death, which they will achieve if not stopped in their progress.

DECEMBER 20

Sin's Tyranny

Do you not know that if you present yourselves to anyone as obedient slaves, you are slaves of the one whom you obey, either of sin, which leads to death, or of obedience, which leads to righteousness?

ROMANS 6:16

Sin has no right to rule in people's souls. People have no power to give sin a right to rule over them. They may voluntarily enslave themselves to it, but this gives sin no right or title. All people originally have another lord, to whom they owe all obedience, nor can anything discharge them from their allegiance. People become servants of sin by their own voluntary subjection to it. But this gives sin no title against the law of God, whose right alone it is to bear sway in people's souls; for all that give up themselves to the service of sin do live in actual rebellion against their natural Lord.

People who live in sin voluntarily wrest themselves from under the rule of the law of God, and give themselves up to be slaves to this tyrant. People reject the rule of God's law, and choose this foreign yoke. The greatest part of mankind visibly and openly profess themselves the servants and slaves of sin. They wear its livery and do all its drudgery.

Yet all have a right in themselves to cast off the rule of sin, and to vindicate themselves into liberty. They may, when they will, plead the right and title of the law of God to the rule of their souls. All people, I say, have this right in themselves, because of the natural allegiance they owe to the law of God; but they have not power of themselves to execute this right, and actually to cast off the yoke of sin: but this is the work of grace. Sin's dominion is broken only by grace.

DECEMBER 21

Religious Sin

On that day many will say to me, 'Lord, Lord, did we not prophesy in your name, and cast out demons in your name, and do many mighty works in your name?' And then will I declare to them, 'I never knew you; depart from me, you workers of lawlessness.'

MATTHEW 7:22-23

Sin represses and overcomes the efficacy of the convictions of the mind. Those who are under the dominion of sin may have light into and conviction of their duty in many things, and this light and conviction they may follow ordinarily, despite the dominion of sin. A tyrant will permit his slaves and subjects ordinarily to follow their own opportunities, but if they interfere with or oppose his interest, he will make them aware of his power. So if people have light and conviction, sin (where it has the dominion) will allow them ordinarily and in many things to comply with them: it will allow them to pray, to hear the word, to abstain from sundry sins, to perform many duties, as is expressly affirmed in the Scripture of many that were under the power of sin, and we see it in experience.

How much work do we see about religion and religious duties, what constant observation of the times and seasons of them, how many duties performed morally good in themselves and useful, by those who, on many other accounts, proclaim themselves to be under the dominion of sin! But if the light and conviction of this sort of person rises up in opposition to the principal interest of sin in those lusts and ways in which it exercises its rule, it will make them conscious of its power.

DECEMBER 22

Insatiable

They have eyes full of adultery, insatiable for sin. They entice unsteady souls. They have hearts trained in greed. Accursed children!

2 PETER 2:14

Sin exercises its reigning power in the imagination with respect to sensuality and uncleanness of life. It is said of some that they have 'eyes full of adultery' and that they 'cannot cease from sin' (2 Pet. 2:14); that is, their imaginations are continually working about the objects of their unclean lusts. These they think of night and day, miring themselves in all filth continually. Jude calls them 'filthy dreamers, defiling the flesh' (Jude 8 KJV). They live as in a constant pleasing dream by their vile imaginations, even when they cannot accomplish their lustful desires.

By this, many wallow in the mire of uncleanness all their days. And by this means, the most cloistered recluses may live in constant adulteries, by which multitudes of them become actually the sinks of uncleanness. This is that which, in the root of it, is severely condemned by our Saviour (Matt. 5:28).

Unbelief, distrust, and hard thoughts of God, are of the same kind. These will sometimes so possess people's imaginations as to keep them away from all delight in God. In these and the like ways may sin exercise its dominion in the soul by the mind and its imagination. It may do so when no demonstration is made of it in the outward life; for by this means people's minds are defiled, and then nothing is clean, all things are impure to them (Titus 1:15). Their minds being thus defiled, they defile all things to them—their enjoyments, their duties, all they have, and all that they do.

DECEMBER 23

Mourning Sin

The LORD is near to the brokenhearted and saves the crushed in spirit.

PSALM 34:18

Constant self-abasement, condemnation, and abhorrence of sin, is another duty that is directly opposed to the interest and rule of sin in the soul. No frame of mind is a better antidote against the poison of sin. 'Whoever walks in integrity walks securely' (Prov. 10:9). God has a continual regard to mourners, those who are 'brokenhearted and crushed in spirit' (Ps. 34:18). It is the soil where all grace will thrive and flourish.

A constant due sense of sin as sin, of our interest in it by nature and in the course of our lives, with a continual painful remembrance of some such instances of it as have had peculiar aggravations, issuing in a gracious self-abasement—this is the soul's best posture in watching against all the deceits and incursions of sin. And this is a duty which we ought with all diligence to attend to.

To keep our souls in a constant frame of mourning and self-abasement is not inconsistent with those consolations and joys which the gospel tenders to us in believing. It is the only way to let them into the soul in a due manner. It is such mourners, and those alone, to whom evangelical comforts are administered (Isa. 57:18).

One of the first things that sin does when it aims at dominion is the destruction of this frame of mind; and when it actually has the rule, it will not suffer it to enter.

DECEMBER 24

Sweet Liberty

For sin will have no dominion over you, since you are not under law but under grace.

ROMANS 6:14

It is an unspeakable mercy and privilege to be delivered from the dominion of sin. Nothing is more sweet, precious, and valuable to a soul in conflict with sin and temptation, than to hear that sin shall not have the dominion over it. Ah! What would some give that it might be spoken to them with power, so as that they might steadfastly believe it and have the comfort of it? 'Fools make a mock of sin' (Prov. 14:9 KJV) and some glory in the service of it, which is their shame; but those who understand anything aright, either of what is present or what is to come, know that this freedom from its dominion is an invaluable mercy.

It appears to be so from the causes of it. It is that which no one can, by their own power and the utmost of their endeavours, attain. People may grow rich, or wise, or learned by their own powers; but no one by them can shake off the yoke of sin. If a person had all the wealth of the world, they could not by it purchase this liberty; it would be despised. And when sinners go to the place where the rich man was tormented, and have nothing more to do with this world, they would give it all, if they had it, for an interest in this liberty (Luke 16:24). It is that which the law and all the duties of it cannot procure.

DECEMBER 25

Christ's Glory

I count everything as loss because of the surpassing worth of knowing Christ Jesus my Lord.

PHILIPPIANS 3:8

The glory of our Lord Jesus Christ is revealed in the Scripture, and proposed as the principal object of our faith, love, delight, and admiration. His glory is incomprehensible, and his praises are unutterable. Some things an illuminated mind may conceive of it; but what we can express in comparison of what it is in itself, is even less than nothing. But as for those who have forsaken the only true guide to this, endeavouring to be wise above what is written, and to raise their contemplations by fancy and imagination above Scripture revelation (as many have done)—they have darkened counsel without knowledge, uttering things which they understand not, which have no substance or spiritual food of faith in them.

However, that real view which we may have of Christ and his glory in this world by faith—however weak and obscure that knowledge which we may attain of them by divine revelation—is inexpressibly to be preferred above all other wisdom, understanding, or knowledge whatsoever. So it is declared by him who will be acknowledged a competent judge in these things: 'I count everything as loss because of the surpassing worth of knowing Christ Jesus my Lord' (Phil. 3:8). He who does not, has no part in him.

If our future blessedness consists in being where he is, and beholding his glory, what better preparation can there be for it than in a constant contemplation of that glory in the revelation that is made in the gospel, that we may be gradually transformed into the same glory?

DECEMBER 26

Eternal Glory

But rejoice insofar as you share Christ's sufferings, that you may also rejoice and be glad when his glory is revealed.

1 PETER 4:13

In the contemplation of the glory of Christ, people will find rest for their own souls. It will be made evident how slight and inconsiderable all these things are from where our troubles and distresses do arise. For they all grow on the root of an over-valuation of temporal things. Unless we can arrive at a fixed judgment that all things here below are transitory and perishing, reaching only to the outward self, or the body (perhaps to the killing of it)—we must spend our lives in fears, sorrows, and distractions. One real view of the glory of Christ, and of our own concernment in it, will give us a full relief in this matter.

For what are all the things of this life? What is the good or evil of them in comparison to an interest in this transcendent glory? When our minds are possessed with thoughts of it, when our affections reach out after its enjoyments, let pain and sickness and sorrows and fears and dangers and death say what they will, we shall have in readiness the means to combat and overcome them. They are all outward, transitory, and passing away, whereas our minds are fixed on those things which are eternal, and filled with incomprehensible glory.

A due contemplation of the glory of Christ will restore and compose the mind. This will lift the minds and hearts of believers above all the troubles of this life, and is the sovereign antidote that will expel all the poison that is in them, which otherwise might perplex and enslave their souls.

DECEMBER 27

Victory

Into your hand I commit my spirit; you have redeemed me,
O LORD, faithful God.

PSALM 31:5

There are sundry things required of us, that we may be able to encounter death cheerfully, constantly, and victoriously. For want of these, or some of them, I have known gracious souls who have lived in a kind of bondage for fear of death all their days. The soul is now parting with all things here below, and that forever. It must alone by itself launch into eternity. It is entering an invisible world, which it knows no more of than it has received by faith. God seems on purpose so to conceal it from us, that we should have no evidence of it, at least as to the manner of things in it, but what is given to faith by divine revelation.

Whatever the state of this invisible world, the soul can undertake nothing of its own conduct after its departure from the body. It knows that it must be absolutely at the disposal of another. Therefore, no one can comfortably venture on and into this condition, but in the exercise of that faith which enables them to resign and give up their departing soul into the hand of God, who alone is able to receive it, and to dispose it into a condition of rest and blessedness. In this, as in all other graces, is our Lord Jesus Christ our great example. He resigned his departing spirit into the hands of his Father, to be owned and preserved by him, in its state of separation: 'Father, into your hands I commit my spirit' (Luke 23:46); as did the psalmist, his type, in a similar condition (Ps. 31:5). This is the last victorious act of faith.

DECEMBER 28

Far Better

My desire is to depart and be with Christ, for that is far better.

PHILIPPIANS 1:23

We must be ready to comply with the times and seasons in which God would have us depart and leave this world. Many think they shall be willing to die when their time is come; but they have many reasons, as they suppose, to desire that it may not be yet—which, for the most part, arise merely from fear of death. Some desire to live that they may see more of that glorious work of God for his church, which they believe he will accomplish. So Moses prayed that he might not die in the wilderness but go over Jordan and see the good land and that goodly mountain and Lebanon, the seat of the church, and the worship of God, which God thought fit to deny him. And this denial of the request of Moses, made on the highest consideration possible, is instructive to all in similar cases (Deut. 3:23-27).

Others may judge themselves to have some work to do in the world, in which they suppose the glory of God and the good of the church are concerned; therefore, they wish to be spared for a season. Paul did not know clearly whether it would be best for him to abide a while longer in the flesh on this account (Phil. 1:22-24); and David often deprecates the present season of death because of the work which he had to do for God in the world. Others rise no higher than their own private interests or concerns with respect to their persons, their families, and goods in this world. They would see these things in a better or more settled condition before they die, and then they shall be most willing so to do. But it is the love of life that lies at the bottom of all these desires.

DECEMBER 29

Sun Rising

He declares his word to Jacob, his statutes and rules to Israel. He has not dealt thus with any other nation.

PSALM 147:19-20

God was known under the Old Testament by the revelation of his word and the institution of his worship. The church then knew him; yet so that they had an apprehension that he dwelt in 'thick darkness' where they could not have any clear views of him (Exod. 20:21; Deut. 5:22; 1 Kings 8:12; 2 Chron. 6:1). And the reason why God so represented himself in darkness to them was to instruct them in their imperfect state, in which they could not comprehend that glory which should afterward be revealed. For as he is now made known in Christ, we see that 'he is light, and in him there is no darkness at all' (1 John 1:5).

Until then, darkness in general covered the earth, and gross darkness the people, as to the knowledge of God; only there was a twilight in the church. The day did not yet dawn, the shadows did not 'flee away' (Song 2:17) nor the 'day-star shine' in people's hearts (2 Pet. 1:19). But when the 'Sun of Righteousness' (Mal. 4:2) did arise in his strength and beauty, when the Son of God 'appeared in the flesh' (1 Tim. 3:16) and in the discharge of his office, God himself, as to his being and manner of existence in three distinct persons, with all the glorious properties of the divine nature, was illustriously manifested to those who believe; and the light of the knowledge of them dispelled all the shadows that were in the church, and shone into the darkness which was in the world, so that none continued ignorant of God but those who would not see. In this is the Lord Christ *glorious*.

DECEMBER 30

God's Love

In this the love of God was made manifest among us, that God sent his only Son into the world, so that we might live through him.

1 JOHN 4:9

It is in Christ alone that we may have a clear, distinct view of the glory of God and his excellencies. For him, and him alone, has he appointed the representative of himself to us. The apostle tells us that 'God is love' (1 John 4:8). And a blessed revelation this is of the divine nature; it casts out envy, hatred, malice, revenge, with all their fruits, in rage, fierceness, implacability, persecution, murder, into the territories of Satan. They do not belong to God in his nature or actings; for 'God is love'.

How shall we have a view of this love, of God as love? By what way or means shall we behold the glory of it? It is hidden from all living, in God himself. The wise philosophers, who discoursed so much of the love of God, knew nothing of this, that 'God is love'. Most of people's natural notions about it are corrupt, and the best of them weak and imperfect. Generally, people's thoughts about it are that he is of a flexible and easy nature, one that they may make bold with; as the psalmist declares (Ps. 50:21).

How, then, shall we know, in what shall we behold, the glory of God in this, that he is love? The apostle declares it in the next words: 'In this the love of God was made manifest among us, that God sent his only Son into the world' (1 John 4:9). This is the only evidence given us that 'God is love'. By this alone is the divine nature as such made known unto us—namely, in the mission, person, and office of the Son of God; without this, all is in darkness as to the true nature and supreme operation of this divine love.

DECEMBER 31

His Face

There are many who say, 'Who will show us some good? Lift up the light of your face upon us, O LORD!'

Psalm 4:6

My present business is only to stir up the minds of believers to a due contemplation of the glory of Christ in the sacred, mysterious constitution of his person, as God and man in one. Let us get it fixed on our souls and in our minds, that this glory of Christ in the divine constitution of his person is the best, the most noble, useful, beneficial object that we can be conversant about in our thoughts, or cleave to in our affections. What are all other things in comparison to the 'knowledge of Christ'? In the judgment of the great apostle, they are but 'loss and rubbish' (Phil. 3:8-10). So they were to him; and if they are not so to us we are carnal.

What is the world, and what are the things of it, which most people spend their thoughts about, and fix their affections on? The psalmist gives his judgment about them, in comparison with a view of this glory of Christ: 'Many say, "Who will show us any good?"' (Ps. 4:6). Who will give and help us to attain so much in and of this world as will give rest and satisfaction to our minds? That is the good inquired after. But, says he, 'Lord, lift up the light of your face upon us.' The light of the glory of God in the face of Christ Jesus is that satisfactory good alone which I desire and seek after.

The Scripture reproaches the vanity and folly of people's minds, in that 'they spend their money for that which is not bread, and their labour for that which does not satisfy' (Isa. 55:2). They engage the vigour of their spirits about perishing things when they have durable substance and riches proposed to them.

OWEN'S EPITAPH

Born in the county of Oxford: the son of an eminent divine, but more eminent himself, and justly to be ranked among the most illustrious of the age. Furnished with the aids of polite and solid learning in a very uncommon degree, he led them all in a well-ordered train to the service of his great study, Christian divinity—controversial, practical, and casuistical. In each of these, he excelled others and was ever equal to himself. In the one branch of this most sacred science, he, with powers more than Herculean, seized and vanquished the envenomed monsters of Arminian, Socinian, and Popish errors. In the other, first experiencing in his own breast, according to the unerring rule of Scripture, the sacred energy of the Holy Spirit, he taught the whole economy of that divine influence. Rejecting lower objects, he constantly cherished and largely experienced that blissful communion with God which he so admirably described. Though a pilgrim on earth, he was like a spirit in heaven. In *Experimental Divinity*, all who could have the blessings of his counsels found him as an oracle. He was a scribe every way accomplished for the kingdom of heaven. To many in private dwellings, from the pulpit to more, and from the press to all who were aiming at the heavenly prize, he shone a pure lamp of gospel doctrine. Thus brightly shining he was gradually consumed, not unobserved by himself and his afflicted friends, till his holy soul, longing for the fuller fruition of its God, quitted the ruins of a body depressed by constant infirmities, emaciated by frequent diseases, but chiefly worn out by severe labours, and so no further suitable for the service of God: a fabric, till thus reduced, most comely and majestic. He left the world on a day rendered dreadful to the church by the powers of the world, but blissful to himself by the plaudit of his God, the 24th August 1683, aged sixty-seven.

CHRISTIAN
HERITAGE

Daily Readings

The
Early
Church
Fathers

Edited by

Nick
Needham

Daily Readings–the Early Church Fathers

Nick Needham

The early church fathers have always had a special place in Christian theology. As the first interpreters of the gospel, we often find in their words a sense of the gospel's sheer freshness and reality. More than this, they were the thinkers who first hammered out the full meaning of what Scripture says about the Trinity and the person of Christ. Their sayings, presented here by Nick Needham, are more than just relevant – they present the opportunity to kindle within us something of that same healthy and godly spirit.

ISBN: 978-1-5271-0043-5

The
Puritans

Edited by

Randall J.
Pederson

(spine) Daily Readings

(spine, top) HERITAGE

Daily Readings–the Puritans

RANDALL J. PEDERSON

As you draw daily from the wisdom of the Puritans, you will find renewed joy for your daily service. This beautifully presented gift edition has 12 months of readings from Richard Baxter; John Bunyan; Stephen Charnock; Jonathan Edwards; John Flavel; William Gurnall; William Guthrie; Matthew Mead; John Owen; Samuel Rutherford; Thomas Watson; Thomas Vincent.

ISBN: 978-1-8455-0978-1

Daily Readings

George Whitefield

Edited by

Randall J. Pederson

Daily Readings–George Whitefield

RANDALL J. PEDERSON

The first devotional compiled solely from Whitefield's works and provides an excellent introduction to the spirituality of this eighteenth century evangelical. In this carefully edited edition, Randall Pederson has chosen passages based upon George Whitefield's letters and sermons that will encourage, inspire and challenge the reader each day. Bible passages are based upon the ESV.

ISBN: 978-1-8455-0580-6

CHRISTIAN HERITAGE

Daily Readings

Matthew Henry

Edited by

Randall J. Pederson

Daily Readings–Matthew Henry

Randall J. Pederson

This beautifully present gift edition is a new selection of Matthew Henry's writings that will nourish your spiritual life. Matthew Henry is one of the best known of our spiritual ancestors. His commentary on the whole Bible is still a staple book for those seeking understanding of God's word to the world. In this carefully edited edition, Randall Pederson has chosen passages that will encourage, inspire and challenge the reader each day. Bible passages are based upon the English Standard Version of the Bible.

ISBN: 978-1-8455-0509-7

LEE GATISS

Light
after
Darkness

HOW THE REFORMERS
REGAINED, RETOLD AND RELIED
ON THE GOSPEL OF GRACE

Light after Darkness

How the Reformers regained, retold and relied on the gospel of grace

LEE GATISS

The stories of Ulrich Zwingli, William Tyndale, Martin Luther, John Calvin and Thomas Cranmer remind us of the glorious truths which warmed the hearts and fired the souls of passionate and imperfect people, and how they tried to share the good news of Jesus Christ in their generation. Will it strengthen and inspire passionate and imperfect Christians today to emulate their clarity, their courage, and their compassion for the lost?

This is a fabulous recounting of the lives of five key figures of the European Reformation. It is a recounting that also reveals that if these lives had not been lived, western history and the story of the Church would be completely different. This is usable history at its best.

Michael A. G. Haykin
Professor of Church History and Biblical Spirituality,
The Southern Baptist Theological Seminary, Louisville, Kentucky

With realism, clarity, and his characteristic twinkle, Lee Gatiss shows just how profoundly and practically relevant the stories and issues of the Reformation remain today. Our churches will be more healthy and fruitful if they can learn these lessons.

Michael Reeves
President and Professor of Theology,
Union School of Theology, Bridgend, Wales

ISBN 978-1-5271-0333-7

Christian Focus Publications

Our mission statement –

STAYING FAITHFUL

In dependence upon God we seek to impact the world through literature faithful to His infallible Word, the Bible. Our aim is to ensure that the Lord Jesus Christ is presented as the only hope to obtain forgiveness of sin, live a useful life and look forward to heaven with Him.

Our Books are published in four imprints:

CHRISTIAN
FOCUS

popular works including biographies, commentaries, basic doctrine and Christian living.

CHRISTIAN
HERITAGE

books representing some of the best material from the rich heritage of the church.

MENTOR

books written at a level suitable for Bible College and seminary students, pastors, and other serious readers. The imprint includes commentaries, doctrinal studies, examination of current issues and church history.

CF4•K

children's books for quality Bible teaching and for all age groups: Sunday school curriculum, puzzle and activity books; personal and family devotional titles, biographies and inspirational stories – Because you are never too young to know Jesus!

Christian Focus Publications Ltd,
Geanies House, Fearn, Ross-shire,
IV20 1TW, Scotland, United Kingdom.
www.christianfocus.com